Lisa Mara Batacchi

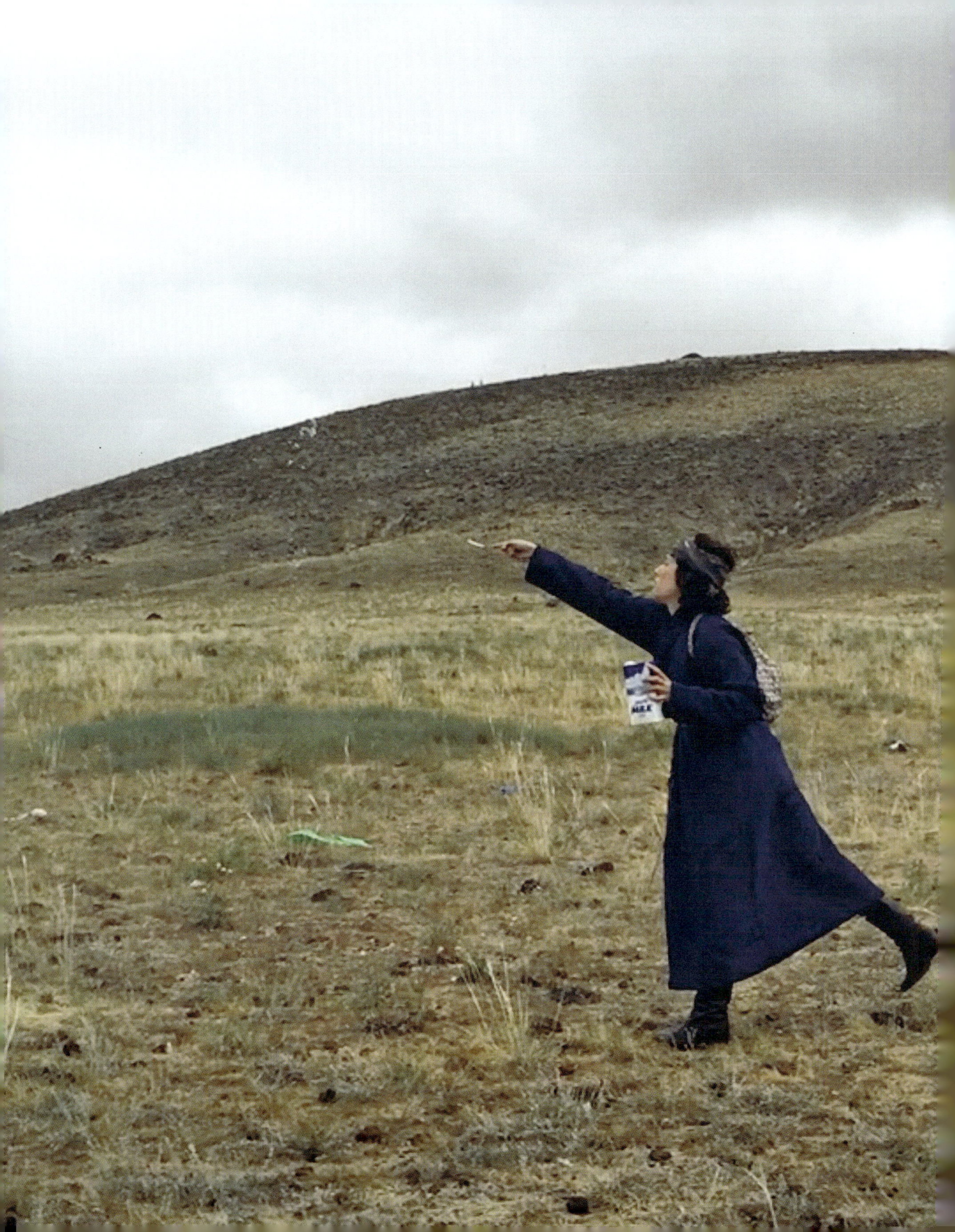

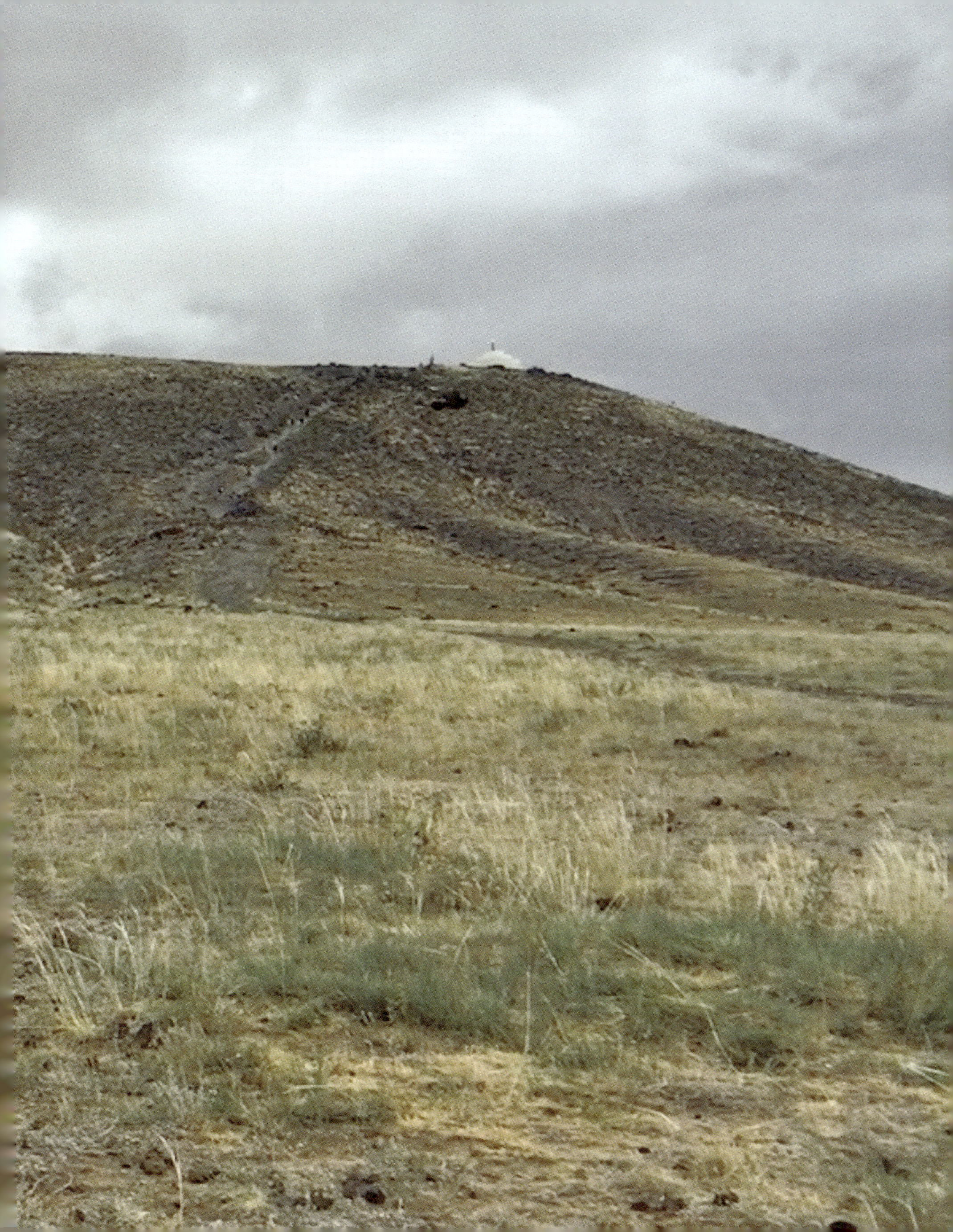

*

Lisa Mara Batacchi
The Time of Discretion

Edited by
Veronica Caciolli

SilvanaEditoriale

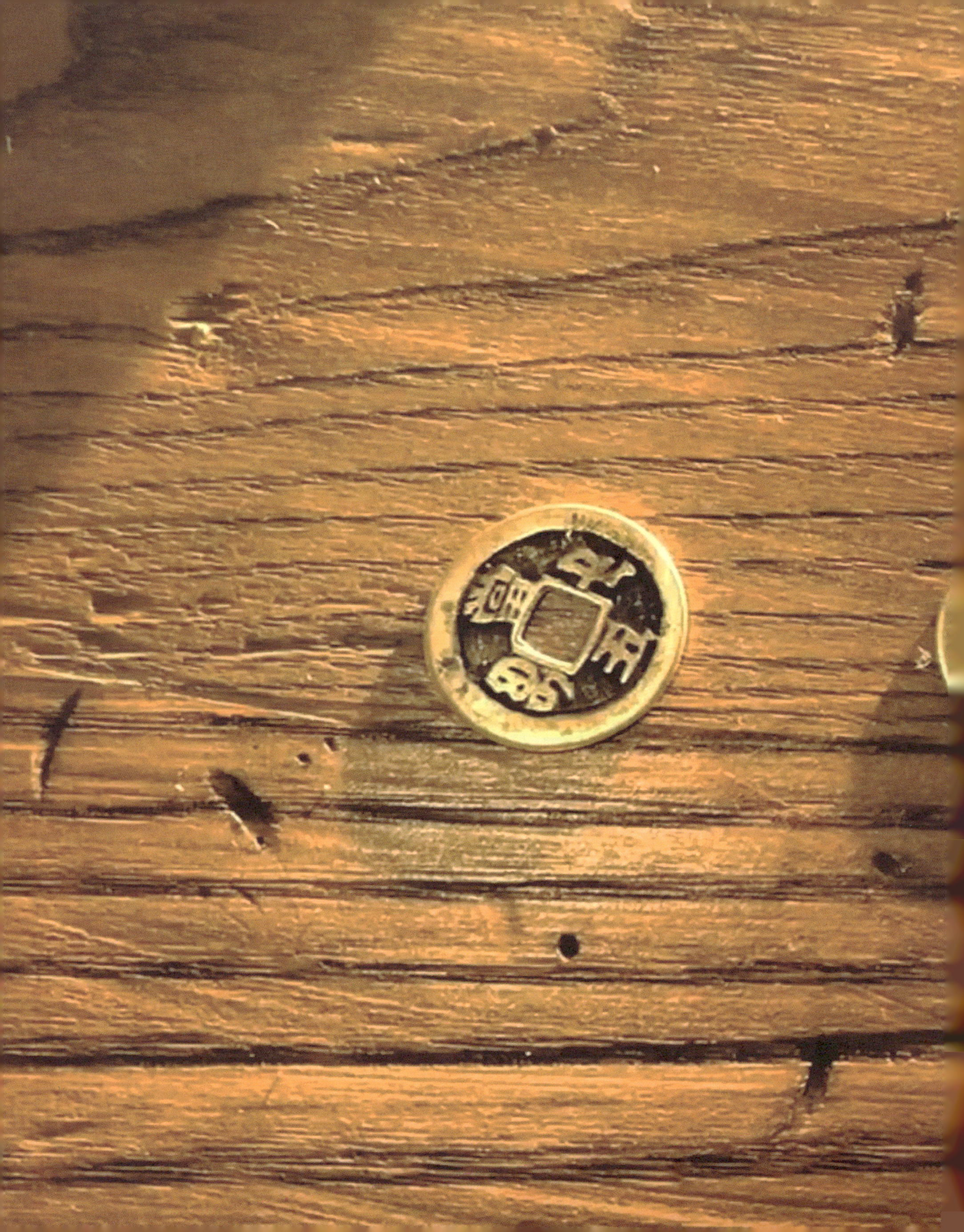

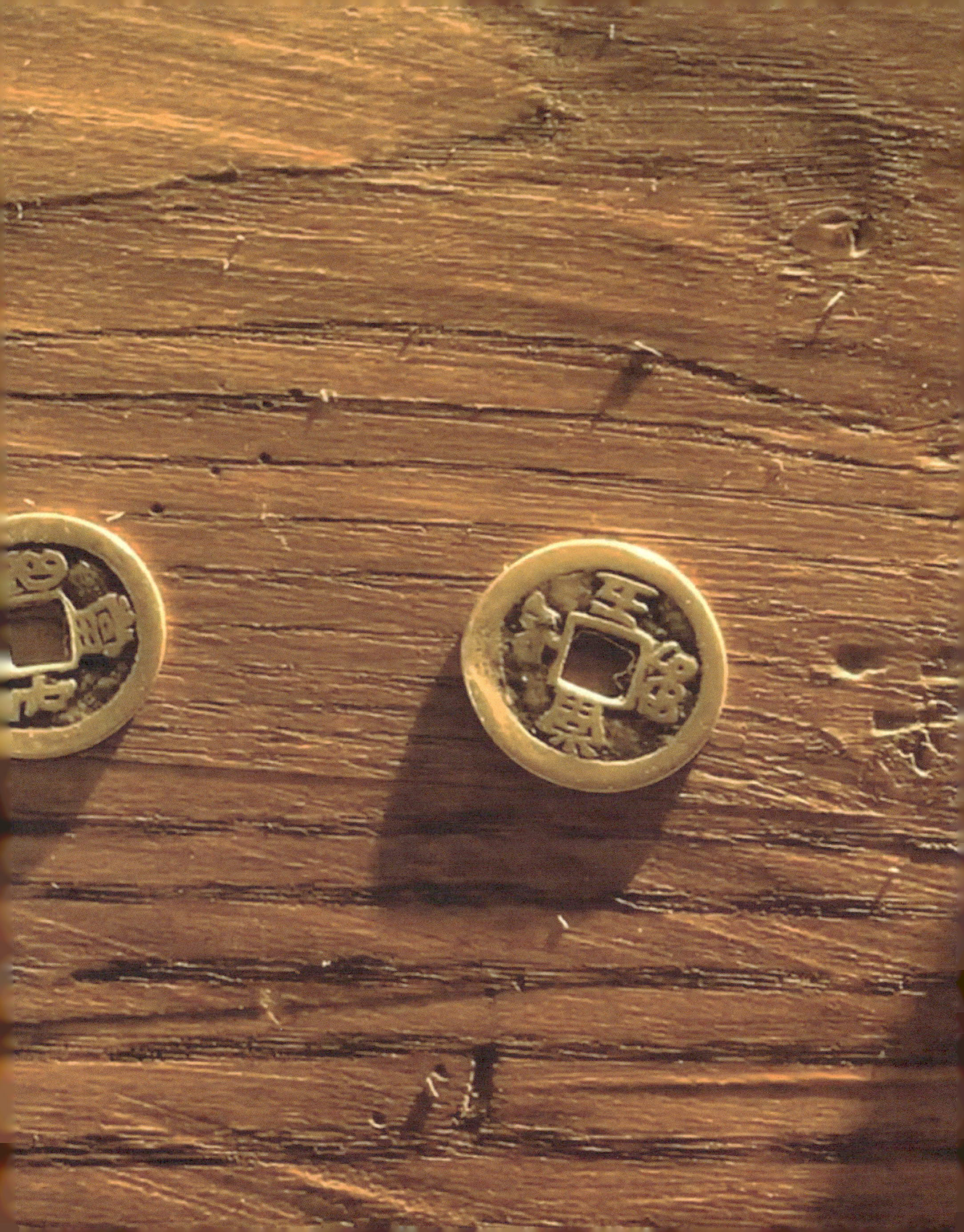

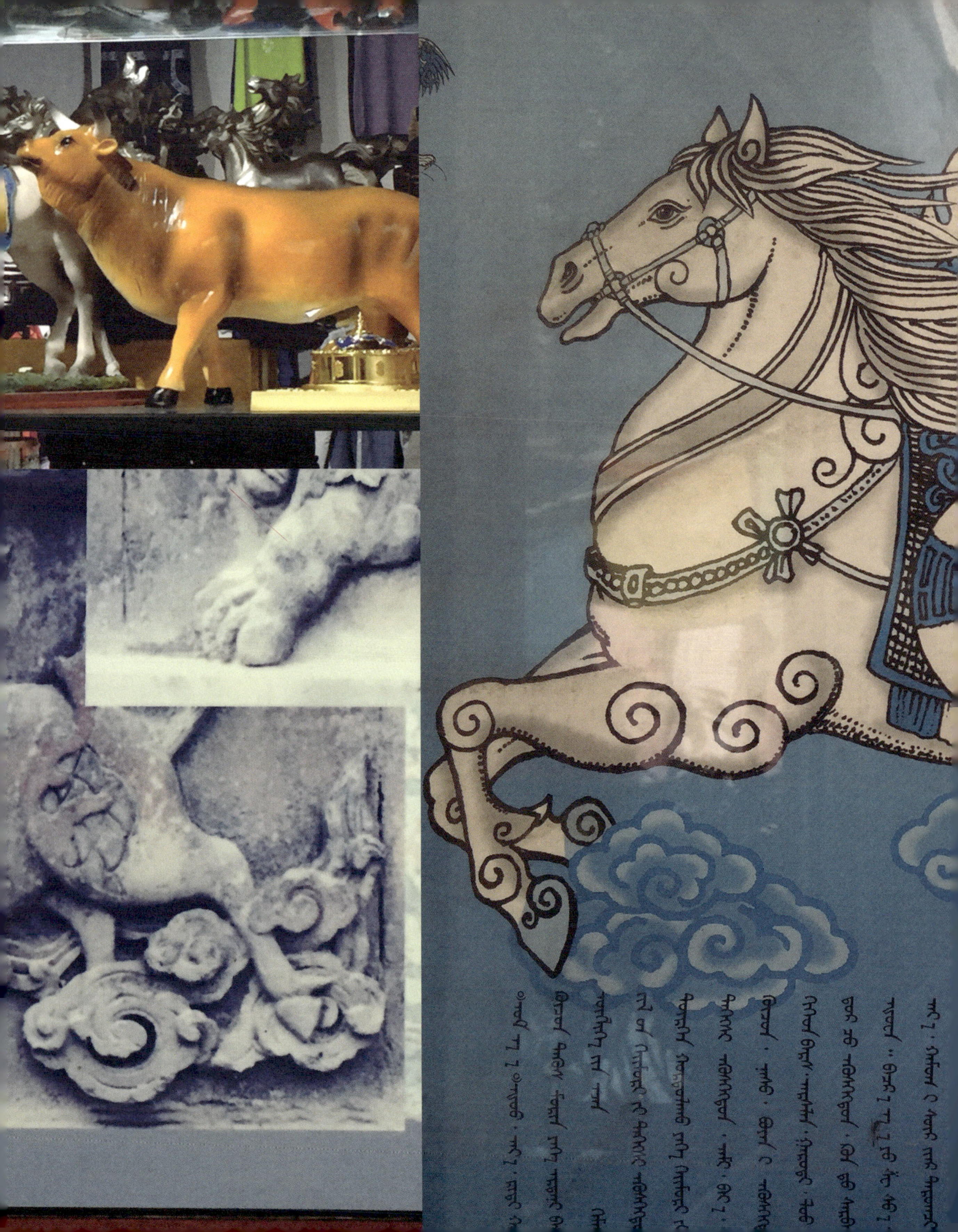

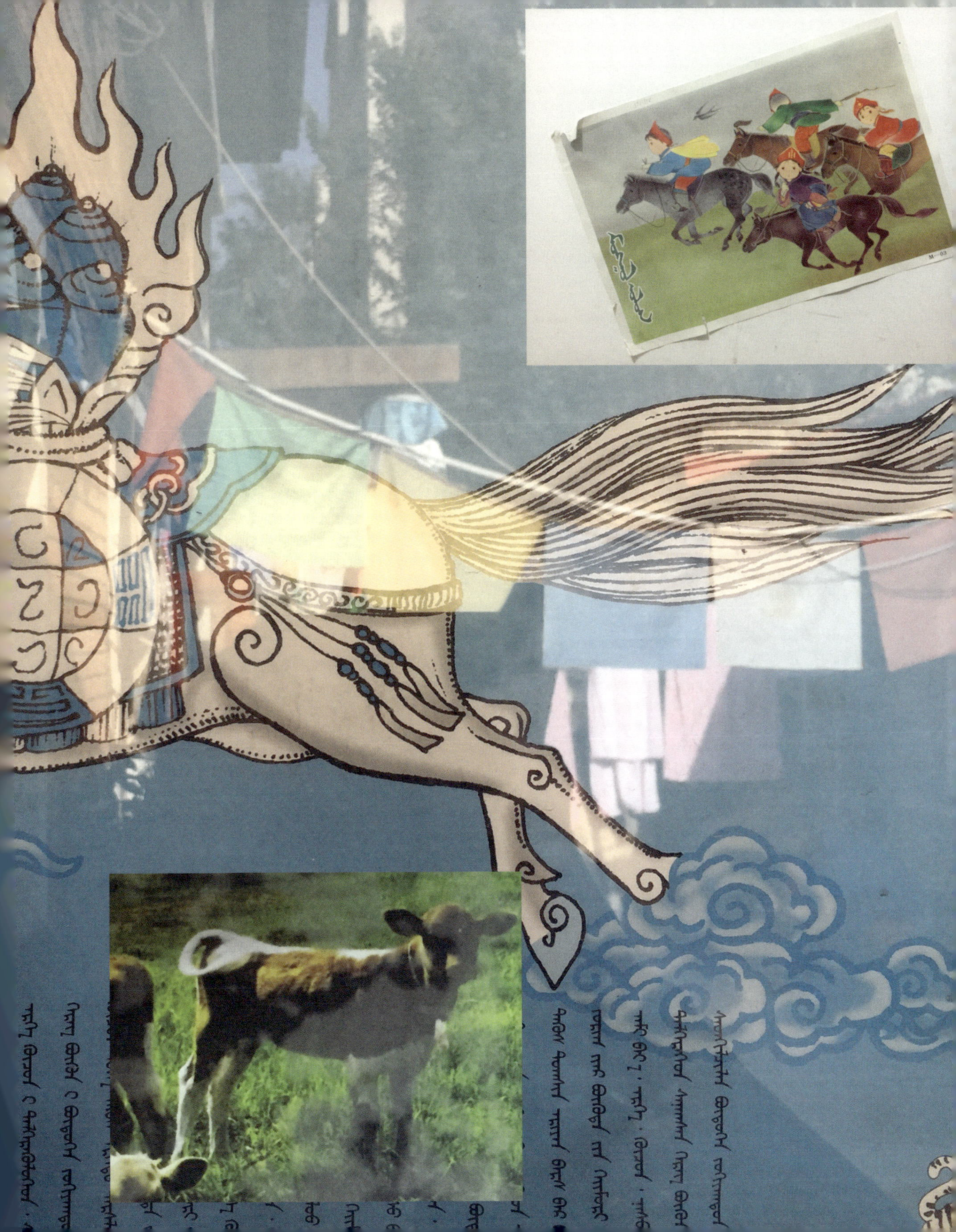

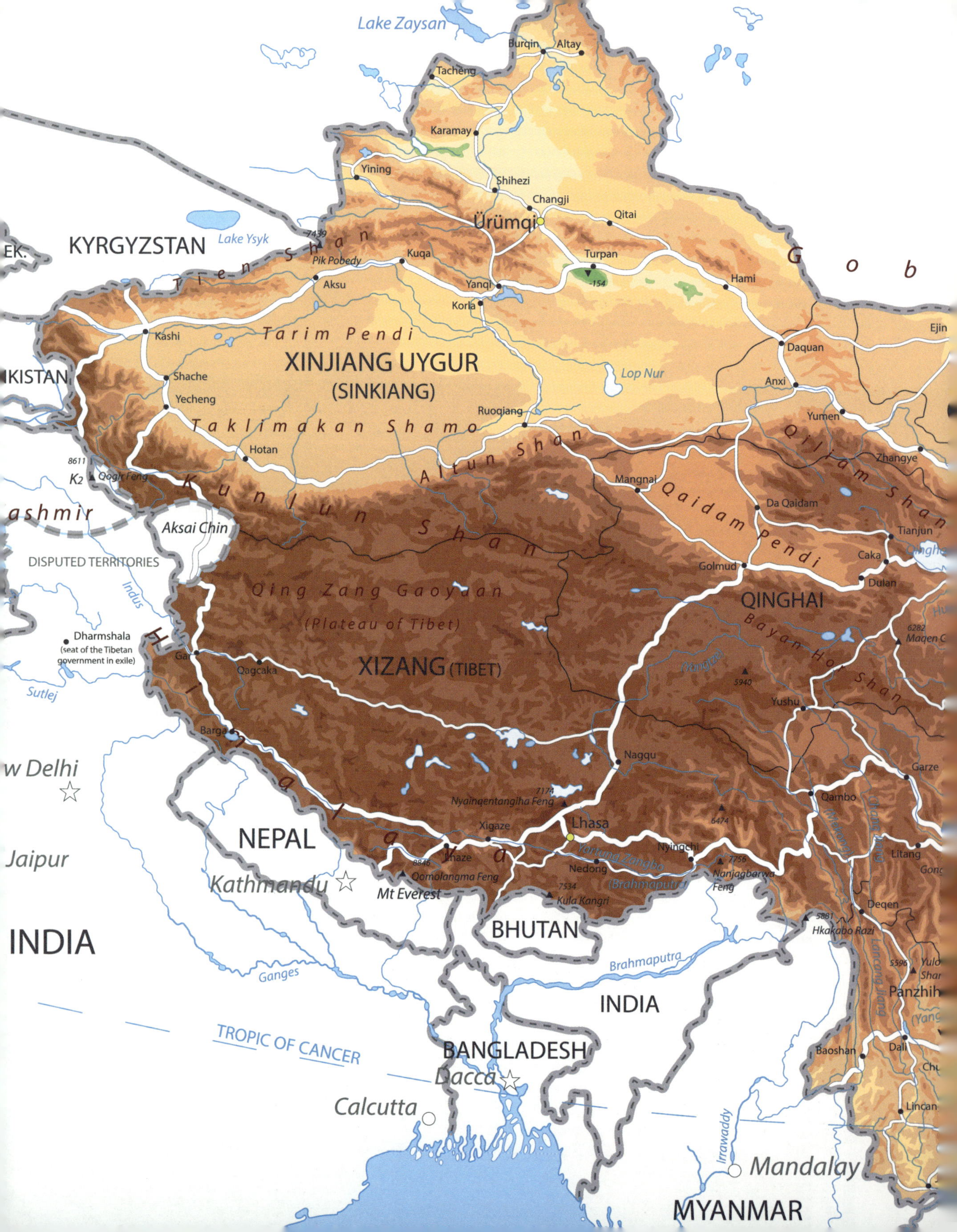
Lake Zaysan
Burqin
Altay
Tacheng
Karamay
Yining
Shihezi
Changji
Ürümqi
Qitai
Lake Ysyk
KYRGYZSTAN
Tien Shan
7439
Pik Pobedy
Kuqa
Turpan
-154
Hami
Gobi
Aksu
Yanqi
Korla
Kashi
Tarim Pendi
Ejin
Daquan
XINJIANG UYGUR
(SINKIANG)
Lop Nur
Shache
Yecheng
Anxi
Yumen
Ruoqiang
Taklimakan Shamo
Qilian Shan
Altun Shan
Hotan
Zhangye
8611
K2
Qogir Feng
Mangnai
Kunlun Shan
Qaidam Pendi
Da Qaidam
Kashmir
Aksai Chin
Tianjun
Caka
DISPUTED TERRITORIES
Golmud
Dulan
Indus
Qing Zang Gaoyuan
QINGHAI
(Plateau of Tibet)
Bayan Har Shan
6282
Maqen
Dharmshala
(seat of the Tibetan government in exile)
Gar
XIZANG (TIBET)
Qagcaka
5940
Sutlej
Yushu
Himalaya
Barga
Nagqu
Garze
New Delhi
7174
Nyainqentanglha Feng
Qambo
NEPAL
6474
Lhasa
Xigaze
Jaipur
Yarlung Zangbo
Nyingchi
Litang
8846
Lhaze
Nedong
7756
Kathmandu
Qomolangma Feng
Mt Everest
7534
Kula Kangri
(Brahmaputra)
Nanjagbarwa Feng
Deqen
5881
Hkakabo Razi
BHUTAN
INDIA
Brahmaputra
Lancang Jiang
5596
Ganges
Panzhihua
INDIA
TROPIC OF CANCER
BANGLADESH
Baoshan
Dali
Dacca
Calcutta
Lincang
Irrawaddy
Mandalay
MYANMAR

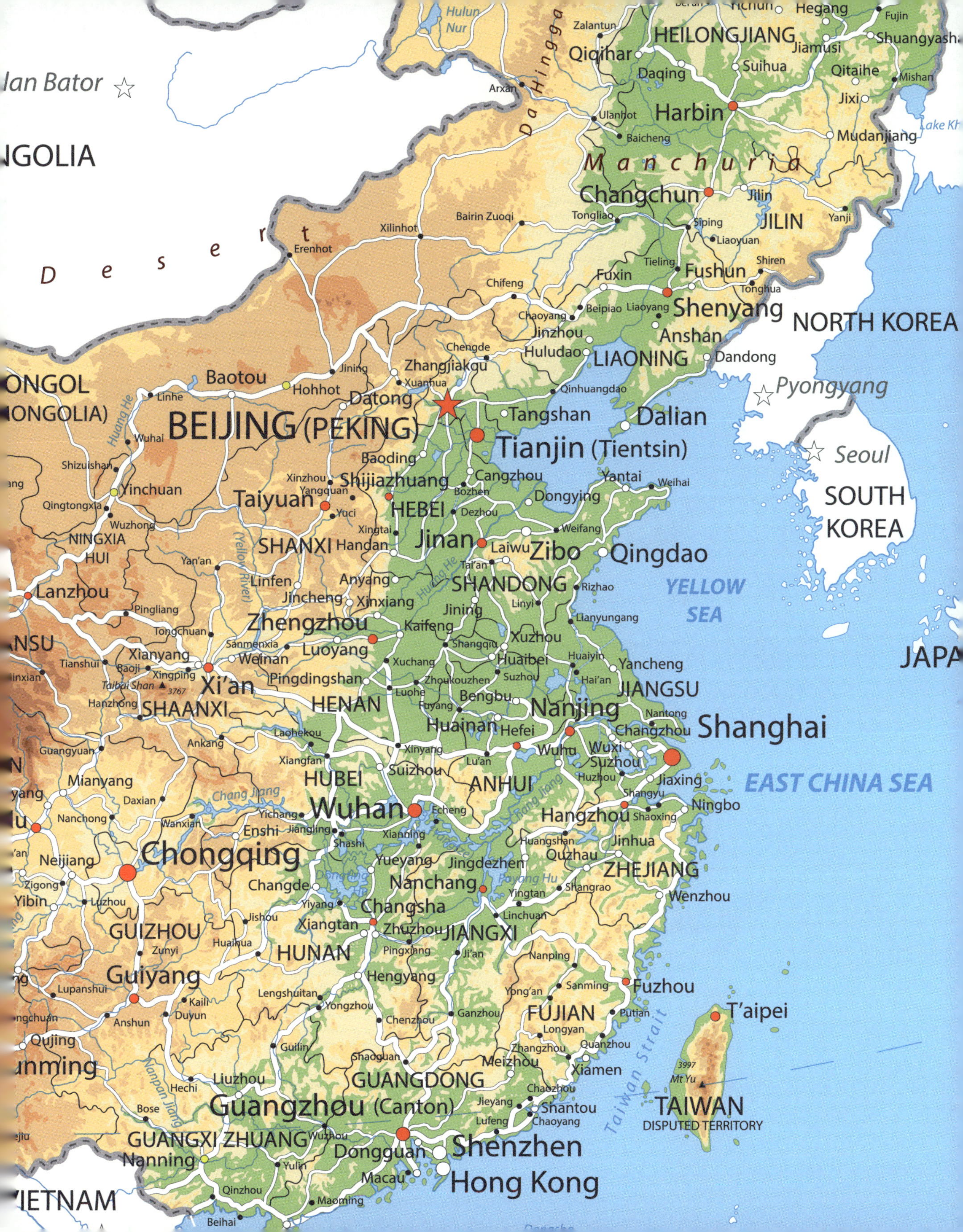

Hulun Nur
Hegang
Fujin
Zalantun
Da Hinggan
HEILONGJIANG
Qiqihar
Jiamusi
Daqing
Suihua
Qitaihe
Mishan
Arxan
Jixi
Harbin
Ulanhot
Baicheng
Mudanjiang
Manchuria
Changchun
Jilin
Bairin Zuoqi
Tongliao
Siping
JILIN
Yanji
Liaoyuan
Xilinhot
Desert
Erenhot
Tieling
Shiren
Fushun
Fuxin
Tonghua
Chifeng
Beipiao
Liaoyang
Shenyang
NORTH KOREA
Chaoyang
Jinzhou
Anshan
Chengde
Huludao
LIAONING
Dandong
Baotou
Jining
Zhangjiakou
Hohhot
Xuanhua
Qinhuangdao
Pyongyang
Linhe
Datong
Tangshan
Dalian
Huang He
BEIJING (PEKING)
Wuhai
Tianjin (Tientsin)
Seoul
Baoding
Shizuishan
Cangzhou
Yantai
Weihai
Xinzhou
Shijiazhuang
Yinchuan
Yangquan
Bozhen
Dongying
SOUTH KOREA
Qingtongxia
Taiyuan
Yuci
HEBEI
Dezhou
Wuzhong
Xingtai
Weifang
NINGXIA HUI
SHANXI
Handan
Jinan
Laiwu
Zibo
Qingdao
Yan'an
Ta'an
Yellow River
Linfen
Anyang
SHANDONG
Rizhao
YELLOW SEA
Lanzhou
Jincheng
Xinxiang
Linyi
Pingliang
Jining
Zhengzhou
Kaifeng
Lianyungang
Tongchuan
Sanmenxia
Luoyang
Shangqiu
Xuzhou
Xianyang
Weinan
Tianshui
Baoji
Xi'an
Xuchang
Huaibei
Huaiyin
Yancheng
Xingping
Taibai Shan
3767
Pingdingshan
Zhoukouzhen
Suzhou
Hai'an
Luohe
Fuyang
Bengbu
JIANGSU
Hanzhong
SHAANXI
HENAN
Nanjing
Nantong
Huainan
Hefei
Changzhou
Shanghai
Laohekou
Ankang
Wuhu
Wuxi
Guangyuan
Xiangfan
Xinyang
Lu'an
Suzhou
Suizhou
Huzhou
Jiaxing
EAST CHINA SEA
Mianyang
Daxian
HUBEI
ANHUI
Chang Jiang
Shangyu
Ningbo
Nanchong
Wanxian
Yichang
Enshi
Wuhan
Echeng
Hangzhou
Shaoxing
Jiangling
Shashi
Xianning
Huangshan
Jinhua
Chongqing
Neijiang
Yueyang
Jingdezhen
Quzhou
ZHEJIANG
Zigong
Changde
Nanchang
Poyang Hu
Shangrao
Yibin
Luzhou
Yiyang
Changsha
Yingtan
Wenzhou
Jishou
Xiangtan
Zhuzhou
JIANGXI
Linchuan
GUIZHOU
Huaihua
Zunyi
HUNAN
Pingxiang
Ji'an
Nanping
Guiyang
Hengyang
Sanming
Fuzhou
Lupanshui
Kaili
Lengshuitan
Yong'an
Duyun
Anshun
Yongzhou
FUJIAN
Putian
T'aipei
Chenzhou
Ganzhou
Longyan
Qujing
Quanzhou
Guilin
Shaoguan
Zhangzhou
3997
Mt Yu
Meizhou
Xiamen
Taiwan Strait
GUANGDONG
Hechi
Liuzhou
Chaozhou
TAIWAN
Bose
Guangzhou (Canton)
Jieyang
Shantou
Nanpan Jiang
DISPUTED TERRITORY
Lufeng
Chaoyang
GUANGXI ZHUANG
Wuzhou
Shenzhen
Nanning
Dongguan
Yulin
Macau
Hong Kong
Qinzhou
Maoming
Beihai

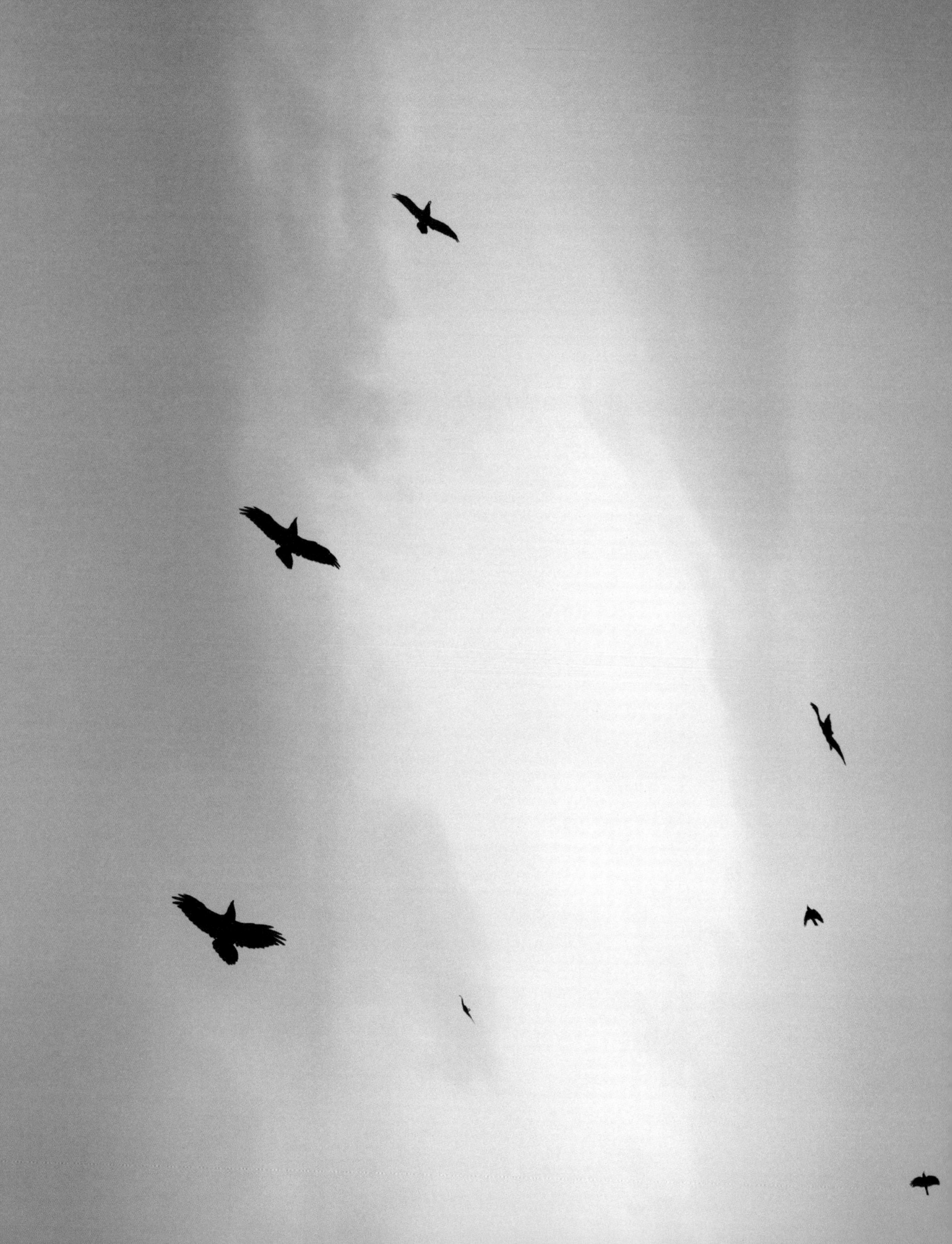

The Time of Discretion

Lisa Mara Batacchi

★

In reality going towards the frontiers of time or space is only the metaphor for a principle which everything stands on. The journey towards the essence of existence is projected, to make itself slightly apprehensible, into a journey towards the extreme frontiers of the existent. The search for the most distant therefore represents the search for the nearest to us, more intimate to the world than the world itself.

Elémire Zolla, *Che cos'è la tradizione*

Prologue

Following Bruce Chatwin's categories of "settled or wandering writers"[1], as an artist I had to question my role, sometimes feeling paralysed by my cultural and residential origins.
In 2015 I got to know one of the most chaotic parts of India. A bustling city like Bombay with its harsh social, political and economic differences, had sometimes evoked in me the idea of a parallel dimension. Probably not by chance, I had taken with me *Uscite dal mondo* by Elémire Zolla, where I could find some allusions to an enlarged experience of space: certain itineraries can suddenly appear as free spaces, offering a "sensorial fourth-dimension"[2] to the experience.
His thought suggested the possibility of some temporary escapist actions towards the edges of society. Then, the term and meaning of "discretion" came about: in *La Discrétion: ou l'art de disparaître*, Pierre Zaoui speaks of a time of discretion as a time which is nearly always perfect, fleeting and joyful "where there is not oneself nor the other, the perspective widens and the world seems wonderfully various, decentralized, distant, with thousands of escape routes which run towards the infinite"[3]. Being discreet means giving up one's own ego, narcissism or desire for power, which is not a limitation but on the contrary, it can open up a space of freedom between us and the other, a space of love, collaboration and creation.
I outlined a project then, where I could move freely "with time and at ease"[4], to possibly learn some ancient techniques for weaving, natural dyeing and embroidery, used mainly for cultural purposes.
The Time of Discretion finally took shape thanks to the invitation to participate in the 2016 Land Art Mongolia Biennale: *Catching the Axis. Between the Sky and the Earth* was the theme of the fourth edition curated by Valentina Gioia Levy.
I started thinking about carrying out a textile work, using a precise chromatic shade (of blue) which could represent that axis. I later discovered that the natural indigo color batik is still produced in southern China by the ethnic group of the Miao, who I decided to reach.

A Possible Future

The "new missionaries of materialism"[5] are making the diversity of this great world give up, and the sky is growing further from the earth. While some people's light gets weaker, making them "shadow-people", this world needs kind words from "people of light"[6] to soften their harshness.
The economic activity and technologies are bringing about a transformation of our species and

⋆

relationships, of the climate and ecosystems; so severe apparently, to make our horizon increasingly uncertain.
What does the future hold then?
I deliberately decided to find possible answers through the consultation of an ancient Chinese oracle, the *I Ching*, and I asked:
Will human beings be able to decrease this accelerating materialism and reconnect with the natural cycles of our planet? If so, when, how?
I interpreted Hexagram 40 in this way:
The world is going through a difficult time where we cannot hope for great changes, but a very strong and liberating rain will come, from which new seeds on the earth will sprout again in the future.
And its changes from Hexagram 2:
In our century the world will be able to rise again if humanity can advance with a different equilibrium. To do this, human beings must search for the creative and spiritual energy of the horse, which represents the egotistic male urge, balanced by the feminine devotion of the cow and its spatial energy which can nourish our planet.

A New Balance

The *I Ching* sentences led me to reconsider some symbols: the sky, the masculine, the egotistic, the innate creative element of the horse and its association with a continuous restless movement.
As well as: the earth, the feminine, devotion, spatial energy, a more stable spirit but constant in time, innate in the cow; and their possible relationships.
The reconstruction of the balance between these basic elements is urging humanity, as an encouragement to get back to a slower-horizontal mobility through the decrease of the vertical-fast one, by once again connecting deeply the spiritual with the spatial, as a final redemption.
I imagined then a synthesis of the two figures in a horse-cow running with its spiritual and spatial pace among the constellations as if to narrate the hopeful course of our history, from the past to the future.
However, additional suggestions still had to come from the Mongolian Steppe and the Chinese mountains.

Ghost Horses

Before the Biennale, I first passed through Ordos and Hohhot in Chinese Inner Mongolia to then go down to the south-west of China and finally to return up with the Trans Mongolian Railway from Beijing to Ulaanbaatar, the Mongolian capital.
Ordos, at the foot of the Gobi Desert, was the first setting I saw in Chinese Inner Mongolia. Here the government, which owns the mines and distributes the resources both inside and outside the country, has left room for enormous financing to create large infrastructures. About ten years ago "ORDOS 100" was created, as a project started off together with the Museum of Contemporary Art in Ordos, which consisted in asking 100 architects/artists to present proposals for modern buildings and public art for the city.
Ethnic minorities have always lived in all the isolated and desert areas, but after the 1950s the central planners saw these regions both as a mining source to be exploited and as convenient territories to encourage the surplus of the Han families (Chinese ethnicity) to relocate[7].

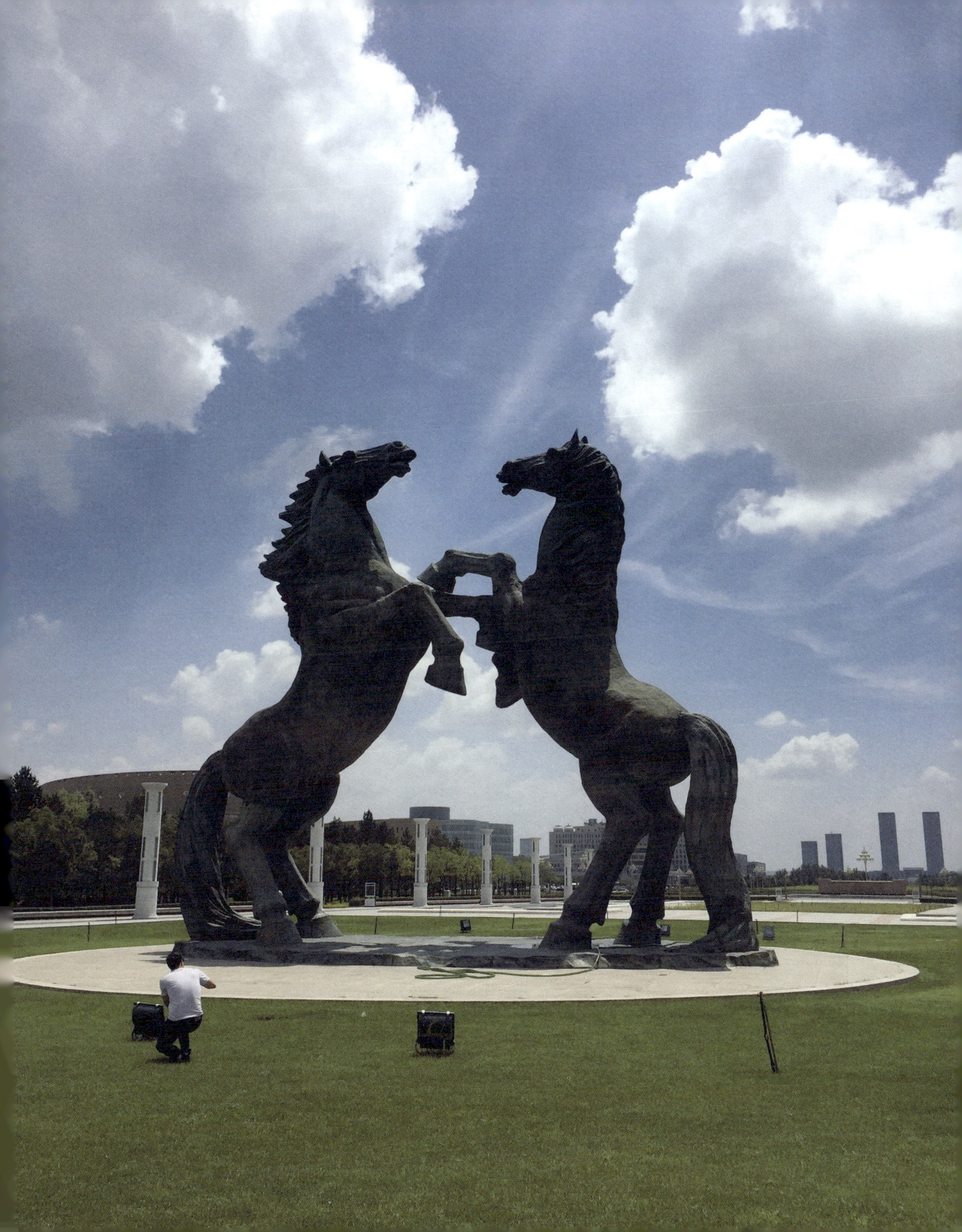

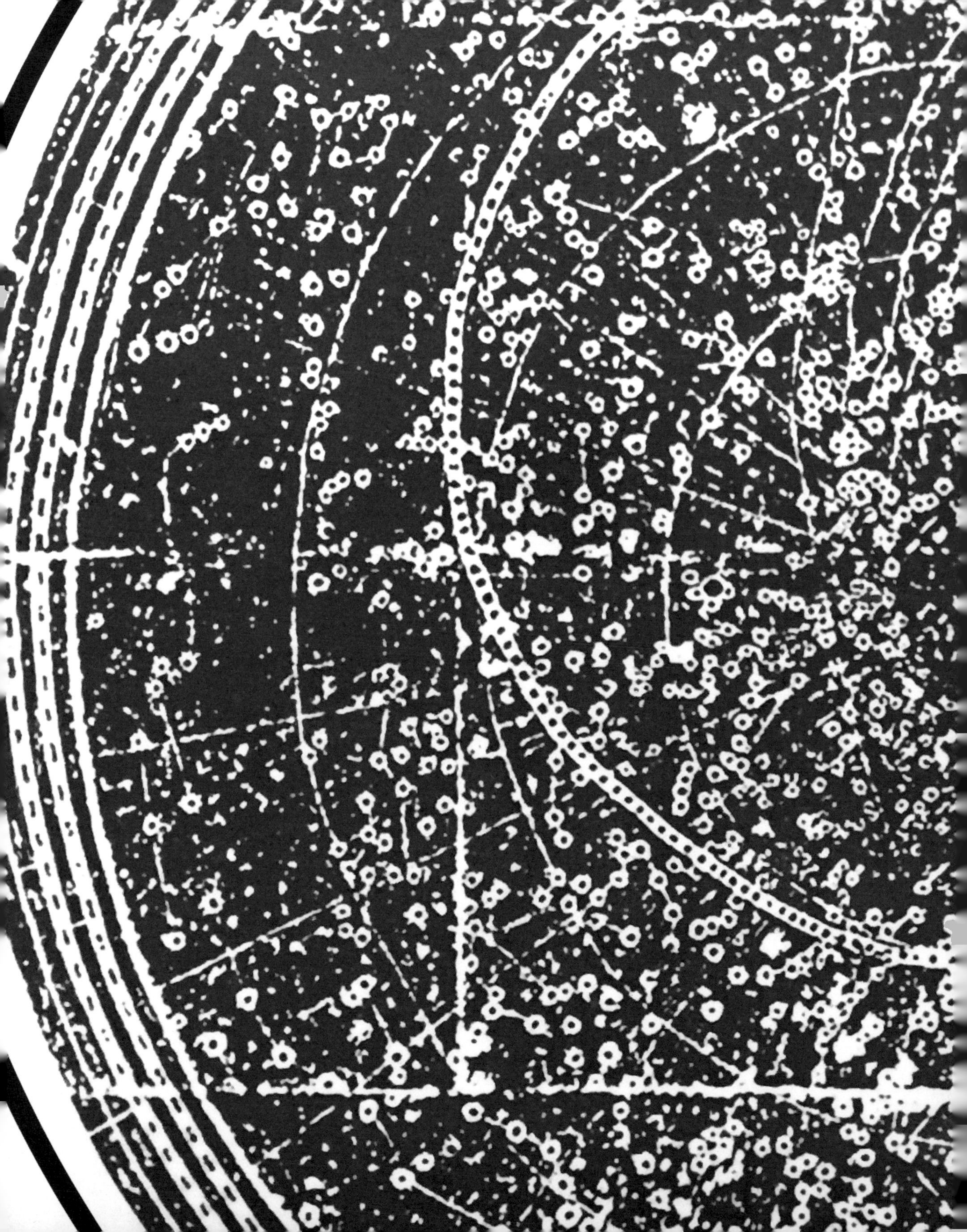

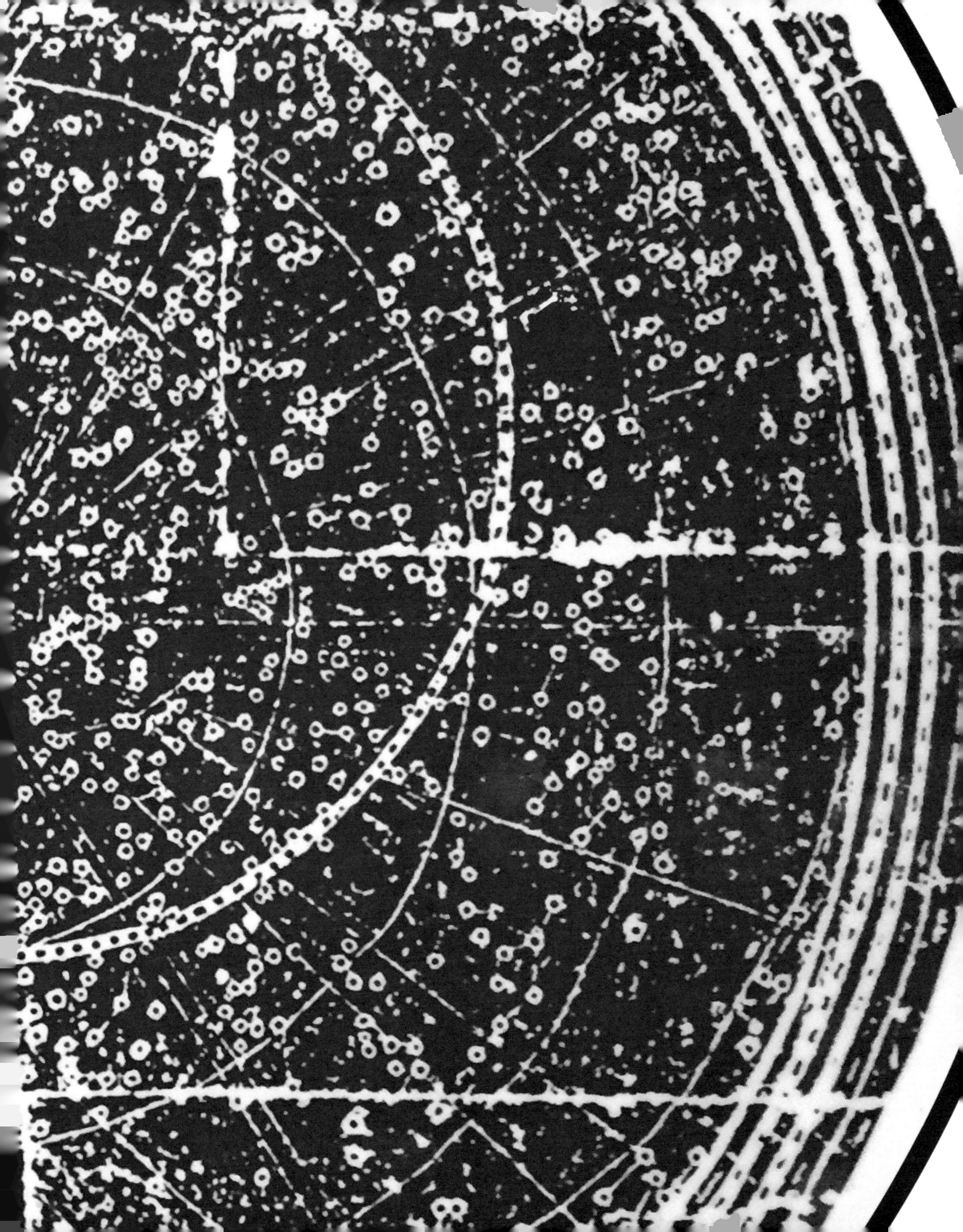

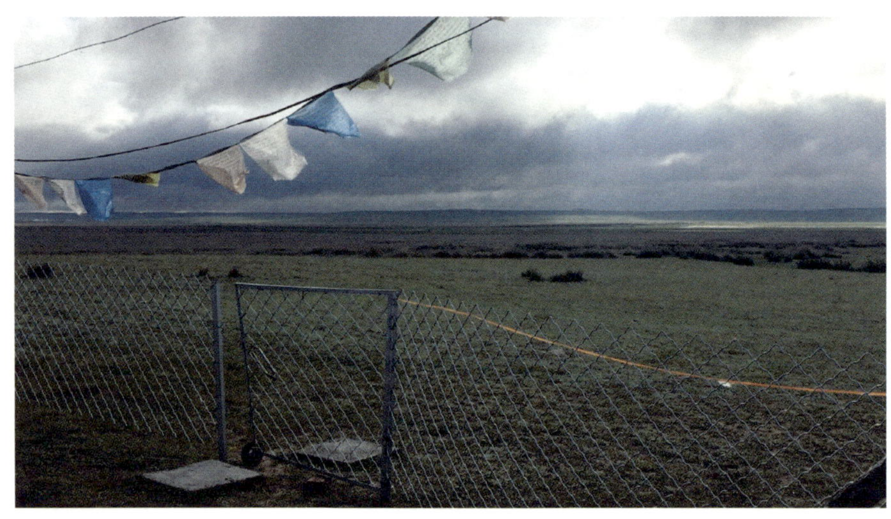

Grass Land, Inner Mongolia, China, July 26th, 2016
still from *The Time of Discretion* (film archive), 2016/2018

On the opposite page: still from the short film *The Time of Discretion*, 2019
HD, color, sound, 24:53 min

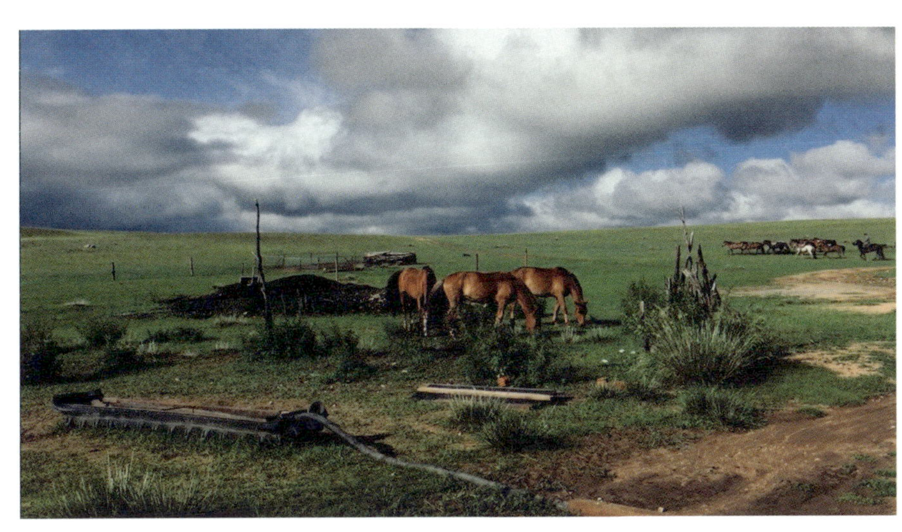

*

Despite all this, the city has more structures than people and remains more or less a ghost-town, surrounded by the desert. Besides, Ordos is no longer so rich, as the resources from coal are thinning out; furthermore, this modern city does not correspond to their inhabitants' lifestyle causing strong visual contrasts.
The two main squares are populated by very large-scale bronze figures. In the first one, there are two horses in the centre, facing each other, rising into a vertical position towards the sky with a dramatic visual impact, while in the other square, many running horses show a pace which simulates the different phases of a gallop.
The Mongolians consider this animal sacred, as over the millenniums they have established a relationship both of dependence and mystical, blending with it into a single being, characterized by the free movement in the world[8]. The horse has always portrayed their nomadic and intuitive culture, although these ghost-town monuments seem to represent only a partial identity, mainly vague and nostalgic.
The strength of the horse, wonderfully represented by the sculptor, on the other hand seems to transmit the incredible egotistical surge of the Chinese Government, which through the appropriation of that symbol, shows off its power as a great and extremely expanded People's Republic.

The Economic Miracle

I caught a train from Ordos to Hohhot and stayed at the Anda Guest House. The owners suggested I should go on an excursion by coach with a small group of people, to visit the Grassland prairies, spending two nights in a yurt together with a Mongolian family. Once I arrived, I realized that the traditional Mongolian tents no longer exist; there are only touristic ones left, with cement bases rather than wooden ones.
Thanks to an Italian girl who spoke Chinese in the group that I was with, I was able to interview one of the women who was hosting us about the possible loss of their "nomadic spirit". The woman (Angir) told us that the government was using political propaganda on the outskirts of the city, by means of large advertising posters focused on the alleviation of poverty: the promise of supporting the remote areas which had still not been touched by the economic miracle. However, she said that since 1982 the Chinese Government has fragmented the territory, marking the borders and obliging the Mongolians to settle down in brick buildings on land which from then on had to be bought from the government itself.
There have been many setbacks in progress for the Mongolian people, in particular Angir told me, although with some apprehension, that the children (including her son) mainly study Chinese culture at school, and they grow up insecure, with very few ties to their original history. She also told me that Chinese rules have led their lives to uncertainty, only making people believe in an economical hierarchy.
Rather attracted by a certain kind of "regression", the moment had arrived to experience the other side of China: the poorer areas, in the south-west of the vast country, where most of the ethnic minorities live[9].

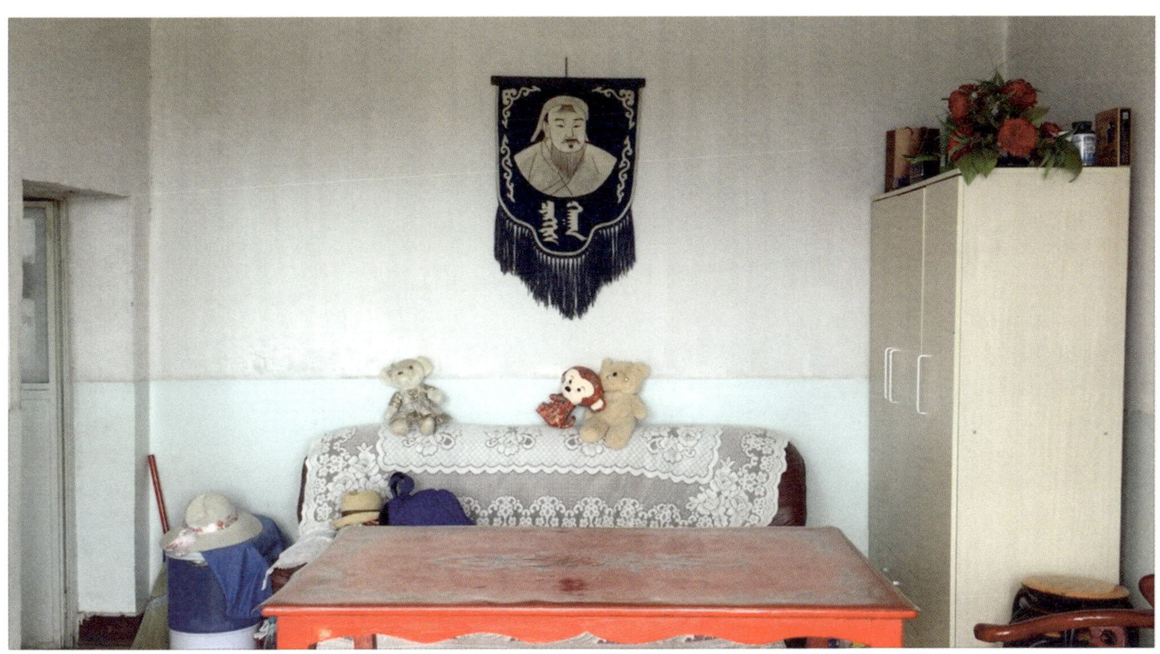

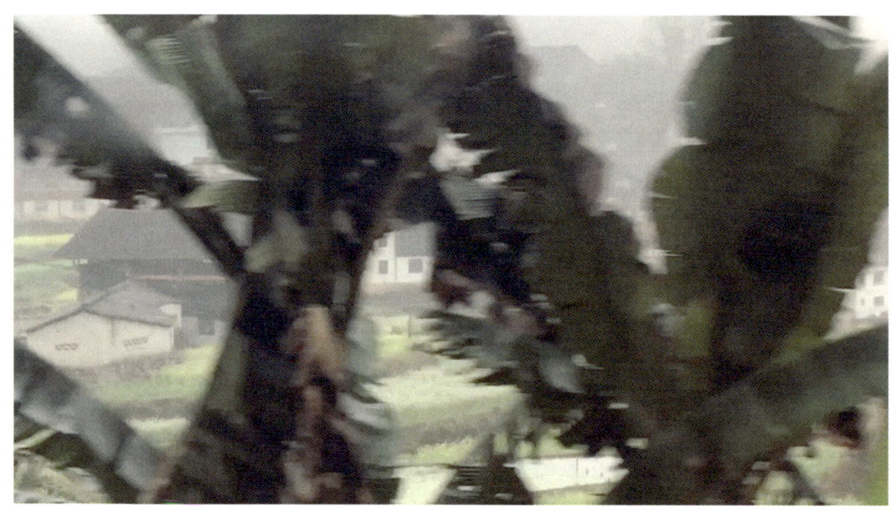

Qiandongnan Prefecture, Guizhou Province, south west China, 30th July, 2016
stills from the short film *The Time of Discretion*, 2019
HD, color, sound, 24:53 min

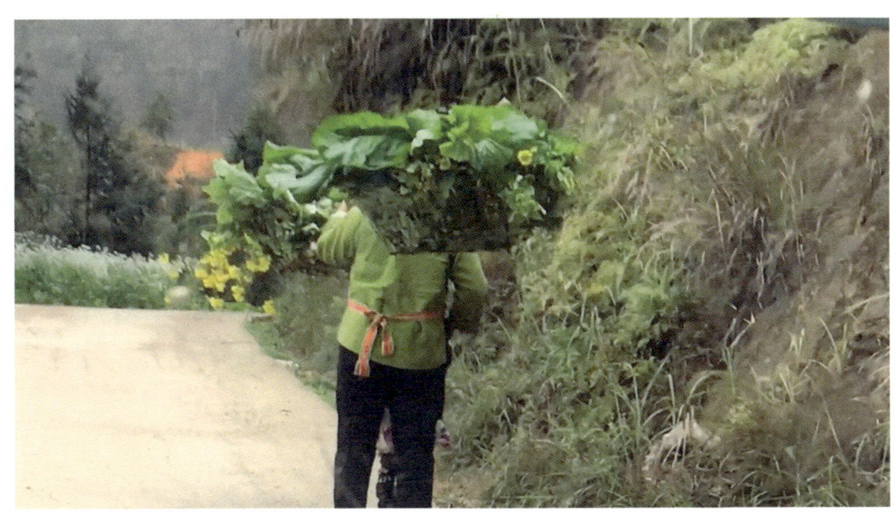

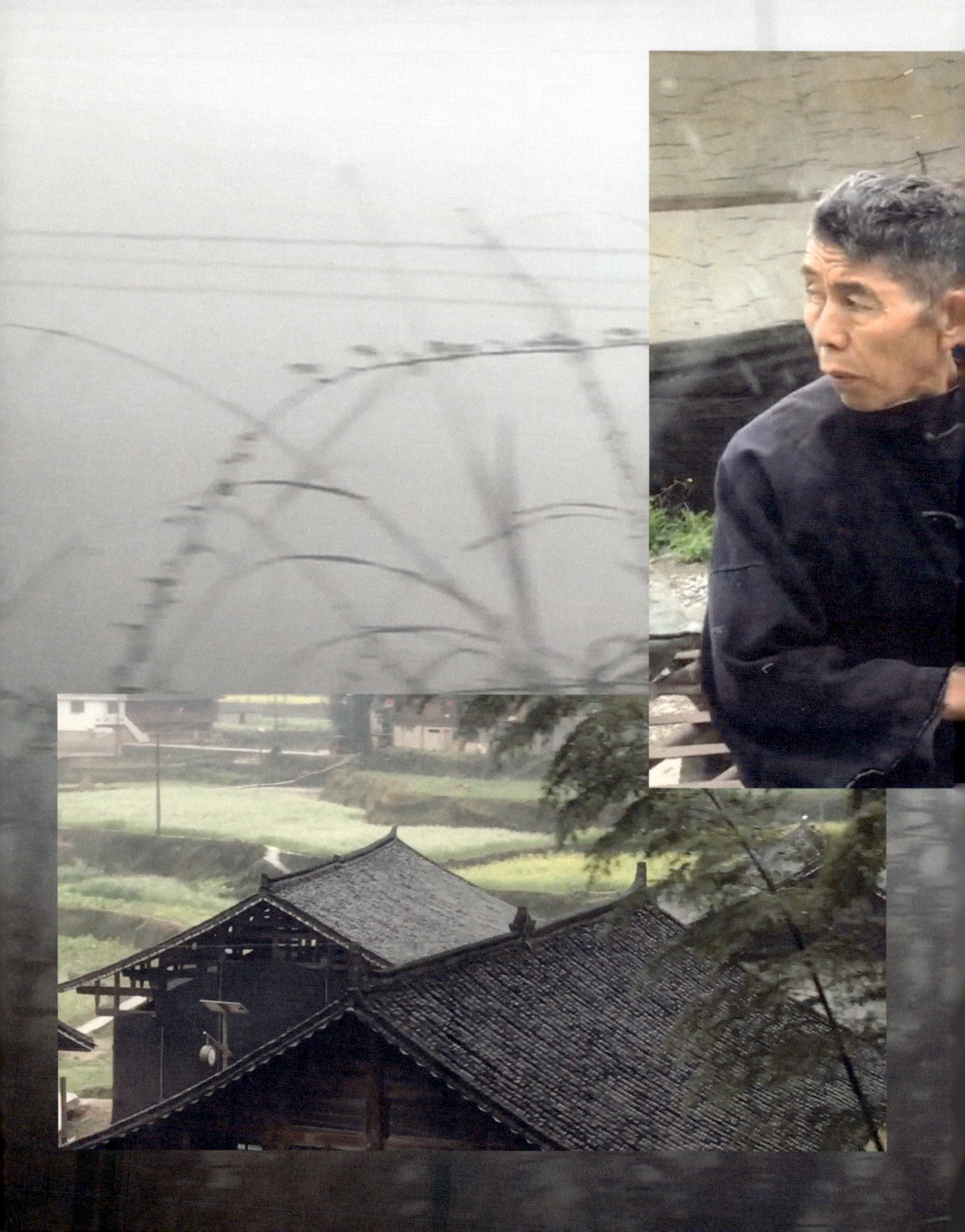

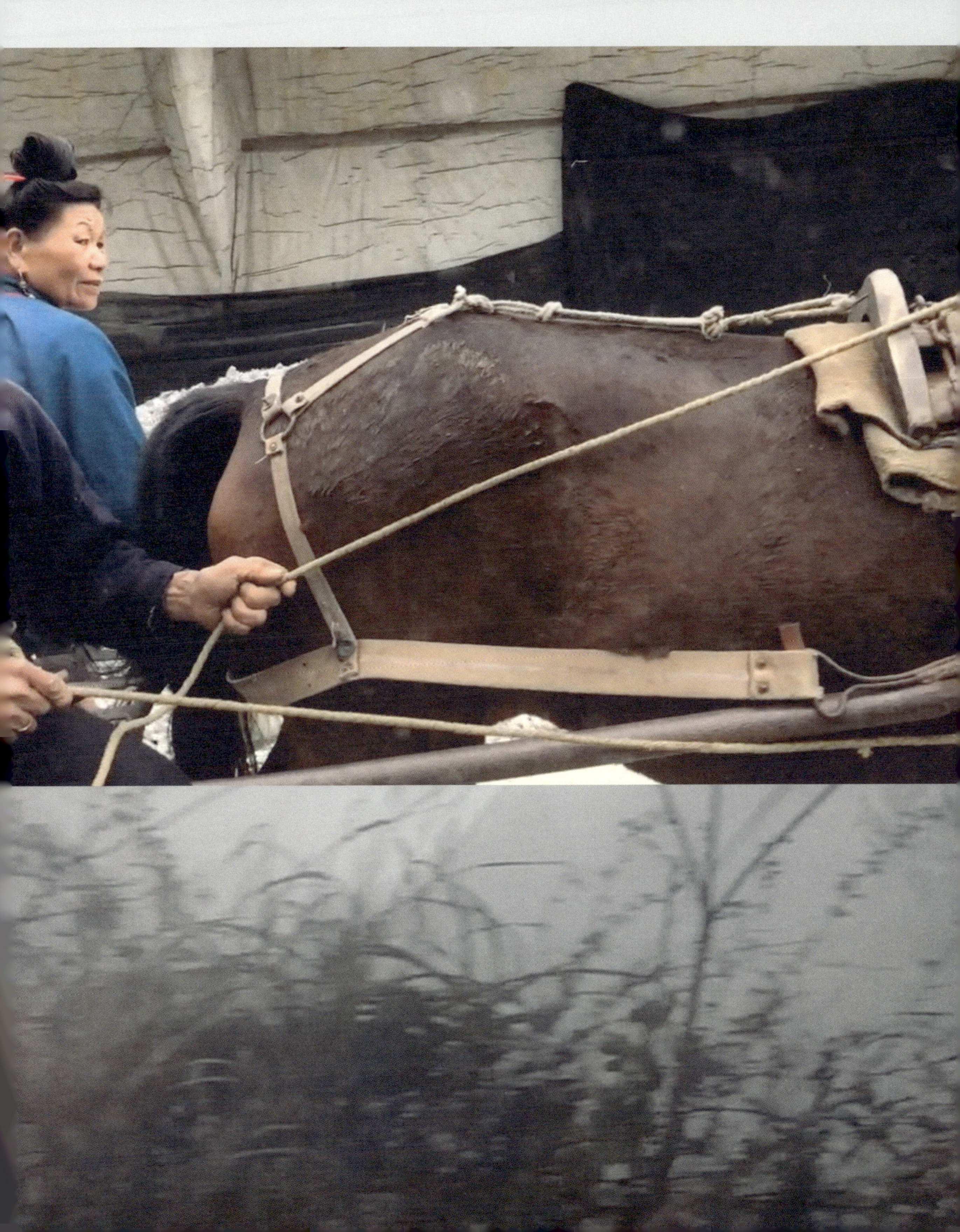

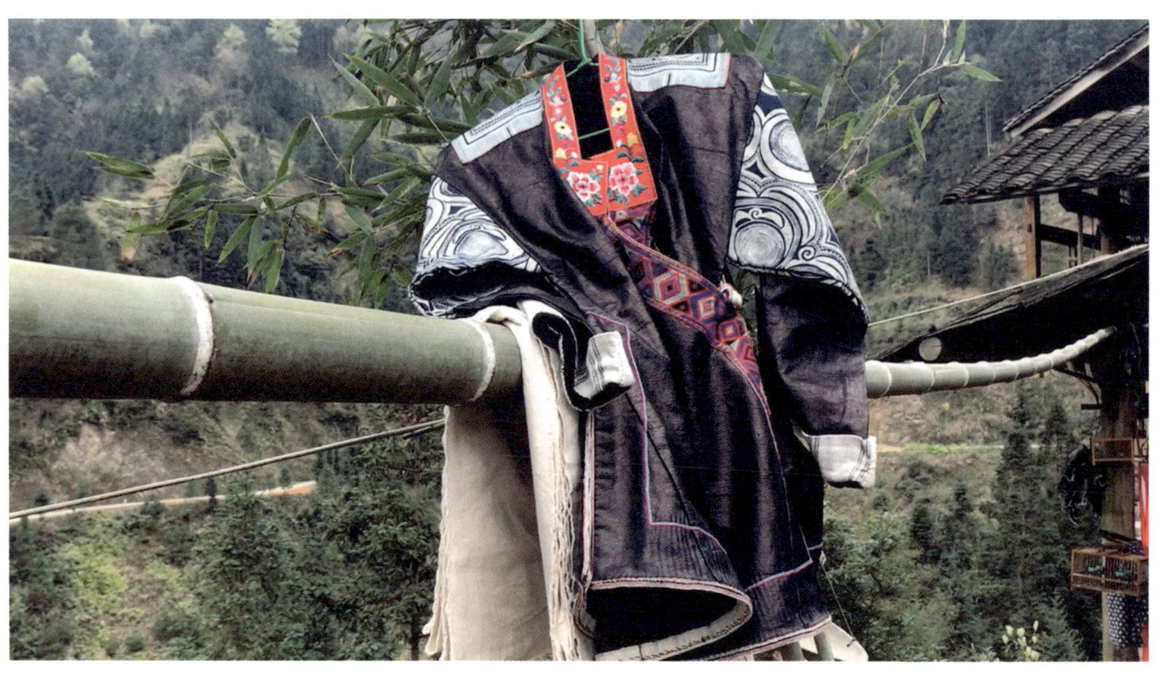

★

The Miao People

The origins of the Hmong people (usually called Miao in China[10]) go a long way back in time. From oral traditions, legends and funerary rituals, western scholars have speculated that they come from "the far north", the Arctic. This thesis was enriched by additional stories about the land they used to inhabit: a dark place for half a year, full of stars and snow, where the earth is connected to the sky[11]. Following these stories, two scholars (Savina 1924; Quincy 1988) have theorized instead that their original land was in high-latitude areas like Siberia, northern Mongolia and the most northern borders of Chinese territory[12]. However, this theory has been contested by other key scholars in Hmong and Asian Studies as there is no firm evidence of a legacy between Mongolians and Hmong/Miao people. Additional scholars (Mottin 1980: 16; Clarke 1907: 252) have claimed that the Hmong arrived in today's China about 3000 BC, even before the Chinese Han ethnic group[13]. They used to inhabit northern China, later settling down in south-western China, about two-thousand years ago[14]. The Miao people started another migration to Indocina in the early nineteenth century; later, in the aftermath of the Vietnam war, they escaped to the US (Minnesota, Wisconsin, California)[15] and to France, Canada, Australia and French Guiana[16].

Despite this long Miao/Hmong diaspora, today this ethnic minority can still be found in south-west China (mainly in Guizhou Province but also in Yunan, Guanxi, Guandong, Hunan, Sichuan and Hainan Island)[17] and in smaller communities in Vietnam, northern Thailand, Laos and Myanmar. They live mainly in the mountains, far from civilization. Keith Quincy, though, adds a further division: the "raw [Hmong] Miao" who never left the mountains and the "cooked Miao" who have instead been gradually assimilated into the dominant culture by settling in the lowlands[18].
From a cultural point of view, as the Miao don't have literature to narrate their origins, the Chinese probably used this term as a connotation of "barbarians"[19]. An often-recurring legend claims that some thousands of years ago, the Miao had their own written language but ever since the Chinese made it illegal, the women have hidden their alphabet in the embroidery and folds of their skirts[20].
Therefore, it is possible that the Miao, or rather the illiterate or pre-literate, have adopted an avant-garde method, opposing the state government by defending their cultural identity in a "*post-litteram* dimension"[21].
Using this subtle strategy of resistance, the Miao textiles hold together their cosmological world, with profound narrative, spiritual and sensorial sense. Actually, political, genealogical and historical texts are nothing but a way of profiling human beings and consequently obliging them to correspond, with taxes, property and sedentary life, to the construction of a Nation[22].

Rural and Ritual Life

Urged by the desire to track down also some cultural, philosophic-religious and historic-social elements of the Miao, on a cold and rainy winter day[23] I found myself on a coach together with Miao

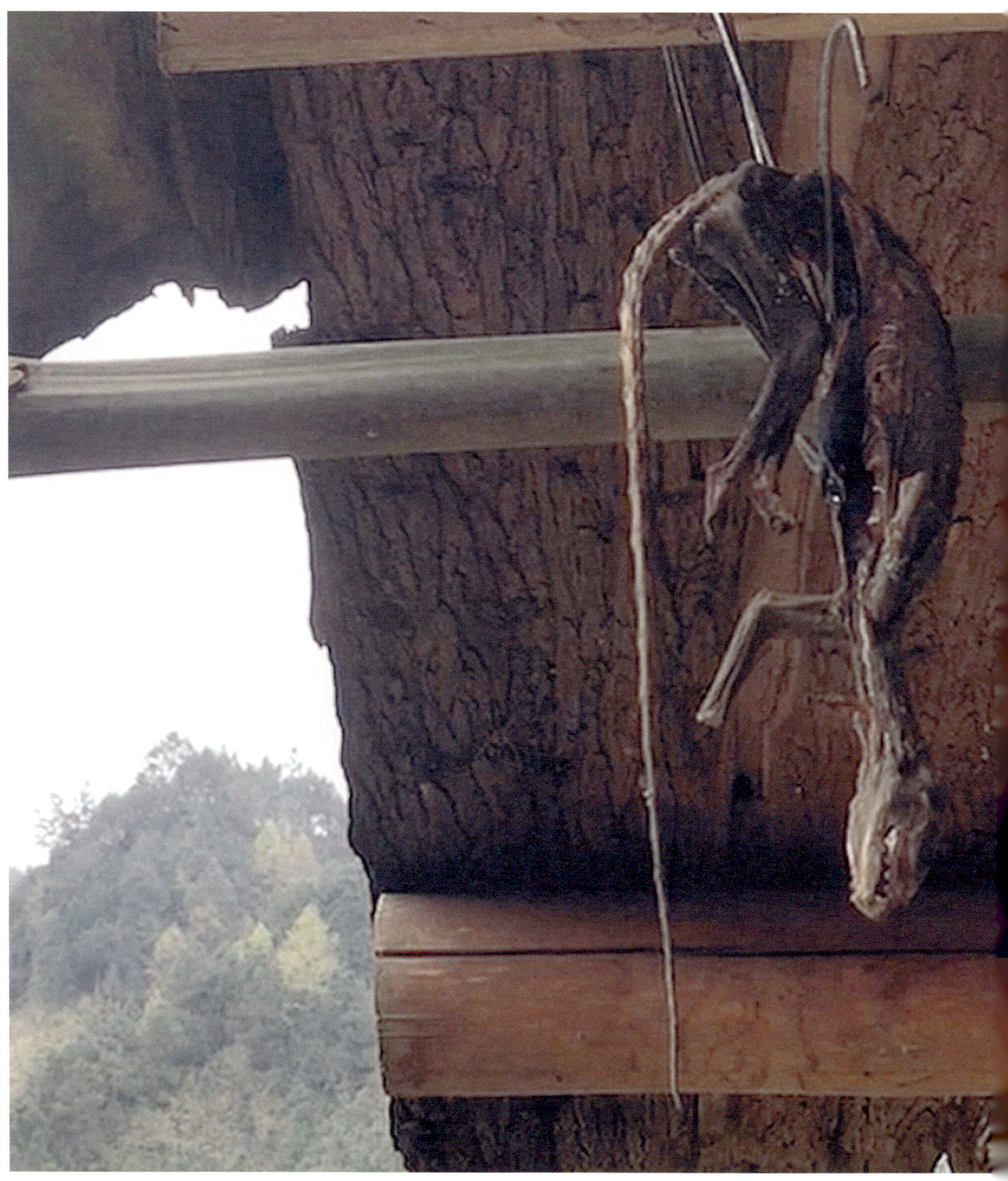

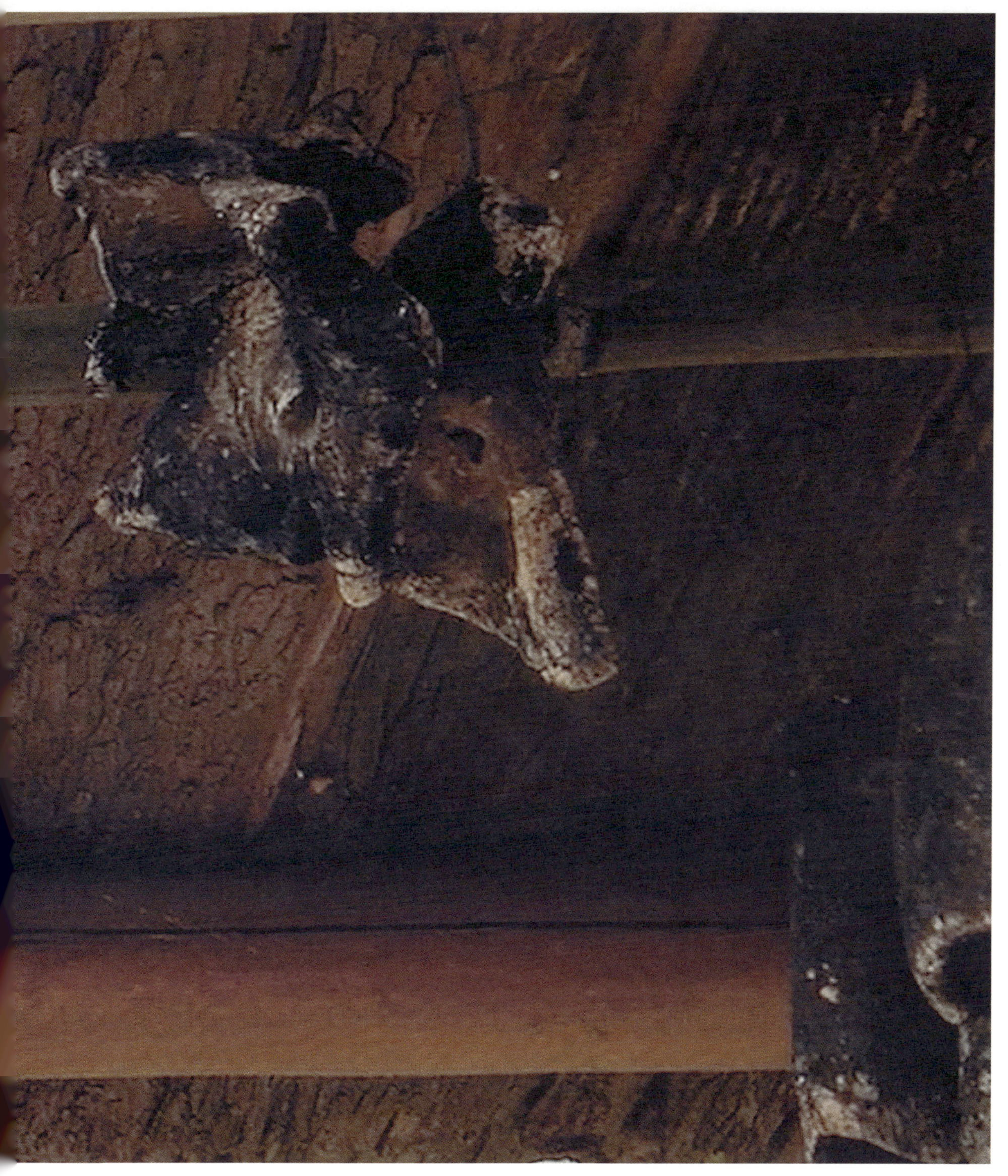

★

men and women. In fact, Chunyen Yang, a lady I was in contact with, had sent them to pick me up in the Danzhai County to take me to a remote mountain village where she lived, which was two hours away. At every turn in the road the landscape became more and more filled with trees and fog but after a good stretch of dirt road we reached the small village. I was Chunyen's guest, she is an artisan batik worker, who with her husband, a woodworker, lived in a wooden house with large terraces overlooking the greenery. The structure was in traditional Miao style, built by her husband, however, it was not insulated, nor were there window fixtures or toilets; they kept warm in winter with braziers. They had warned me about the cold and humidity at night and so I took two electric heaters as a gift. I had also taken some books about their ethnic group with me so that I could further my knowledge during my stay, as the Miao women only speak their tribal language. Chunyen was the only woman in the community who had ventured outside the village to look for work and had returned. She had learnt Chinese and used Wechat to keep up a relationship with the outside world. Through this app, with some of her Miao "sisters", Chunyen shared quite impressive vocal messages: their conversations were sung[24]. Together instead, we shared a clumsy and unrepeatable language to understand each other, with the help of the automatic translator.

One morning I found *Memory on Hands* on the kitchen table, probably the only English book in the house. Leafing through it, I found out that for the Miao women, the blue indigo flower is a bridge between humans and the spiritual world. Just like every batik artisan, every day Chunyen is used to mixing her own indigo. She believes in their own legends which I found in that book: if some bubbles come to the surface, it means that the herbal mixture is alive and that she will be protected by her guiding spirits, who will lead her back to her ancestors after her death[25].

The anthropologist Sadae Torimaru describes "The Miao world" as animated by entities that live in an isolated space, in between sky (the heavenly) and earth (the mundane) where butterflies identify their legendary ancestors, birds represent a heavenly messenger and rice seeds refer to a good life and wealth. Furthermore, flowers are associated with the nurturing of wilderness and water-buffaloes are considered noble creatures. All these symbols, like many others, are placed, rather than in the woven fabrics, in embroideries or in wax drawings on fabric, to create auspicious patterns considered more as talismans than ornaments[26]. The spiral symbol (that I have seen in the nearby Danzhai County) drawn with wax on garments, used for special ceremonies, I was told it represents instead never-ending life.

In this village, the women had given life to a small workshop in a traditional wooden house where they meet to draw in wax on cloth and create marvellous batiks, a skill they have learnt from their mothers or grandmothers and which they hand down to their daughters. These female artisans adorn themselves with earrings, bracelets, pendants, bas-relief silver hairpins. Even though dressed in their work clothes, their aprons, trousers, shirts have batik motifs and colored embroidery featuring symbolic designs. Their attention to ornaments has become a habit which they learnt when they were young, from the age of six or eight. In *Calling in the Soul: Gender and the cycle of life in a Hmong village*, Patricia

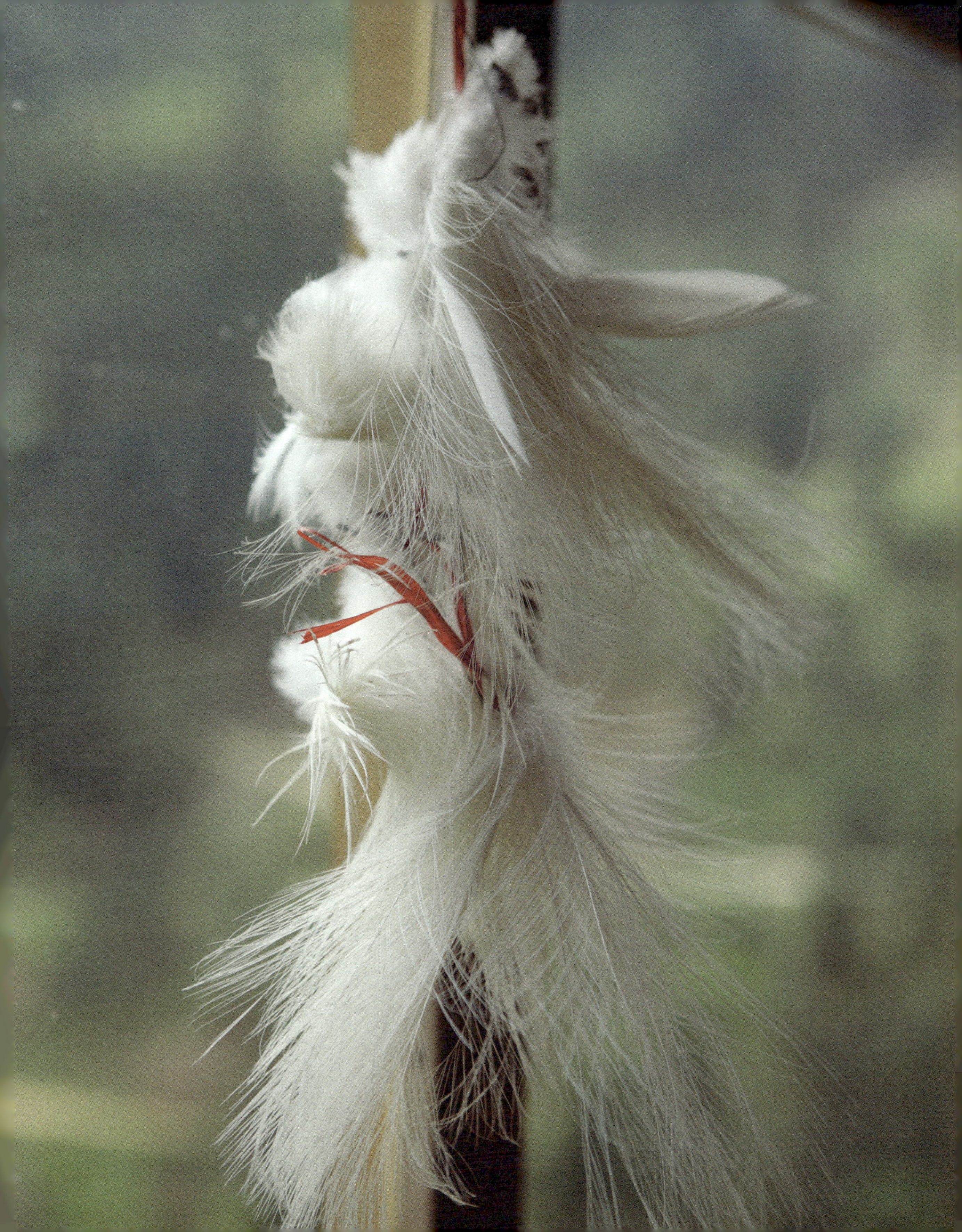

★

V. Symonds explains how together with their mothers, the young girls prepare their clothes and in particular they examine the extravagant ones for when they start looking for a husband. In fact, it is thought that a Miao woman can have more or less fascinating influence over a man (looking for a wife), according to her textile skills and the richness of the embroidery on her clothes; as her ability and patience in the needlework can also predict if she will become a good mother, wife and housekeeper. The specific dresses for weddings, funerals, traditional festivities and the liminal periods of birth and death would be prepared with more dedication and care than the others, resulting in sheer masterpieces[27].

There I had dyed some local yarn of raw cotton in a lighter shade of indigo than their traditional one. With their help, I wanted to carry out some tests on textiles using Chunyen's weaving-loom. I commissioned Chunyen with the first work and simply the process of changing threads was already the demonstration of an astonishing mastery.

My days there were all quiet, only soothed by the voice of the greengrocer amplified by a small rudimental megaphone throughout the valley, every day at the same time. One day though I was woken up by a different and hypnotic sound. I reached the house loggia, where I found a figure with his back to me, dressed in a long black tunic, wearing a straw hat and a basket on his arm containing some cloth. He was singing continuously and rhythmically.

He was the village shaman, he had come to visit Chunyen who had been suffering from hearing problems for some weeks. Chunyen's ceremonial jacket was hung on a tree with a crutch, tied, with a long trailing thread, to the table. The thread itself is a metaphor of the connection between the altar and the shaman's spirit helpers[28]. On the table some sacrificial objects had been arranged: two large round bowls filled with uncooked rice, another smaller one which also contained an egg, some banknotes, two trays with raw fish on them (of an odd quantity), six bowls all upside down except for one. Incense was placed on the rustic altar and around it; still as an offering to the spirits, close by there were a tied suckling pig and a hen in a basket-cage, which would later be cooked and eaten by all those who were there. During his ceremony, the shaman seemed to go into a trance, isolating himself from the people around him. With his mantra which had no beginning or end, like a spiritual "minister" he seemed to search for that intimate communication between physical reality (Earthly Kingdom) and the metaphysical one (Celestial Kingdom)[29].

Contrary to westerners who believe that each human being corresponds to one "soul", the Hmong believe it is composed of twelve souls (guiding plants and animals together with the sun and the moon which form a single vital system)[30]. Illness arrives when one or more souls dissociate from the body. In these cases, the shaman intervenes, thanks to his incessant chant which leads him to reaching a state of dissociated consciousness, visualising the collocation of the dissociated souls and convincing them, through the offerings, to return to the body[31].

The shaman carried out his performance of healer of souls with extreme gentleness, simplicity and dedication as if he wanted to re-establish the necessary faith inside Chunyen, in her future physical recovery.

I had reached that special village thanks to my friend

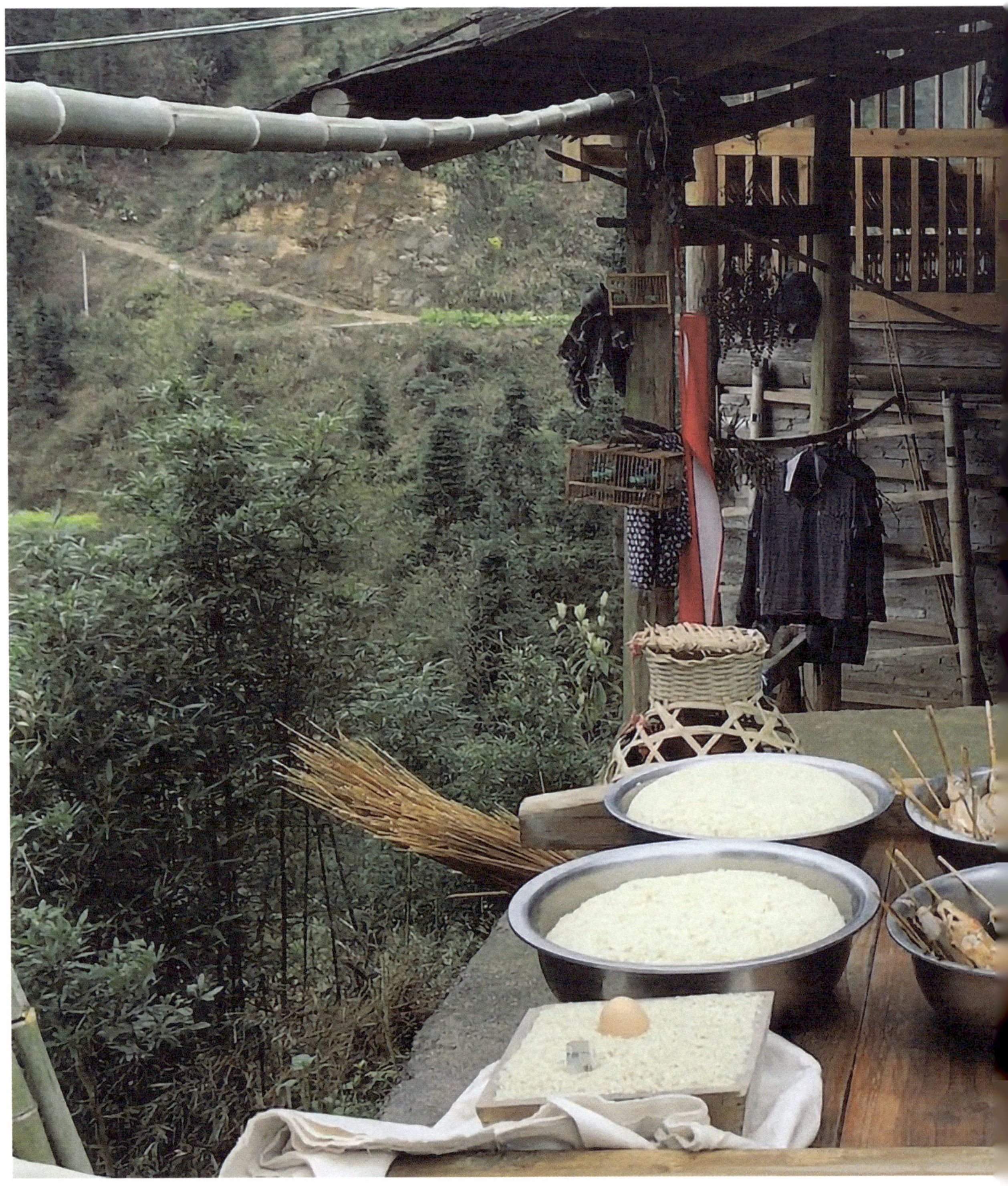

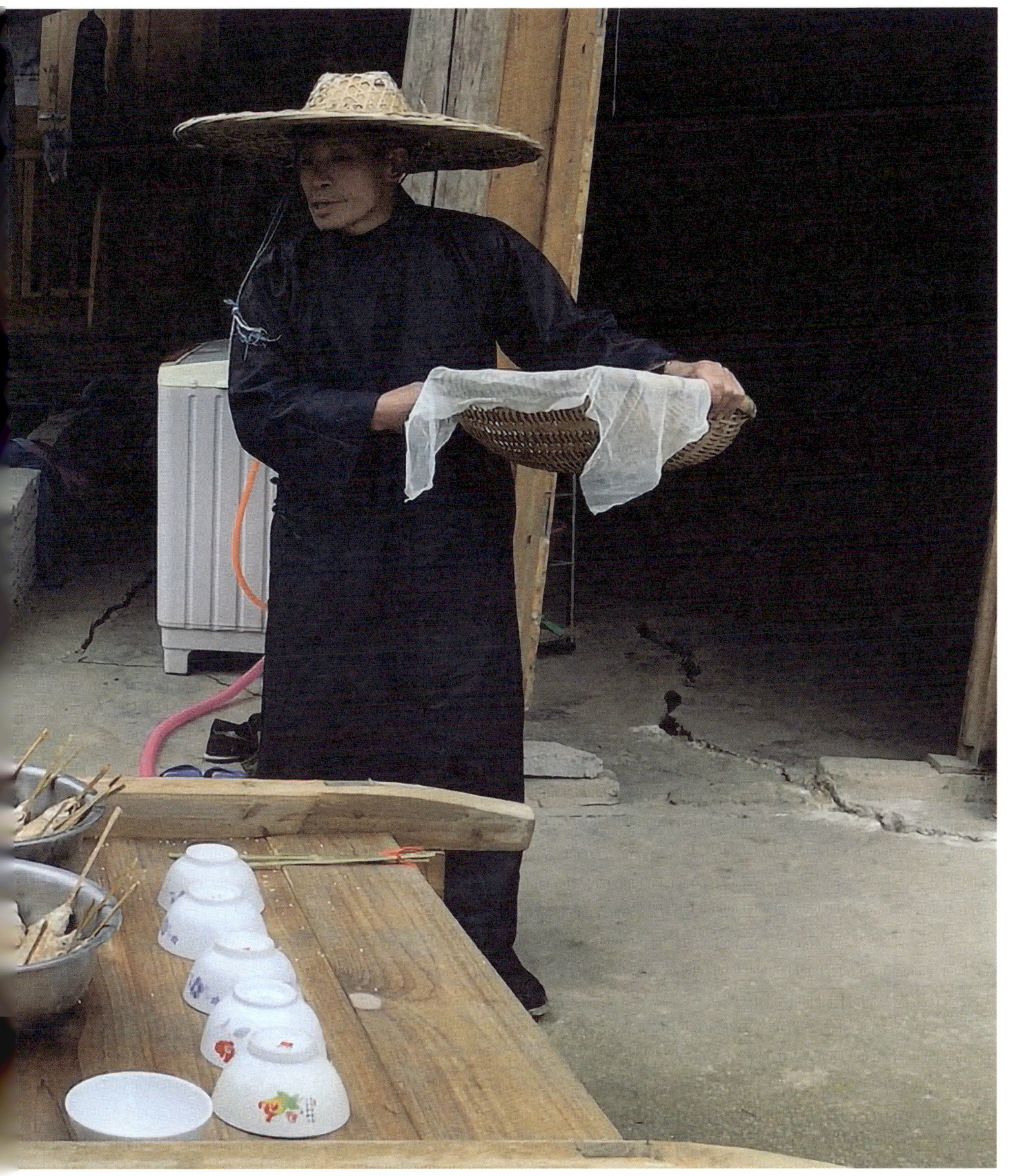

★

Julie Peters Desteract, who had previously visited the Guizhou Province several times a year, until she became a "sister" of the Miao women both from Danzhai and the community of this mountain area. She wanted me to promise I would not reveal the name of this village, as she believes it to be one of the few tiny places left which "modernization" has not invaded yet.

Traces of Taoism

One day, a young American woman got in touch with me on Wechat, her name was Sarah Horowitz, she was a Macalester College graduate and U.S. Fulbright student in China. I learnt that she had passed through the village before and was quite impressed by the untraditional pale-blue yarn on Chunyen's weaving-loom. That's how she got to know about a "foreigner wandering around the county". Sarah invited me to meet up with her for some days in Guiyang at a non-governmental organization, the "Blue Flower Courtyard", where she was working on projects for the protection of local ethnic minorities. On this occasion I met Wang Xiaomei, the director of the NGO, chief correspondent of the Citibank Handicraft Development Program, founder of the Guizhou Anthropology Association: the author, among other books, of *Memory on Hands*. She wanted to know more about my latest project in China and I told her about my *Curtain*'s design, which features some elements connected to numerology and ancient Chinese cosmology: for example, high up and in the centre of the composition there is an eight-pointed star which corresponds to "the eight winds which evoke the surge in all directions of what determined the properties of space and time just like on the compass rose"[32]. On the two sides of the composition there is a repeated element with seven points, as this number symbolizes "the rising of a secret ambition"[33], or a new start to life (despite its excesses and dangers). The central horse-cow is then plunged into a trustful dimension, still always subjected to the changes both of the Yang (male-urged egotism) and the Yin (female-urged devotion), in the Celestial and Earthly Kingdom. After having listened to that, Xiaomei first led me to verifying a few of my intuitions about the Miao culture. She told me that between the two ethnic groups (Han and Miao) there has never been a peaceful coexistence, but it seems that the Miao have absorbed the Taoist culture from the Han. Therefore, after the Maoist Cultural Revolution, China has lost every connection with its ancient traditions and the Taoist culture has been preserved in the impervious mountain areas where all the non-Han ethnic minority groups have been confined. So, the *I Ching* (that I consulted at the very first steps of my project) found its final relevance in the Hmong/Miao culture.

She later brought me some cloth from her collection, an antique Miao batik design called horse-hoof print: abstract (not figurative, like those produced recently by the community for tourists) and meant for ritualistic use; with no component to be changed (otherwise it would fail in its effect). She told me that this pattern can be read as follows: in the centre of the upper square there is a small circle, which represents the place the Miao originated from, that is the North star, where their lives began and where they hope to return after their death. Their ancestors live there, and the Miao people hope to be protected

★

by wearing this cloth, the size of a headscarf, put on their backs during certain festivities. Xiaomei pointed out that it also has a strong tie with the Taoist philosophy, astrology and numerology, due to the repetition of some numbers. Five indicates the Five elements (earth, water, fire, wood, metal) with the earth in the middle. I also noticed that the shape of the hoof is made up of twelve parts and could refer to the "Twelve meridians" in the human body which regulate all the vital circulations[34]. Xiaomei continued telling me specifically about the horse-hoof which illustrates an ancient connection of the Miao with the horse as they had been warriors in the thousands of years of war against the Chinese (Han) and therefore nomads, before becoming sedentary and substituting it with the cow, as the suitable animal for the new rural life. To communicate with the ancestors, during the funeral rituals, in fact, the horse is still the privileged animal for transporting the effigy to a mountain top, attracting the spirits who arrive to welcome the deceased. The body then takes the place of the effigy and is buried to make it join its ancestors in the beyond. So, for the Miao, the horse is the animal which reconnects the dead with the North star.

As for the ancient Mongolian culture: the mare is imagined as a heroine running at the limits of life and death on the golden frontier of the universe[35]. At the end of our meeting, Xiaomei decided to give me that cloth as a gift.

A Team Game

During my first experience in 2016, before acquiring any knowledge about the Miao people, in our difficulty with communications, using gestures, smiles and songs, there had never been a lack of reciprocal curiosity. This led me to retrieve an instinctive feeling of spontaneous interaction, like that of our childhood, based on a simple conviviality. I recognized a certain affinity among us women, as I did not perceive their cultural context as foreign. Instead, we seemed to have established an agreement which was "beyond words", stronger than simple "passing feelings"[36], articulated by the sharing of everyday life and the hard work on my large *Curtain*. Thanks to Ho Min (Gioia), a dear Chinese friend who joined us to support me in the final days of this work, I had been able to interact more deeply with two Miao women, Na Jin Yang and Guang Lian Yang (nicknamed Lala and Napon), in a wonderful and unforgettable female team game. Together we followed a slow process, harmonious, at the same time meticulous and intense which made us stop every now and then to massage each other's shoulders or to dance happily. Thanks to the time spent in their company I had learnt to draw on cloth in hot wax. One evening I finally managed to finish my design and was walking to my place, a small and not very clean but cheap rooming house. Along the way I noticed some small white circles on the street, probably drawn with chalk, with piles of sheets of paper burning inside. It is a widespread ritual in the city of Danzhai, carried out in front of every workplace. It is used to fend off evil spirits and to wish for a flourishing business. I hoped it was a sign of good luck also for my curtain, which the next day was to be gradually immersed in a large vat of indigo, prepared by Lala and four other Miao women: to finally create the various shades of blue that I longed for.

*

[1] Bruce Chatwin, *Anatomy of Restlessness*, London: Jonathan Cape Ltd, 1996.
[2] Elémire Zolla, *Uscite dal mondo*, Milan: Adelphi, 1992.
[3] Pierre Zaoui, *La Discrétion: ou l'art de disparaître*, Paris: Autrement, coll. Les grands mots, 2013.
[4] See "At Ease" chapter in Giorgio Agamben, *The Coming Community*, Minnesota: University of Minnesota Press, 1993 (*La comunità che viene*, Turin: Einaudi, 1990).
[5] Tiziano Terzani, *A Fortune-Teller Told Me*, Glasgow: HarperCollins UK, 1997 (*Un indovino mi disse*, Milan: Rusconi, 1995).
[6] See concepts of "shadow-people" and "people of light" in Gombojav Mend-Ooyo, *Altan Ovoo: The Golden Hill*, En. tr. Simon Wickham-Smith, Ulaanbaatar: self published, 2007, p. 170.
[7] See Stevan Harrell, *Ways of Being Ethnic in South West China*, Seattle: University of Washington Press, 2001, p. 51.
[8] See Mend-Ooyo, *Altan Ovoo*, op. cit.
[9] After three weeks I arrived with my batik to Mongolia where I joined the Biennale group, made up of artists, curators and organizers. We stayed in yurts mounted for us in the Dariganga area, located in a steppe in the south-east of the Gobi Desert, where my performance later took place.
[10] "Miao is the Mandarin term for Hmong", in Xiaomei Wang, *Memory on Hands. The Life Stories of Sister Yang and Sister Li*, Guizhou: Guizhou Educational Press, 2015, p. VI.
[11] Gary Yia Lee, "Cultural Identity in Post-Modern Society: Reflections on What is a Hmong?", *Hmong Studies Journal*, vol. 1, no. 1 (Fall 1996: http://hmongstudies.com/LeeCulturalIdentHSJv1n1.pdf).
[12] Gary Yia Lee, "Diaspora and the Predicament of Origins: Interrogating Hmong Postcolonial History and Identity", *Hmong Studies Journal*, (2008), p. 4.
[13] *Ibidem*, p. 17.
[14] Tomoko Torimaru, *One Needle, One Thread: Miao (Hmong) Embroidery and Fabric Piecework from Guizhou, China*, exhibition catalogue (21 September – 30 November 2008), Honolulu: University of Hawai'i Art Gallery, 2008, p. 7.
[15] Chia Youyee Vang, *People of Minnesota. Hmong in Minnesota*, Minnesota: Minnesota Historical Society Press, 2008, p. 1.
[16] Nicholas Tapp, Gary Yia Lee, *The Hmong of Australia: Culture and Diaspora*, Canberra: Anu Press, 2010, pp. 18–19.
[17] Angela Sheng (ed.), *Writing with Thread: Traditional Textiles of Southwest Chinese Minorities*, exhibition catalogue (21 September – 30 November 2008), Honolulu: University of Hawai'i Art Gallery, 2008, p. 7.
[18] Keith Quincy, *Hmong: History of A People*, Chaney: Eastern Washington University Press, 1988, p. 12.
[19] See Charles F. McKhann's Preface in *The Art of Ethnography. A Chinese "Miao Album"*, Seattle: University of Washington Press, 2006, p. XI.
[20] Geraldine Craig, "Neej Tawg Rog (War-torn People): Linguistic Consciousness in the Hmong Diaspora", in *Textiles and Politics: Textile Society of America 13th Biennial Symposium Proceedings*, Washington, DC, September 18–2, 2012: http://digitalcommons.unl.edu/cgi/viewcontent.cgi?article=1670&context=tsaconf.
[21] *Ibidem*.
[22] James C. Scott, *The Art of Not Being Governed: An Anarchist History of Upland Southeast Asia*, New Haven: Yale University Press, 2009, p. 7.
[23] I made a second trip to Guizhou in 2017.
[24] One of these conversations was recorded and used in my short film *The Time of Discretion*, 2019.
[25] See Wang, *Memory on Hands*, op. cit., p. 278.
[26] Sadae Torimaru, *Spiritual Fabric. 20 Years of Textile Research among the Miao People of Guizhou, China*, Fukuoka City: The Nishinippon Newspaper Co., 2006, pp. 132–135.
[27] Patricia V. Symonds, *Calling in the Soul: Gender and the cycle of life in a Hmong village*, Seattle: University of Washington Press, 2004, pp. 19–20, 49.
[28] Jacques Lemoine, "Commentary: The (H)mong Shamans' Power of Healing: Sharing the Esoteric Knowledge of a Great Mong Shaman", *Hmong Studies Journal*, vol. 12 (2011), pp. 14–15.
[29] Dwight Conquergood, *Establishing the World: Hmong Shamans*, Minneapolis: Center for Urban and Regional Affairs, University of Minnesota, 1989, p. 7.
[30] See Lemoine, "Commentary...", op. cit., p. 7.
[31] *Ibidem*, pp. 6–7.
[32] See the Introduction to, Elisabeth Rochat De La Vallée, *The Symbolism of Numbers in Classical China, Chinese Medicine from the Classics*, tr. Nora Franglen, London: Monkey Press, 2018.
[33] Ibid., chapter seven.
[34] Ibid., chapter twelve.
[35] See Mend-Ooyo, *Altan Ovoo*, op. cit.
[36] See Unni Wikan, *Resonance: Beyond the Words*, Chicago: University of Chicago Press, 2013.

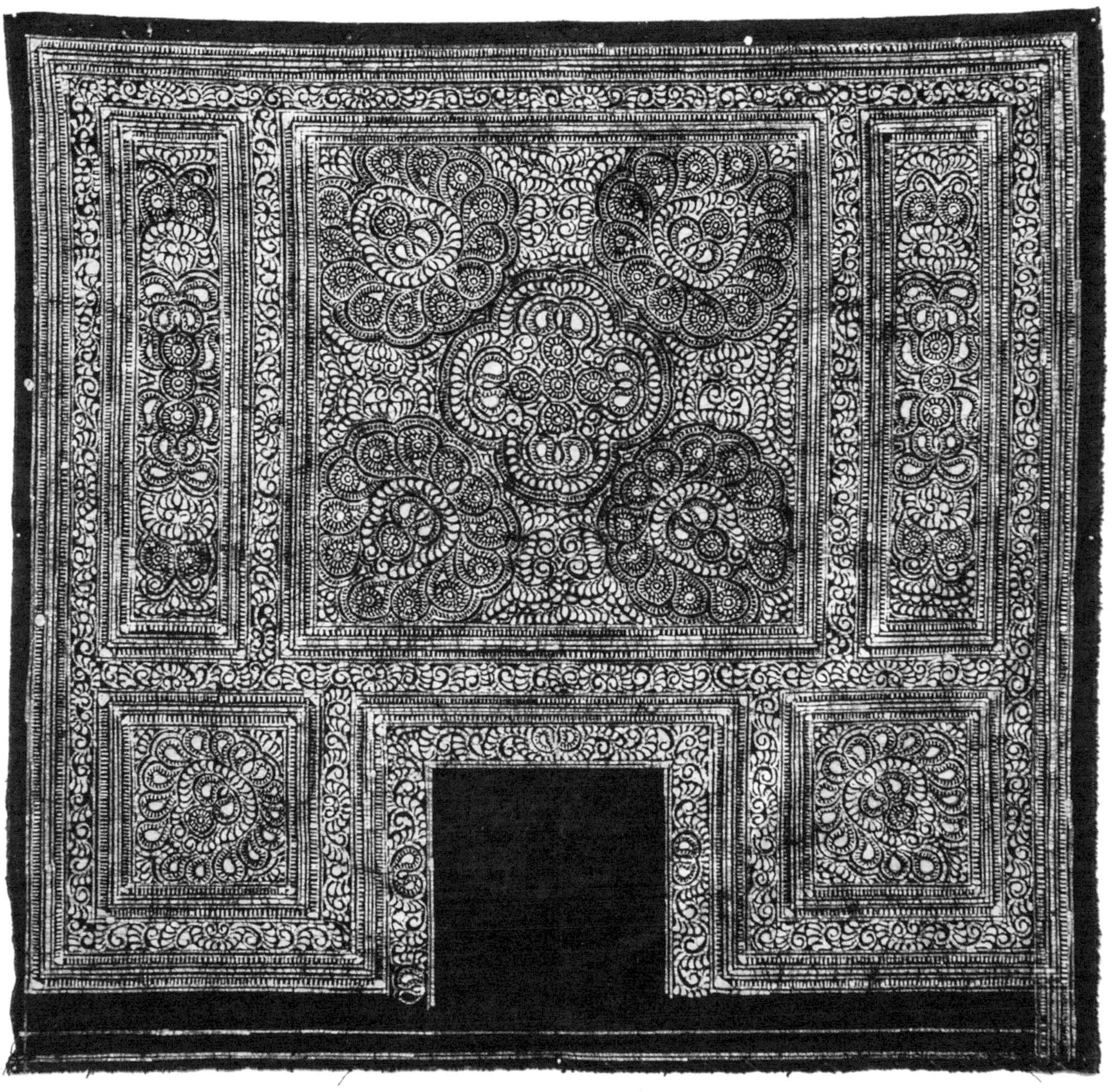

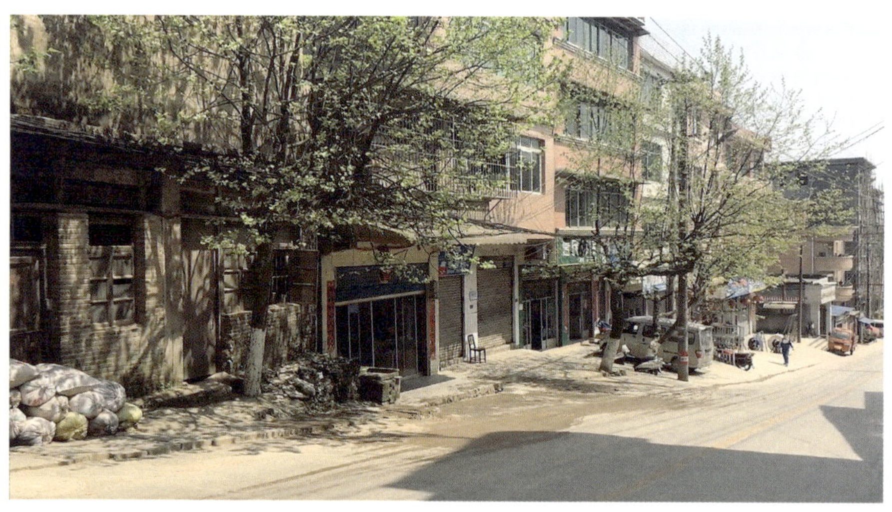

Danzhai County, Guizhou Province, south west China, 31st July, 2016
stills from *The Time of Discretion* (film archive), 2016/2018

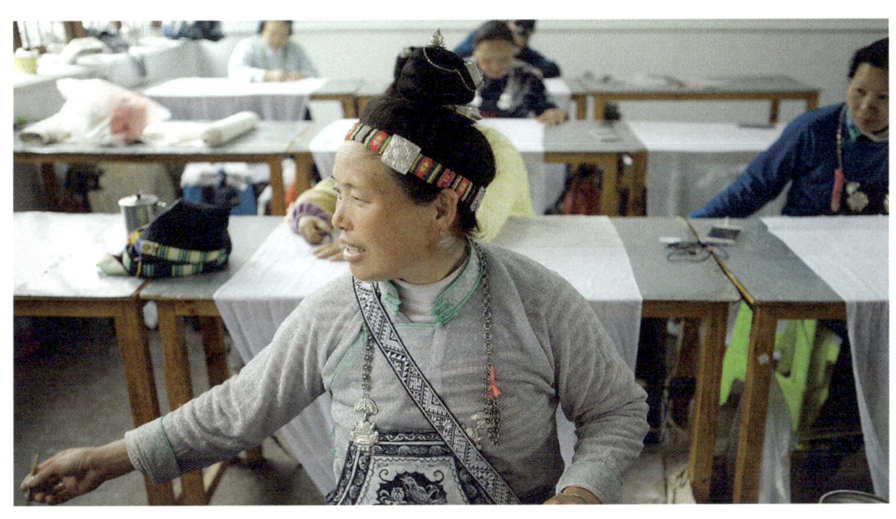

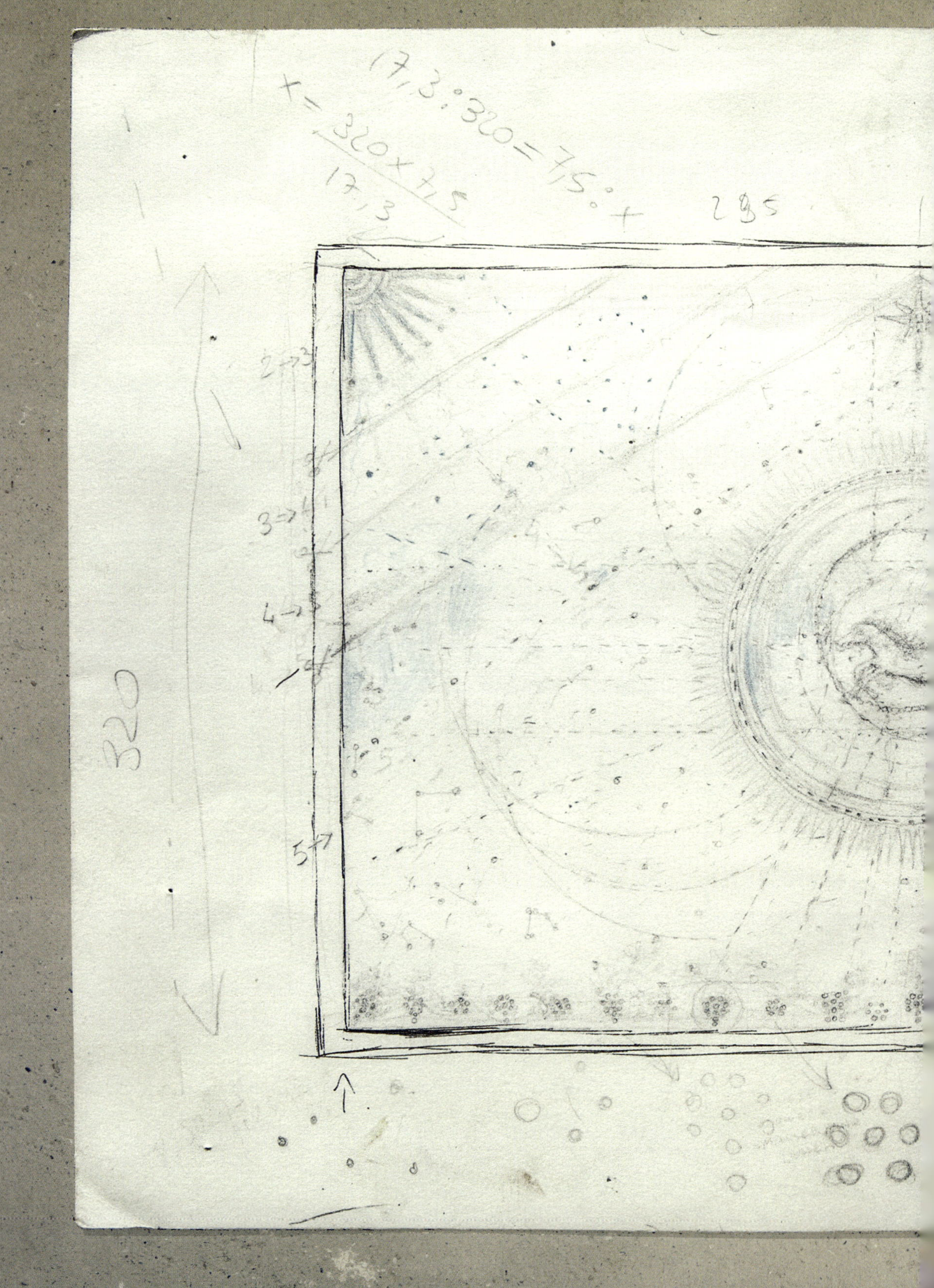

9 12,5

0,5
0,8
– 0,9
23c

arazzi
4,90 x 3,20

Rosa
83,93 x 56,76
~~83,26 x 57,82~~
~~81,14 x 57,33~~

16,78					
18,9	1	4	7	10	13
18,9	2	5	8	11	14
18,9	3	6	9	12	15

3,20
2,34

17,3
276

4 x 4,90 +

3,7
6,5 : x = 3,7 : 80

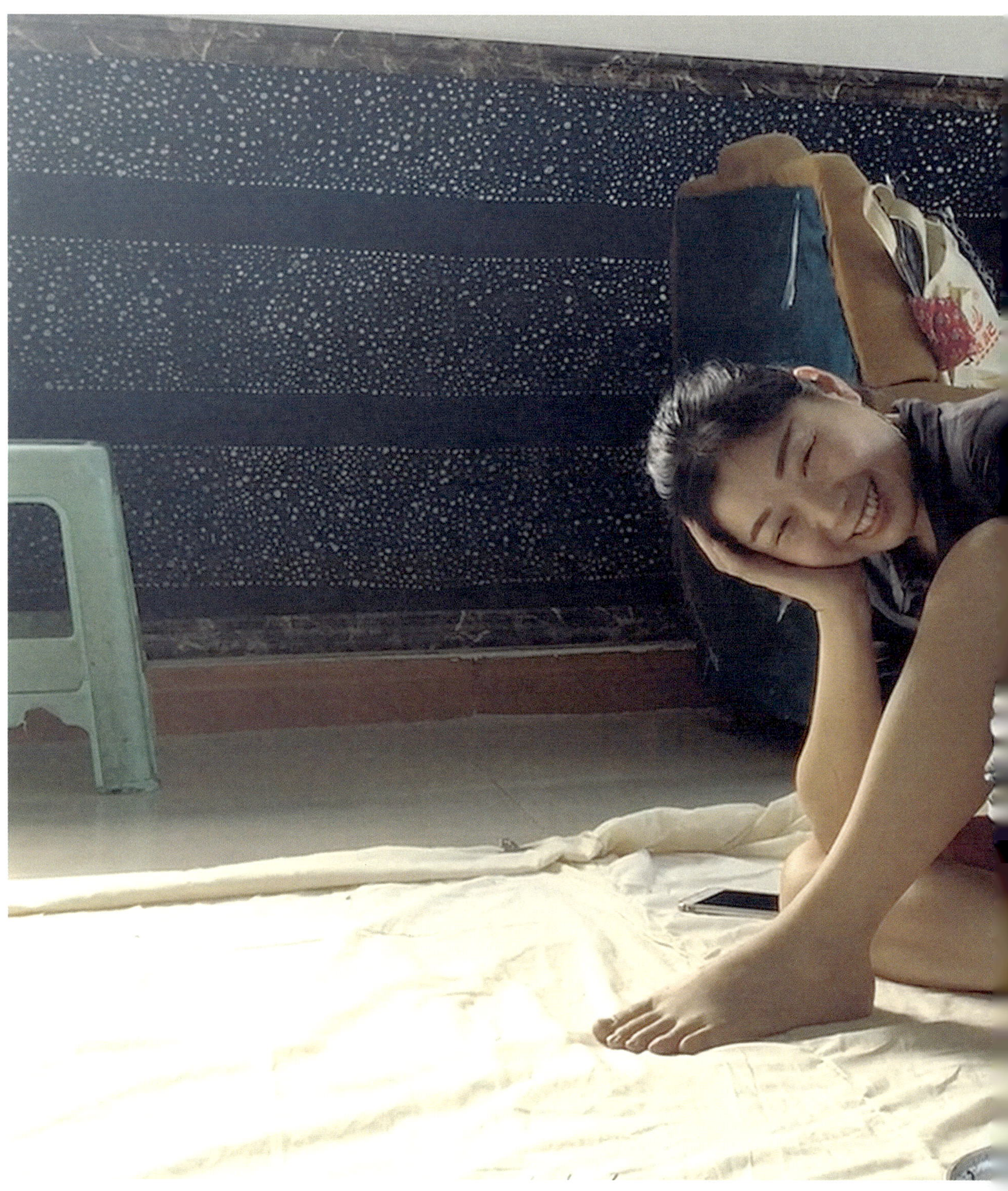

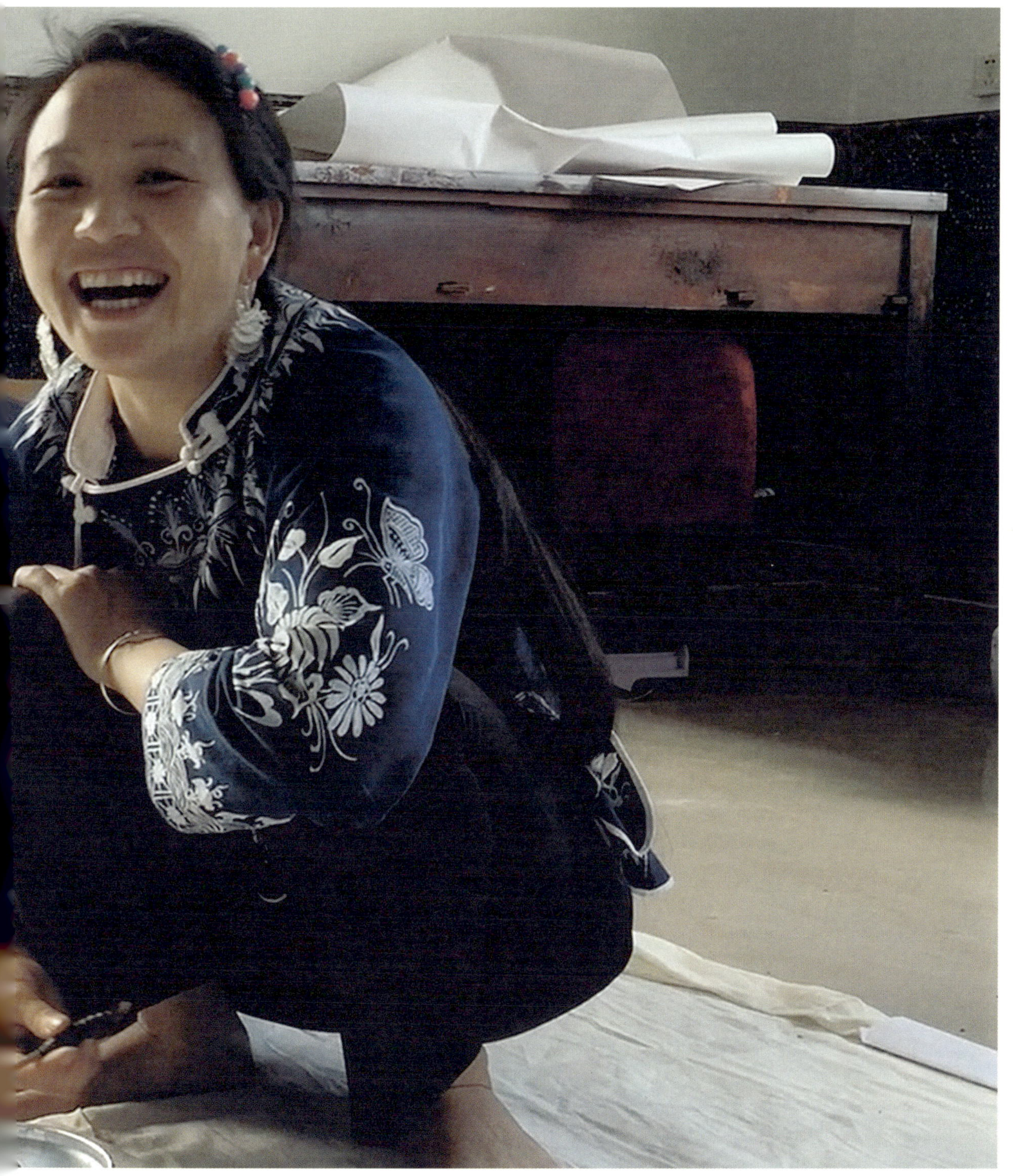

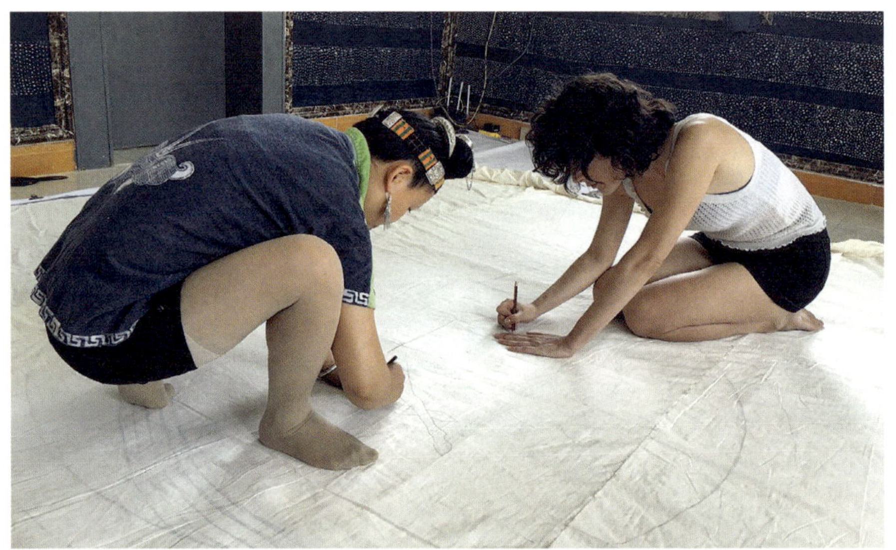

Danzhai County, Guizhou Province, south west China, 8–15th August, 2016

On the following pages: photographic documentation of the production of the work

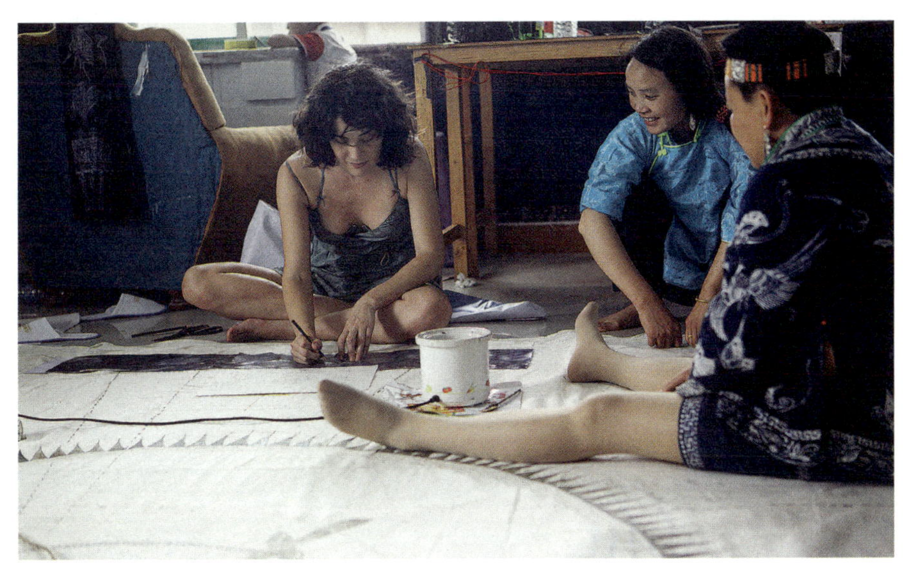

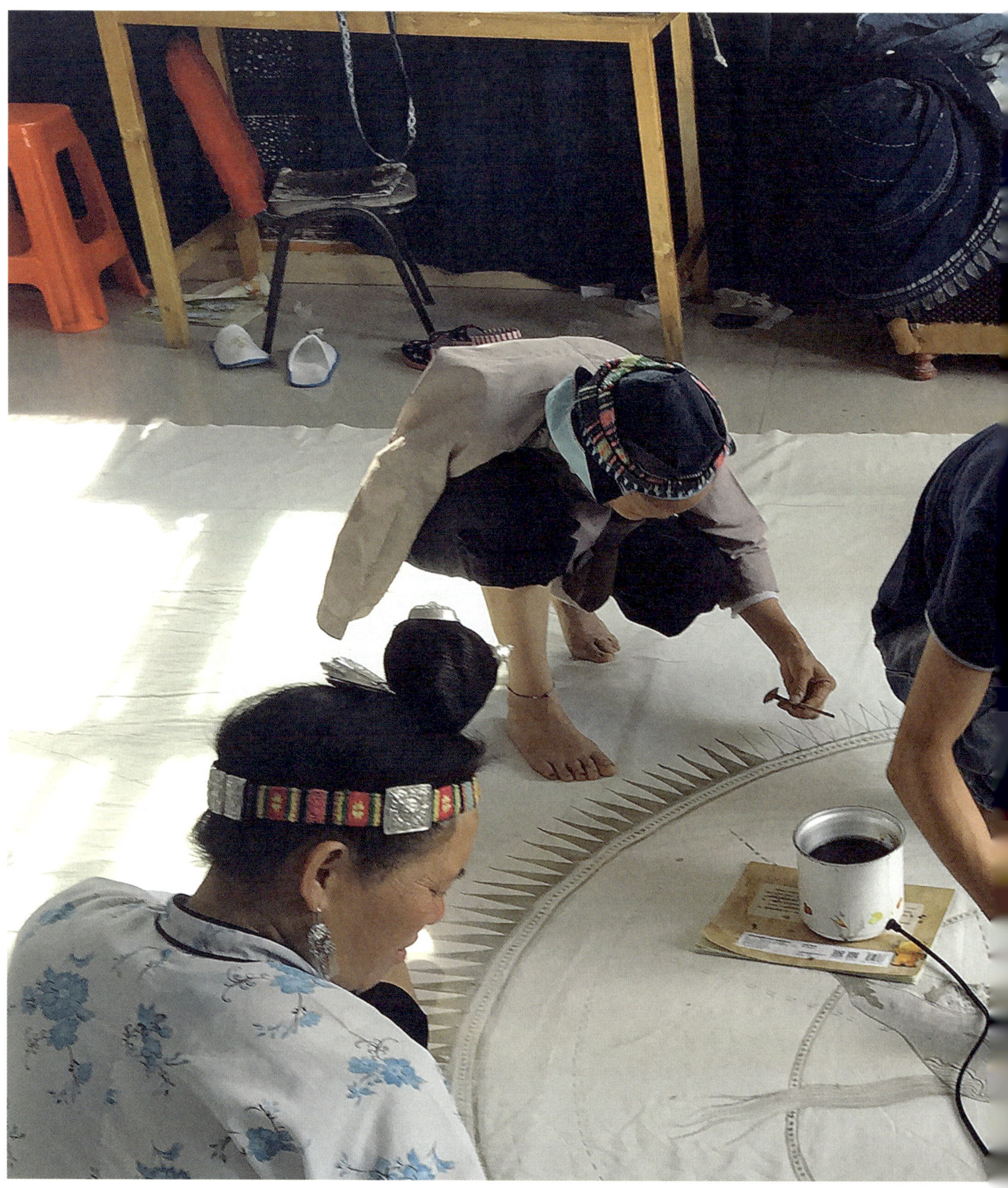

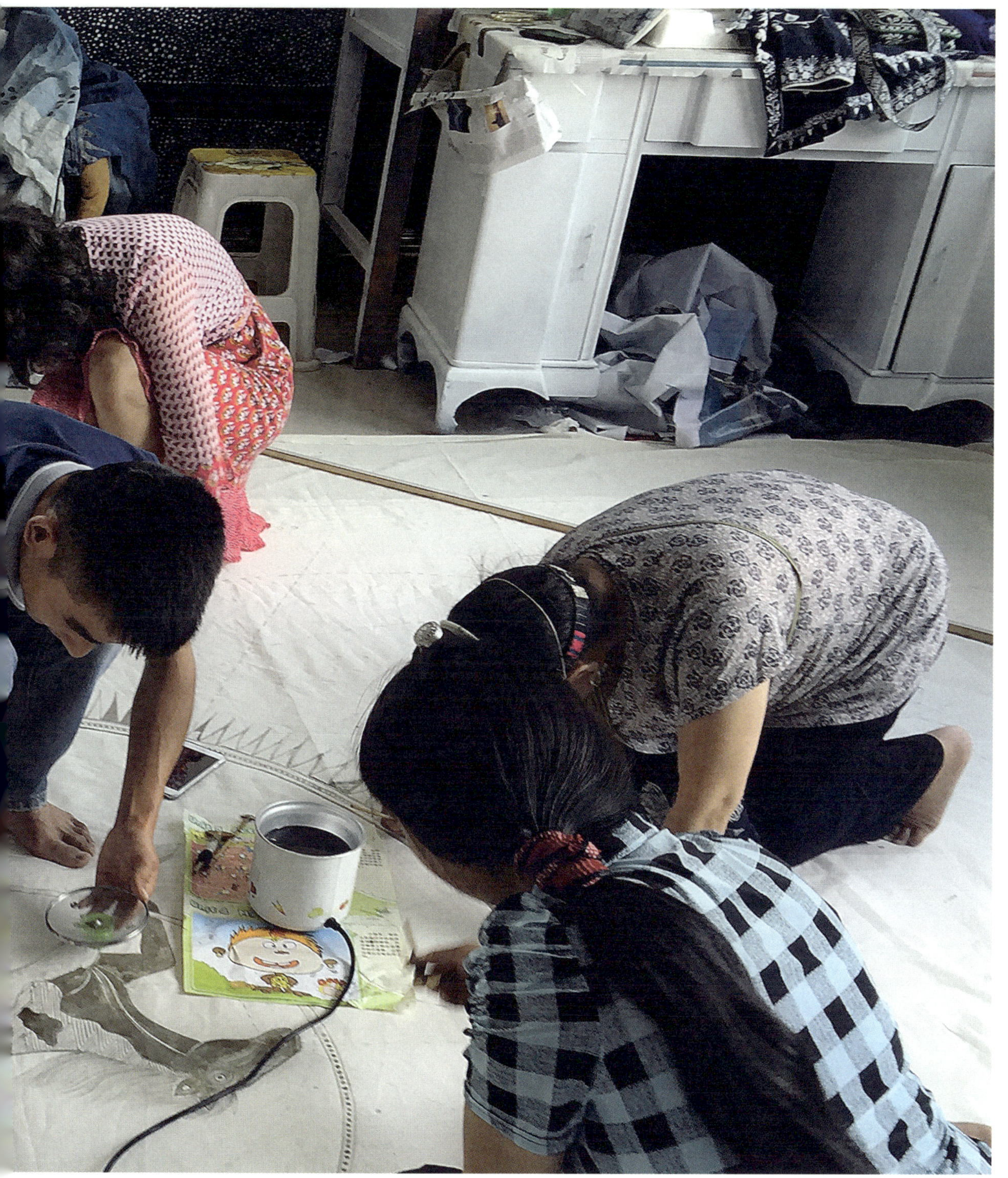

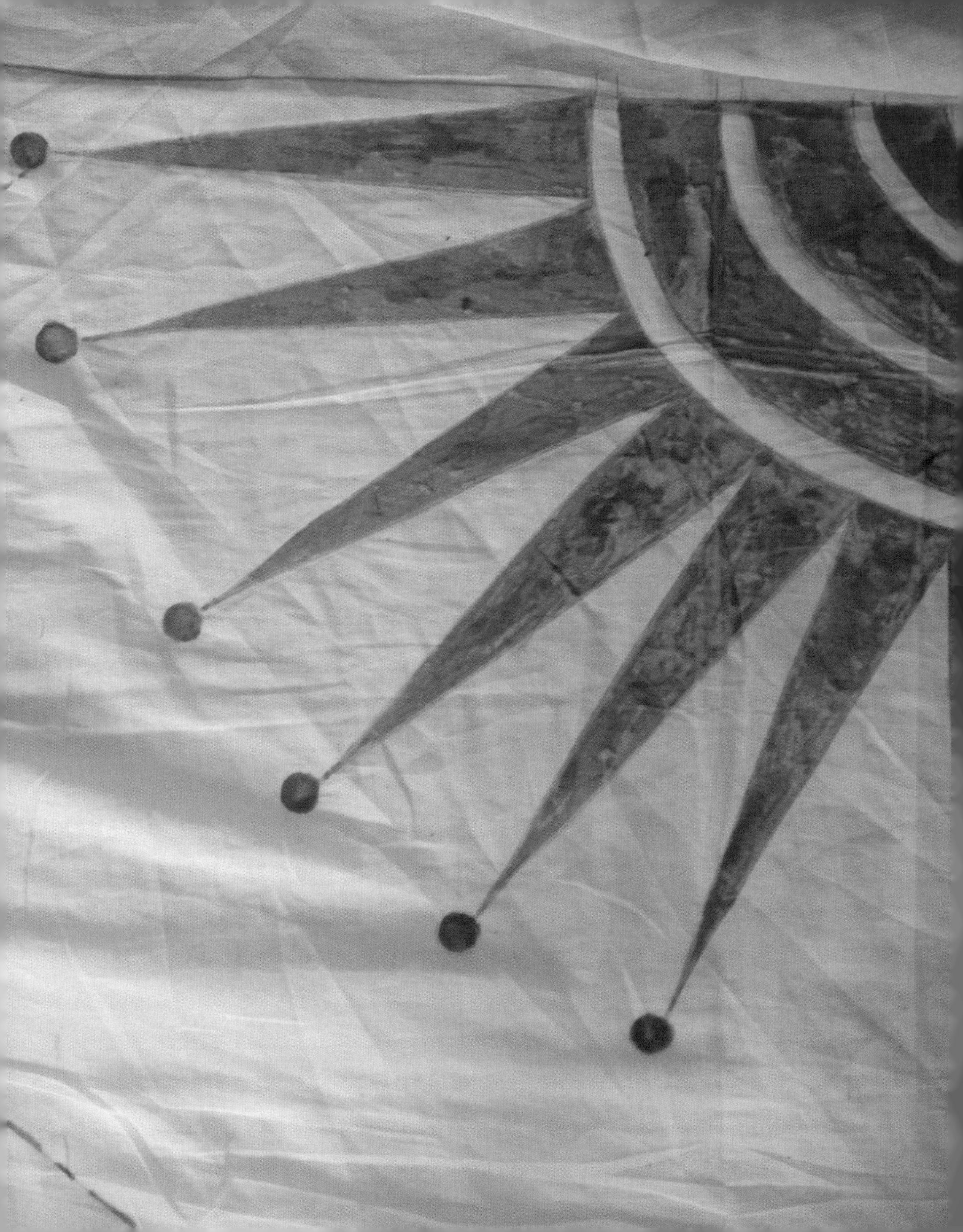

Paina Kal. Timelines for the Art of Lisa Mara Batacchi

Sumesh Sharma

*

In how many ways should we determine the aesthetics of India? India expands itself to an abstraction that cannot be defined by a nation state. Its adherents believe in its singularity as a source of spiritual, aesthetical and intellectual wealth, but this singularity is limited, hiding a diverse geography with a people rich in language and culture: a material history and experience well entrenched in the conscience of the world, a memory of colonization. What is most resplendent of this history are the colonial facades, roundabouts, Corinthian columns, marble statues and the arrangement of roads, bridges and public buildings. In fact, the First War of Independence in 1857 was followed by the establishment of the Sir JJ School of Arts in 1858, in Bombay, by a citizens' charter encouraged by the colonial government. Here children of the artisans who had participated in the revolt were taught the arts of the west. A western academy arts programme was created to teach textile weavers' children how to paint Renaissance perspective and sculpt Greco-Roman figurines depicting Indian mythology.

The foundries of the school crafted the facades of the Neo-Gothic architecture which marked the vista of Bombay, now described as Indo-Saracenic architecture as it was also influenced by Rajput and Mughal aesthetics.

It is here that I introduce the practice of the conceptual visual artist Lisa Mara Batacchi.

A critic or curator may take time to decipher layers that are intimate and rooted in her imagination, in particular, her practice is not what we might expect of an artist from Florence, Italy.

Nor is it essentially the genre of Arte Povera. Rather, if we search for a genealogy of her vocabulary, we may find it in the performances, happenings, temporary sculptures, blow-ups and works of the UFO collective, that consisted of radical architects. Lapo Binazzi, one of the members, calls his practices "discontinuity". Irreverent to Tuscany's architectural traditions they are called Anarchitects.

Similarly, Batacchi's practice is far beyond and distant from classical techniques and histories. But radical propositions by artists such as Lisa Mara Batacchi or Shiva Gor, a Roma artist from India, are unclear territories as they propose and inhabit a radicality that is true, honest and persistent. If we were to define radicality as definable or follow a practice taught in an art school, curatorial course or artist workshop on radical arts, then by default the art work produced by such adherents is informed by a learning of a system rather than a pursuit of dissent. Political art often falls prey to the "Delacroix Parody". Delacroix painted the romantic notion of the French revolution, a mythical rendition of Liberty leading a united France. The revolution has never seen its final bounty until today and utopian representation of political art often falls for the same parody of artists churning out bold statements that they ignore to follow in their secular lives.

Batacchi does not make any tall claims of artistic radicality, rather, when one observes her practice and the course of her career one understands the shifts she has made both aesthetically and ideologically.

A case in point is her residency at the Clark House Initiative, Bombay. *Soulmates (Within Time)* was her solo show at Clark House in 2015 where she collaborated with a Gormati casual labourer Sita Chavan who also had a side business as a tailor to the Banjara Gormati community in Bombay. Not far from Clark House, the vicinity of Cuffe Parade, Colaba are the Ambedkar Nagar slums that have a

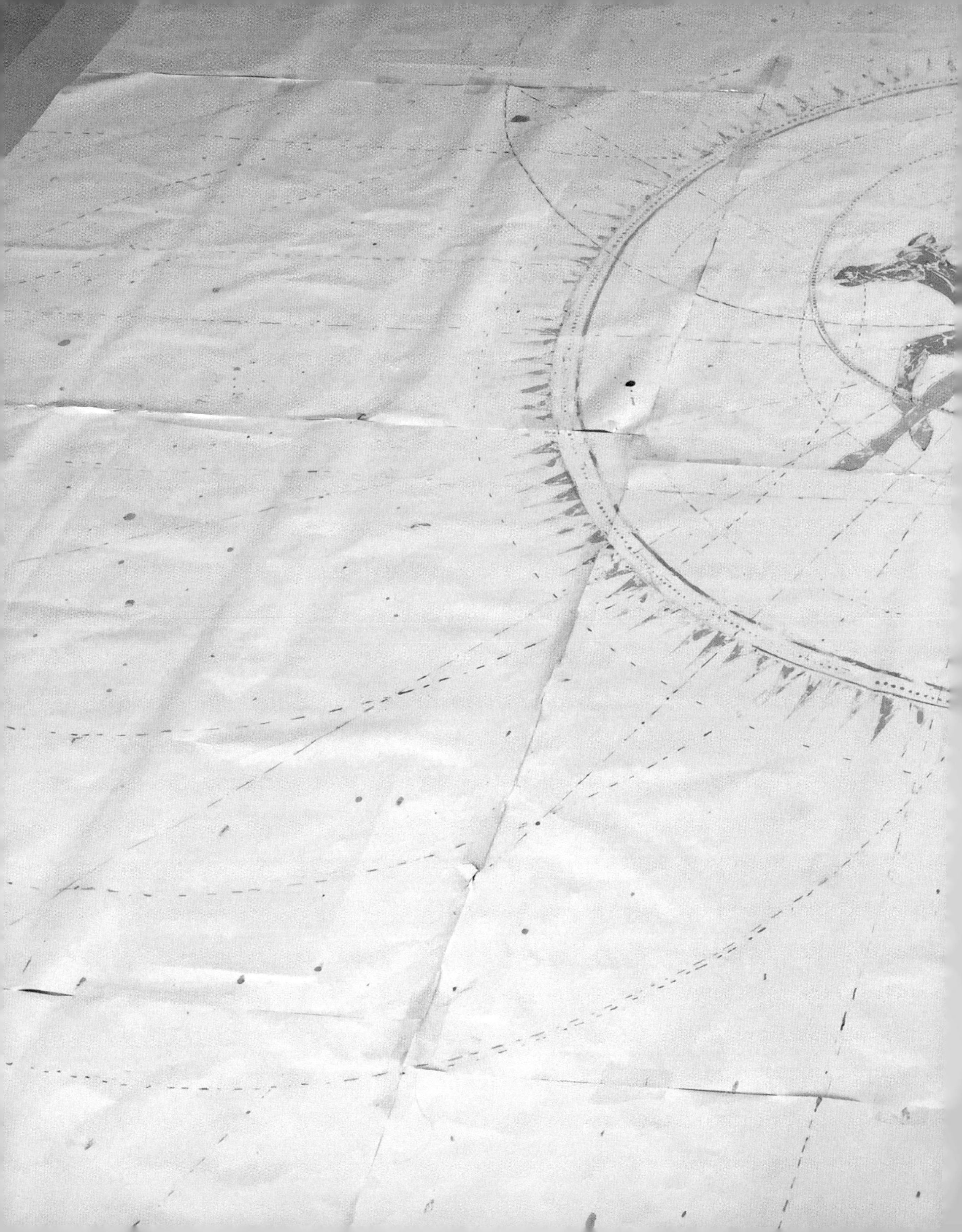

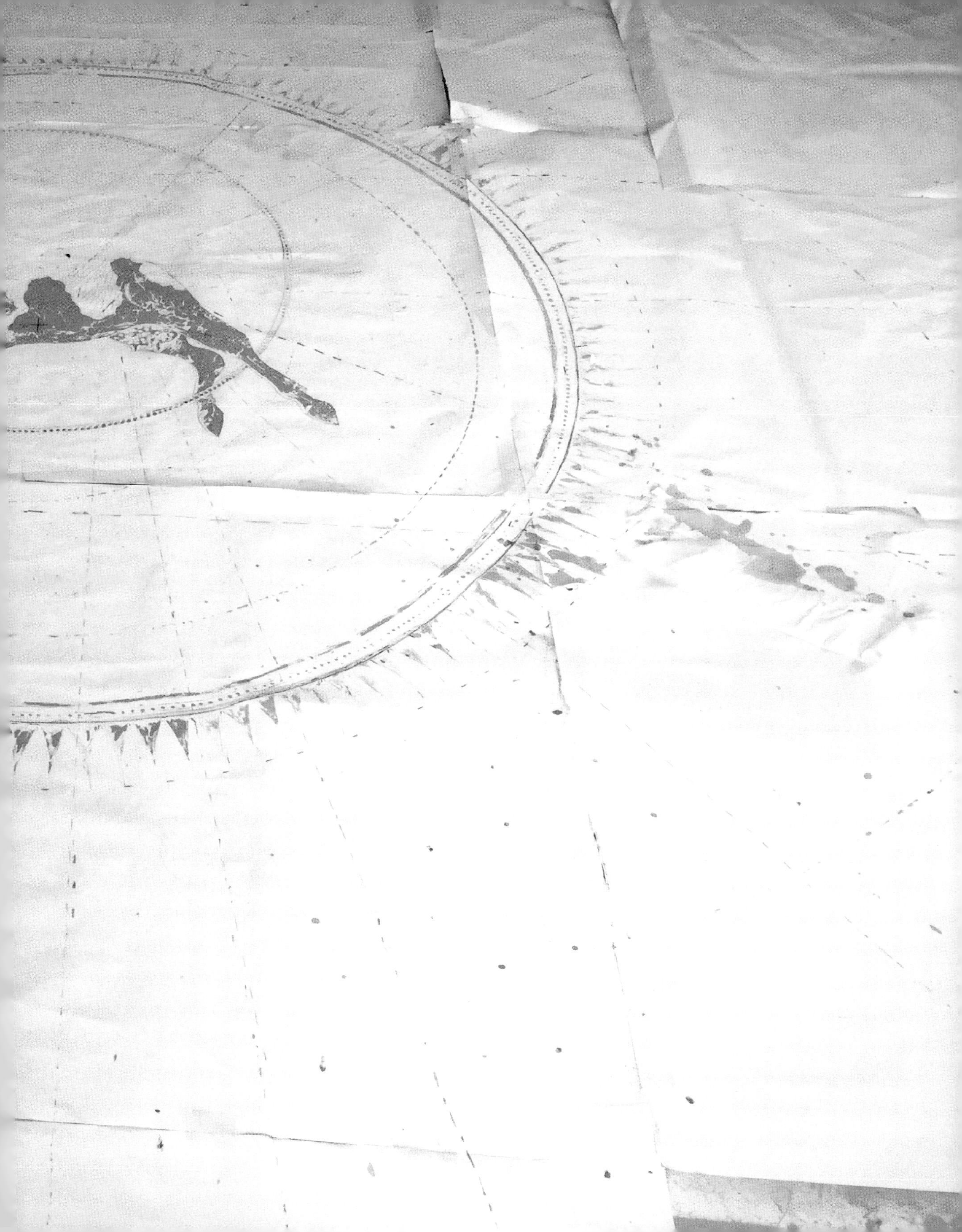

*

sizeable population of Roma or Banjara Gormati community. The Gormati are part of the large Roma community that is spread across Europe, Africa, North and South America.

They are distinguished from the other settled communities by their skirts and bodices that are embroidered and colorful, as well as by their nomadic life. Badshah Naik, a Banjara activist and blogger, observes in his online post dated 2010 "Featuring geometrics and eschewing the floral and animal motifs used in the majority of Indian villages, Banjara embroidery is strikingly different. The viewer's eye is drawn to bold squares, triangles, circles and irregular shapes, all delineated in brilliant contrasting colors. All Banjara embroideries are designed for a nomadic life. These are multipurpose clothing and dowry pieces, not large wall decorations like those made and used by settled village people in most Indian regions"[1].

Batacchi used two blouses that were connected together by different colored cotton laces embroidered by Sita Chavan and her relatives. When worn, the two people were interconnected by the strings that ran from one shirt to the other. An interconnection of history, womanhood and art history.

We do not jot down the names of the millions of women who have invented knots, designs and history in weaving. Weaving might be in vogue now as a conceptual act that readdresses the lack in art history that has been discriminatory towards women, to be really able to address the problem. The collection of textile works needs to move out of the white cube towards the millions of women who enact it as a tradition, vocation or necessity to clothe oneself. Batacchi, calling Sita Chavan her *soulmate,* makes this connection start out with a cause that not only finds a place for Sita Chavan but also for herself in a world which continuously forces anonymity on many women artists.

Lisa has an interesting personal story, she worked as a research assistant for international fashion brands such as the Prada group and Vivienne Westwood, having studied fashion design in Florence. After working for seven years she decided to go into art, having seen the exploitative practices of the fashion industry in its factories in Cambodia. She decided to study at the Academy in Florence and soon after realized that she still had a strong passion for fabrics. The art world in its present form of biennales, fairs and rapid internationalism was preceded by a global trade in textiles: the Silk Road, the Hollandaise and other textile myths are part of this trade. Indian merchants from Sindh called "Sindworkies" as slang for Sindh Workers and Multanis from Punjab would tread up across the Himalayan mountains towards Astrakhan in Russia and Baku in Azerbaijan forming mercantile guilds that traded in textiles.

Their remnants are now found in the forms of scrolls, textiles and paintings in the museums of the ex-Soviet state and abandoned Fire temples of Central Asia. Batacchi, almost following the Silk Road, travelled across China to Inner Mongolia and Ulaanbaatar. Here, for the Land Art Biennale 2016, she made a beautiful installation of cloth dyed in the hue of indigo with one of China's minority-tribe communities.

Indigo is a hue that has been the representative color of most indigenous communities in Asia and Africa and its prized status led to the poverty of millions in the Gangetic plains of India during British Colonization.

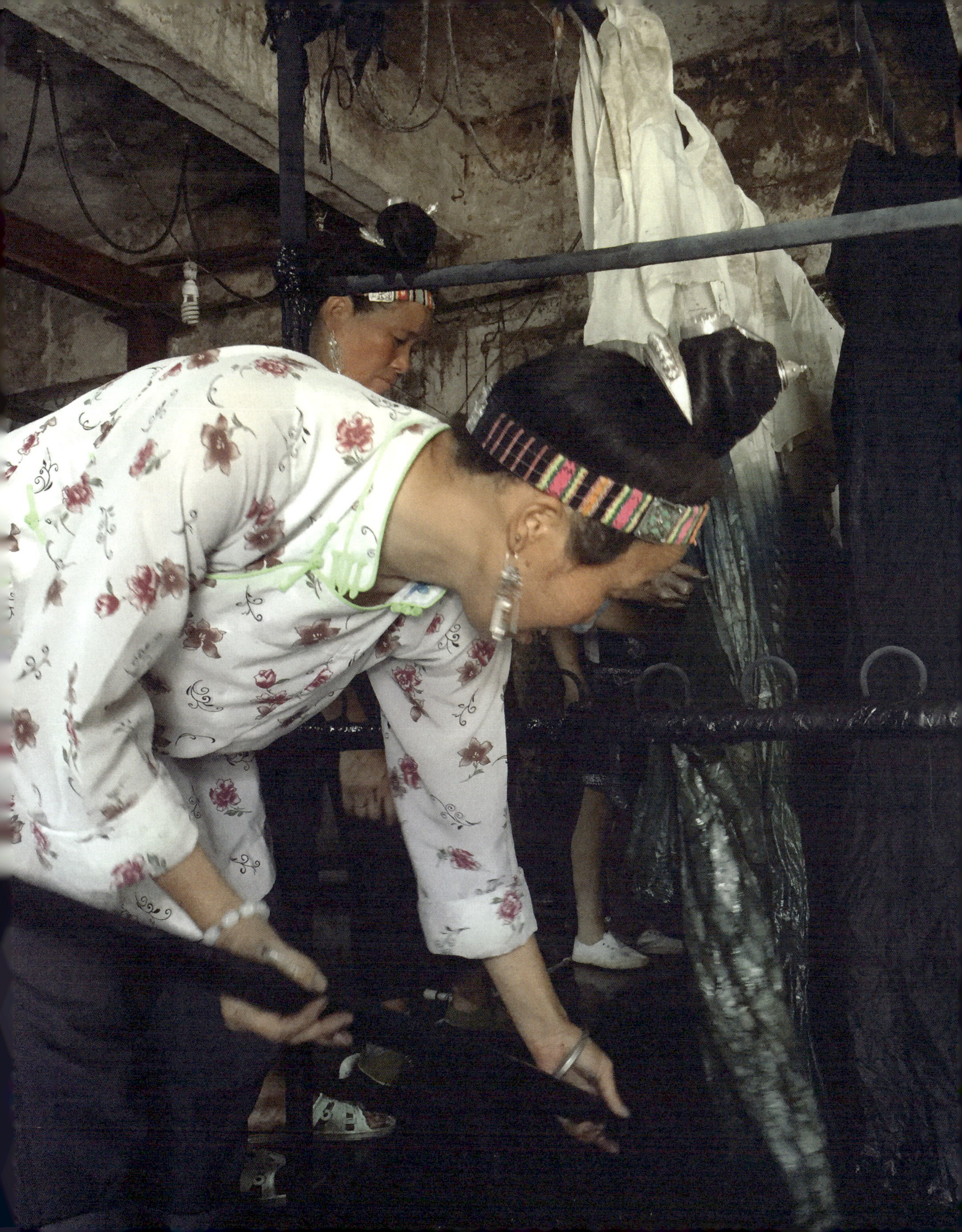

*

Batacchi freeing the indigo into the winds of the Mongolian Steppe initiated a revolt against Marco Polo's yearning, a desire that even Alighiero Boetti failed to resist with his Afghan carpets.
Batacchi in her practice as a conceptual weaver sows poetry into the threads that gather friendship and conversation between people who do not share the same language. The Roma preserved their "Romani Chib" language even after dispersing from India, as their counterparts in South Asia, the Gor, also maintained their distinct culture. Their approach to the spiritual was through dance and ritual and not belief in a set of gods. Rather, they believed in a time system called "Paina". Paina is a meaning of time that does not represent the past or future, the "Paina Kal" represents another time that is not now but of significance and insignificance at the same moment. Art history suffers from "linear time", it cannot deal with time systems that do not respect a Roman-Christian time frame and thus it takes for granted that events proceed in a line stretching from the past through the present and into the future; this fails to record a belief that time repeats cycles endlessly. This modern and western attitude leads to failing to record what does not represent the signifier of that time. Few artists challenge this order, among them is Lisa Mara Batacchi and also Shiva Gor, an artist from the Banjara Gormati community who has been writing and creating art extensively based on the *Paina Kal*, a term that he coined to discuss a time undefined by the scales of linearity.
Rather than dwelling on identity politics, Gor began to consolidate the wisdom of the community to assemble a group of like-minded thinkers, poets and intellectuals to gather strength for their political marginalization.

Even during the forming of the Indian constitution the Banjara Gormati were called aborigines in debates where it was discussed if they were capable enough to be awarded the universal adult franchise or simply the right to vote. The departing colonial government in its gazettes had defined the tribes as "Criminal Tribes" and after much deliberation they were reclassified as "Denotified Tribes", as they were denotified from their legal status as perpetual offenders. Nowadays they have not yet been able to access the fruits of India's positive discrimination policies and they sit on the lowest rung of exploitation and hate. Much like in Europe, the Banjara Gormati are seen as dirty, lazy and unwelcome guests. This is because their lifestyle, that contests the settled civilizations, is at odds with the Protestant-Christian ethic of continuous work. On the other hand, the settled civilization, despite its preaching of democracy and liberty, has formed a society of deceit, jealousy and treachery that has caused numerous unfortunate incidents, including the World Wars, the Holocaust and a continuous history of strife in the regions of the Middle East and Eastern Europe. Colonization was a result of such a culture and the present immigrant crisis is a result of years of economic and political exploitation of ex-colonies and the export of war to distant geographies.
Nowadays amongst the Euopeans live the Romas, refugees from a violent crisis in South Asia around the sixteenth century. Keeping their traditions and accepting the faith to live among people who fear their dark skin, the Roma hold Europe's richest heritage of having moved through all its languages, cuisines, music, religions and folklore while keeping their own. Rightwing fascists who

*

scream out loud against immigration also hound out the Roma from their informal settlements. Police routinely round them up as offenders but somewhere in their music and flowing skirts lies their understanding of time, the relationship with aesthetics and it is here where *Paina Kal* sits.
If artists pursued radicality, then the Roma would be their inspiration as they have the most interesting anarchistic acts even if they were out to pickpocket. The head of the Latvian Roma organization once exclaimed that the Roma will steal your chicken to feed his family but seldom indulges in politics that can destroy lives. Artists constantly invent acts of precarious existence and ephemeral materialism without attempting to involve and learn from the Roma in their midst who have an ever-existing vocabulary.

> *Where is the man who gives life to the stones of the dead, the man who makes the stones and the dead speak?*[2]

Octavio Paz, the Mexican poet and pacifist who was on his way to India as an under-secretary for the Mexican embassy on a boat to Bombay while carrying a print of Goddess Durga and a copy of the Bhagawad Gita, glimpsed on the horizon the Taj Mahal Hotel, Bombay's glamourous enclave on the port built by Indians to provide luxury when they were not allowed into European Hotels. He heard the myth of the architect's plan having been miscalculated and the building being built with its back to the sea. Paz rather believed it was India that had turned its back on Europe.
It is in the same geography that Lisa Mara Batacchi began her sojourn in India living in the district of Colaba.
In the Light of India, Octavio Paz perhaps realized that the supposed imperfections of his home country Mexico, where a great divide existed between the elite, who sought enlightenment in Europe, and just outside Mexico City where the peasants worshiped skulls, the dead and nature. Much like the gods and goddesses of India it was not Christianity that soothed the souls of these once colonized people. Paz at once saw the limits of Hinduism that had been straddled by the burden of caste and had not moved beyond its traditions, like the changes Europe had benefitted from through Enlightenment, Renaissance and the Industrial Revolution. His words were written in 1951, while Ambedkar, the architect of India's constitution, was attacking the newly elected Indian Congress as he felt that if caste was not annihilated through affirmative action so that the so-called untouchables, who identified as Dalits, could not benefit from the real bounties of freedom. Lisa Mara Batacchi came long after the Dalit movement and, even though caste has not yet been wiped out in India, she was able to collaborate with the Banjara Gormati in the Cuffe Parade slums of Bombay. These slums appeared after the government reclaimed land for an urban city project and parts of it were occupied by indigenous groups such as the Kolis (fisherfolk), the landless and communities such as the Banjara Gormati. This act of claiming reclaimed land was a self-organized act of affirmative action on resources that would have landed in the hands of the powerful few.
Perhaps Lisa Mara Batacchi illustrates with her embroideries the visions that Paz had for India as a society linked to its past but more importantly defined by its people and their beliefs in its geography. Since 2015, Batacchi has emerged as a poet

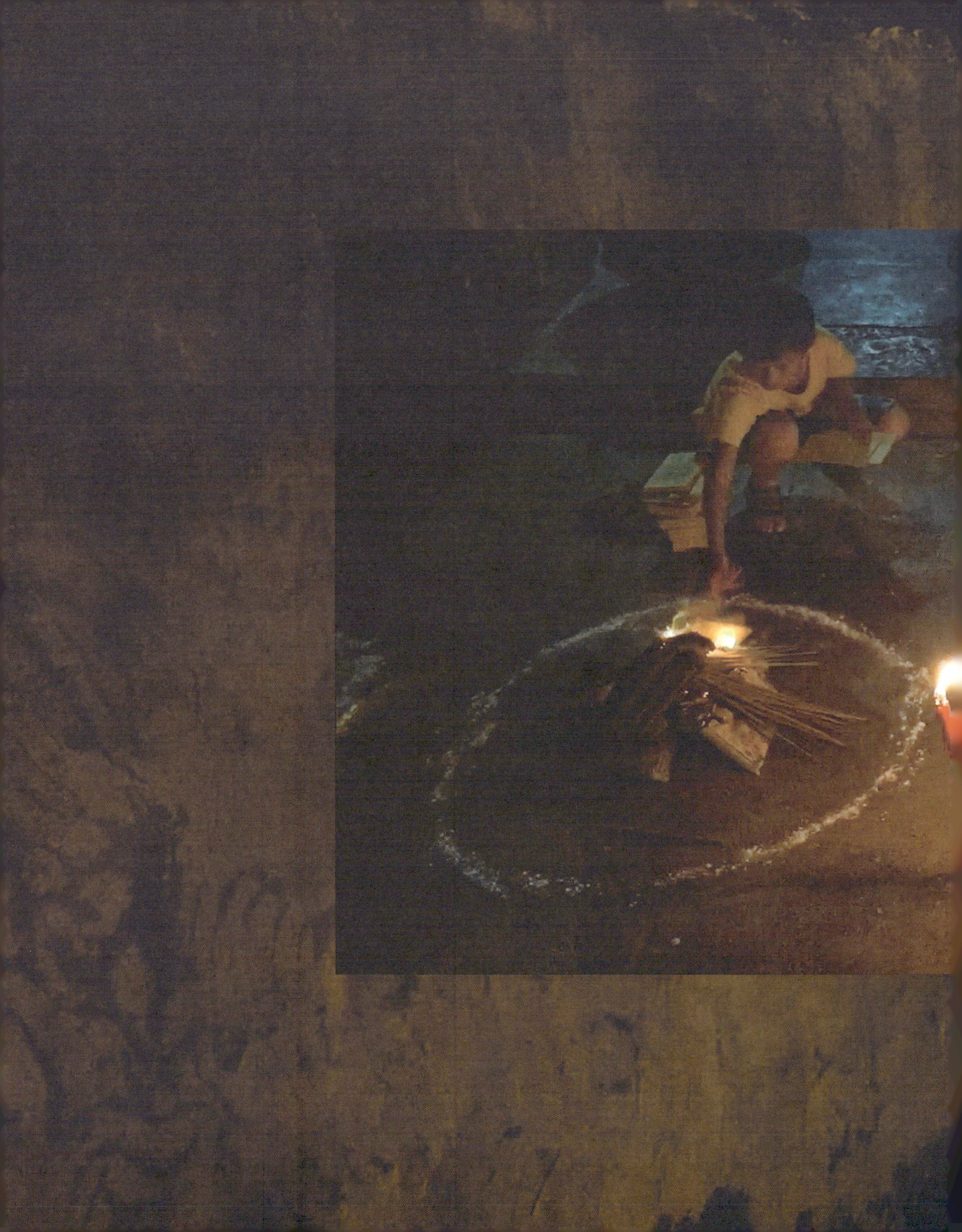

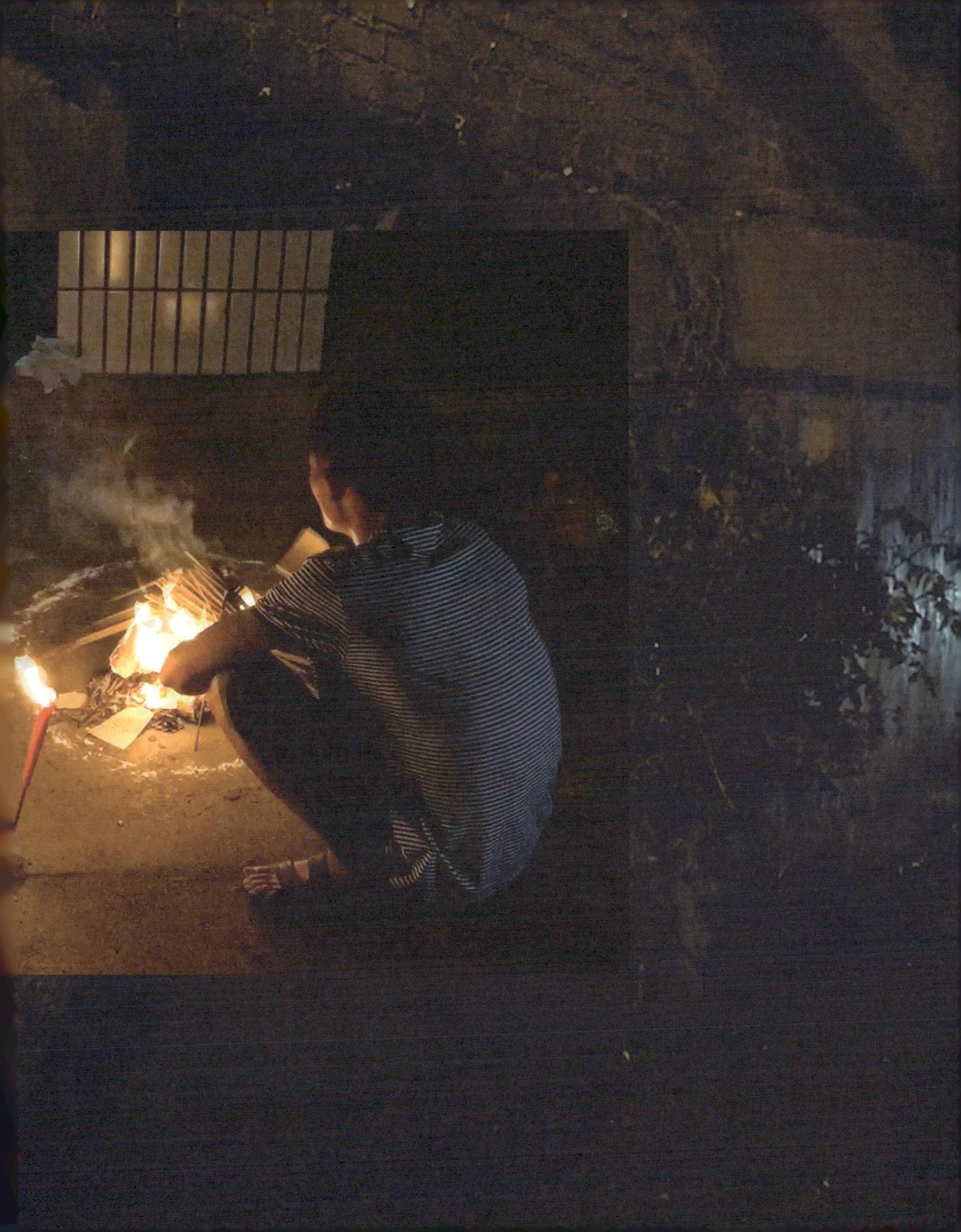

★

who wanders to India and later to Mongolia, China and onwards to Cairo bringing with her a unique aesthetic format and vocabulary in her contemporary art practice which is enjoined by friendship, conversations, and collaborations.

The greatest challenge for art history today is to rid itself of its stance of non-inclusion regarding artisanship and artisans, perhaps it is the only radical departure from the act of neo-capital object making. But more importantly, contemporary art historians should begin to read and decipher the cultures of continuity of handicrafts which artists follow.

Artists such as Lisa Mara Batacchi exist within the time lines that are not defined by tomorrow or yesterday, but rather, are calculated on the present scale with the person they face.

Poetry often does not only form in words but in actions that etch our thoughts. If we begin to define Art from here, its accessibility emerges and shall not need a history, theory or words that I write.

[1] Reema Gehi, "Stitch on the move. A social artist from Italy meets her match in Ambedkar Nagar's Banjara colony to tell the story of life in embroidery", *Mumbai Mirror* (June 14th, 2015), p. 12.

[2] Eliot Weinberger (ed. and tr.), *The Poems of Octavio Paz*, New York: New Directions, 2012, p. 115.

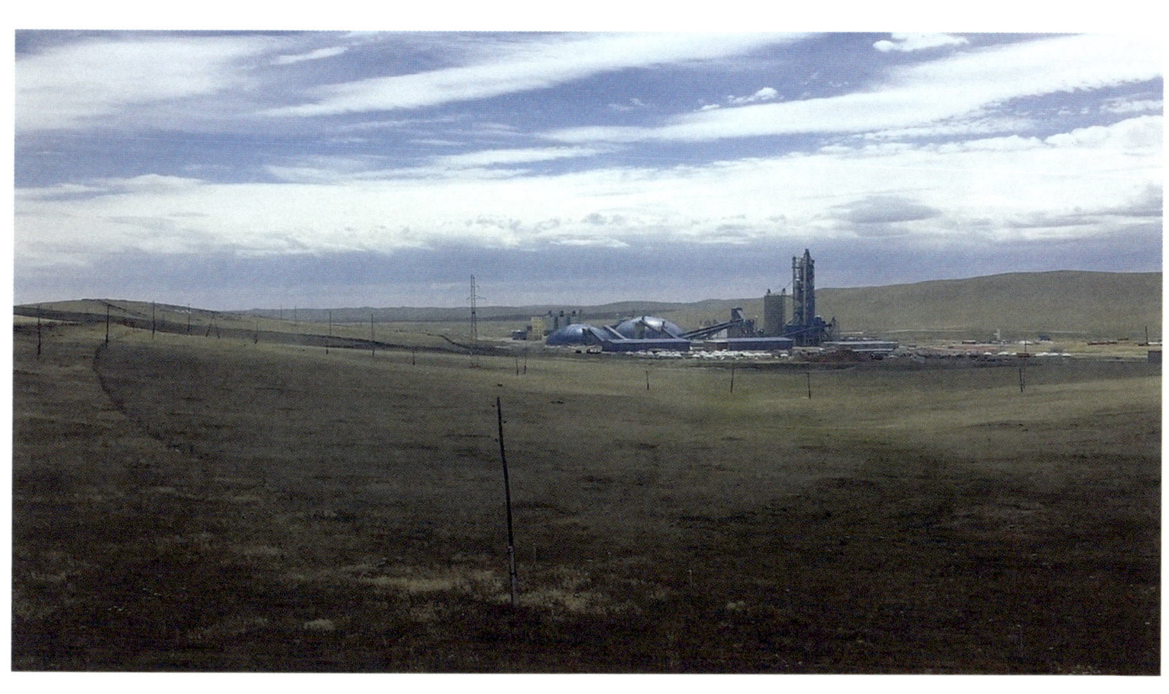

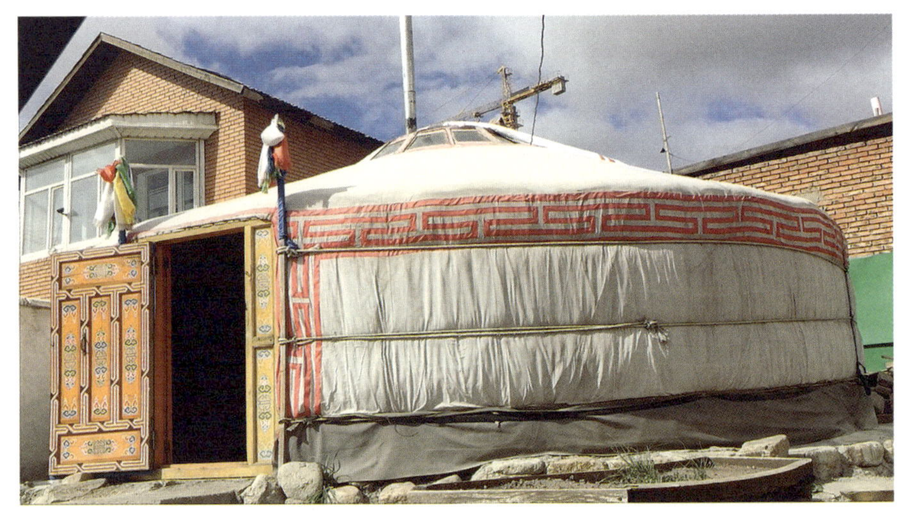

Ulaanbaatar, Mongolia, 20th August, 2016
still from *The Time of Discretion* (film archive), 2016/2018

On the opposite page: still from the short film *The Time of Discretion*, 2019
HD, color, sound, 24:53 min

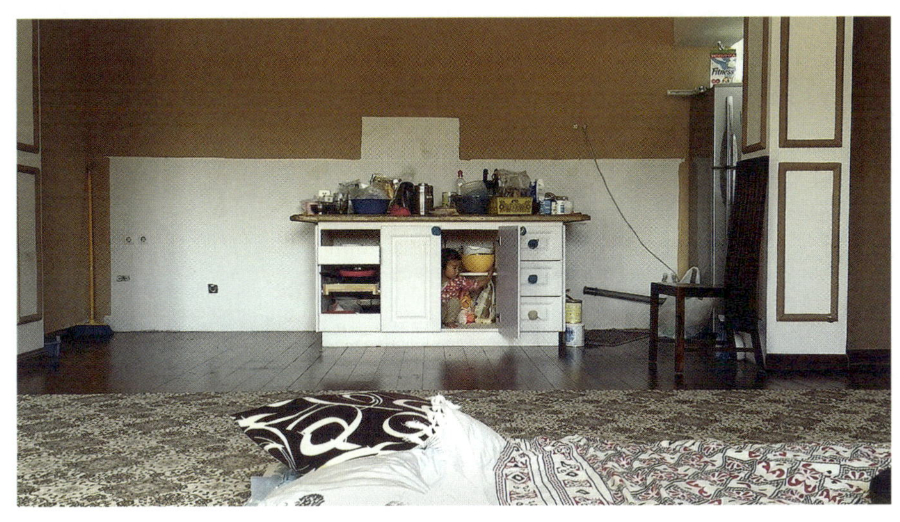
Fitness

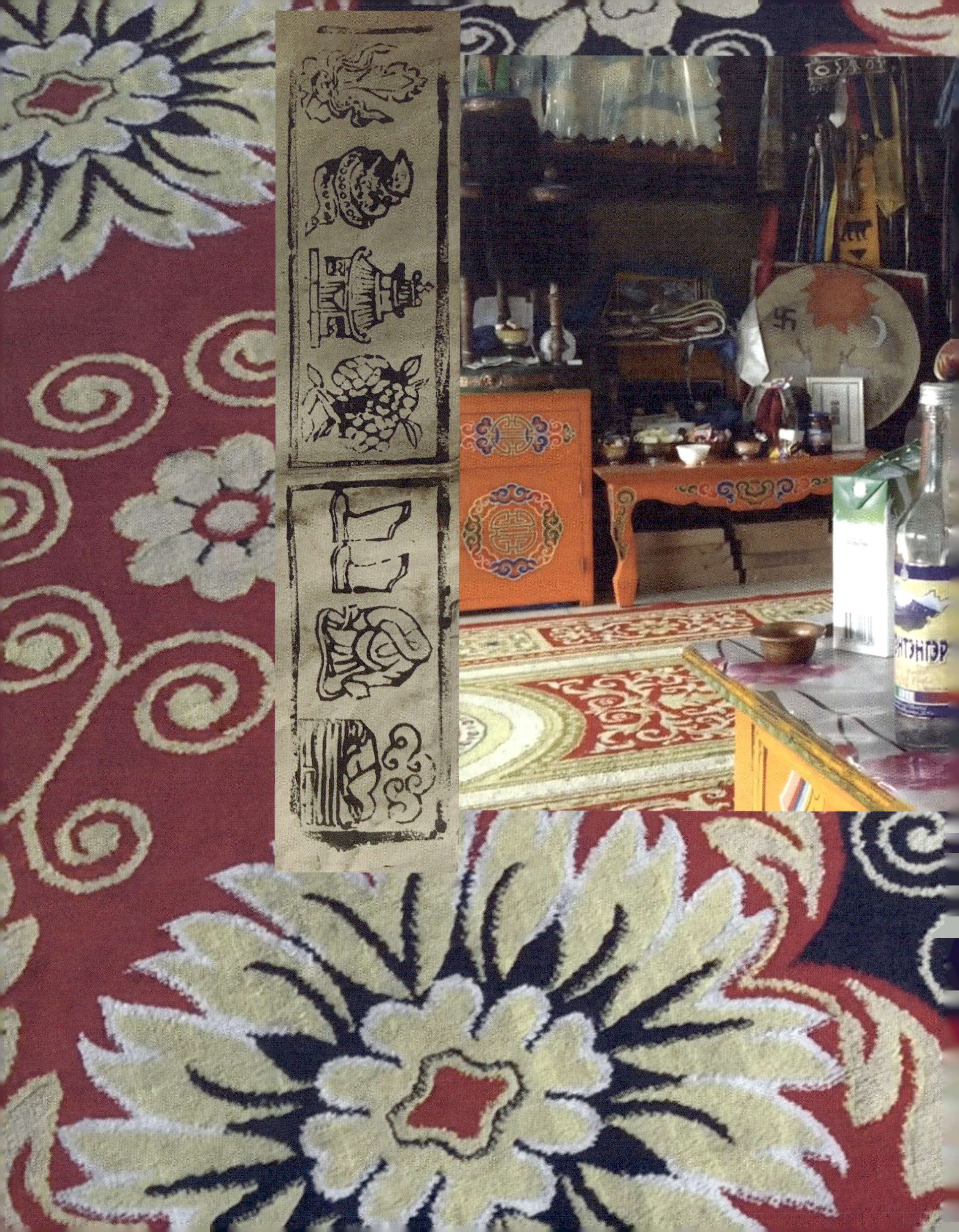

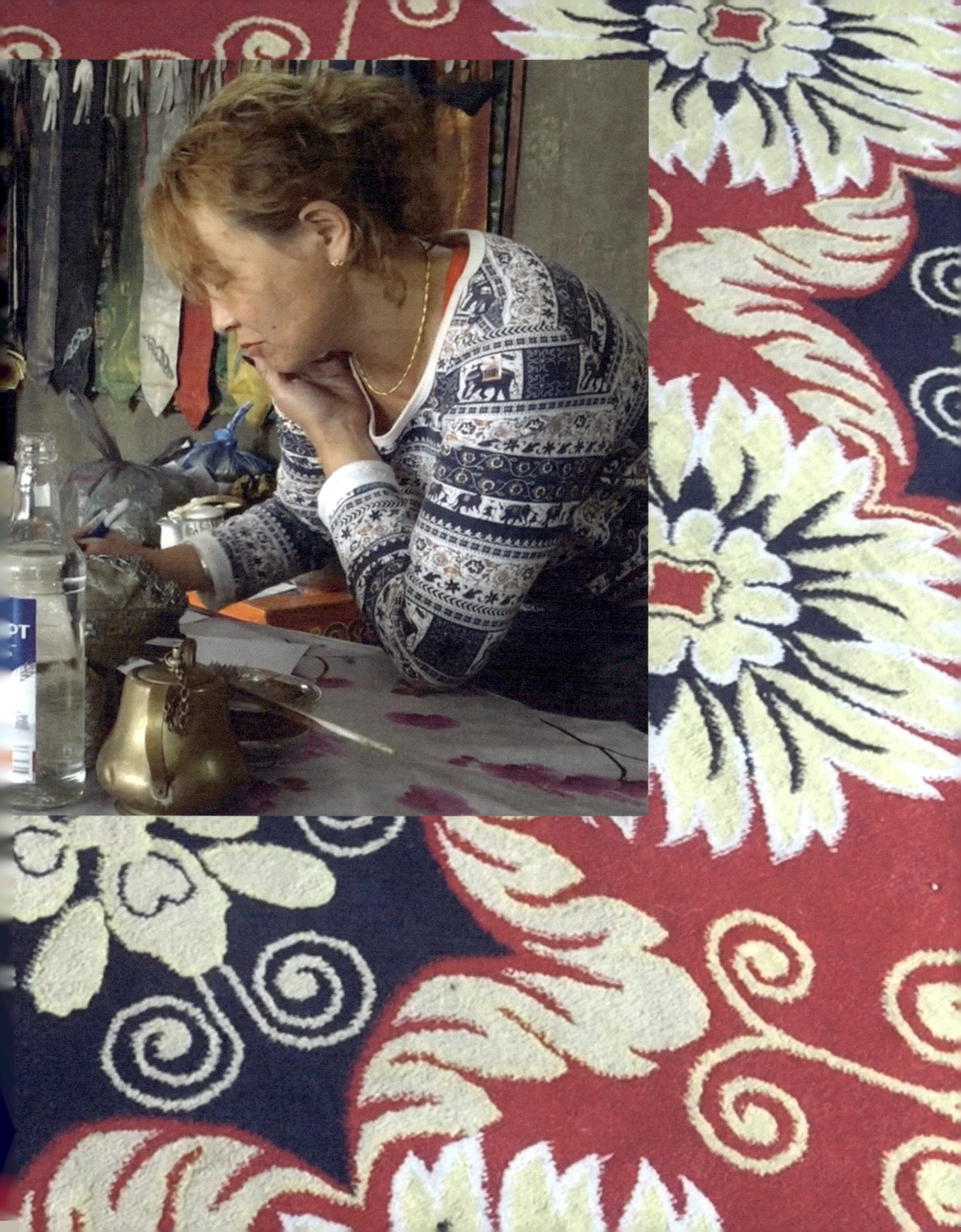

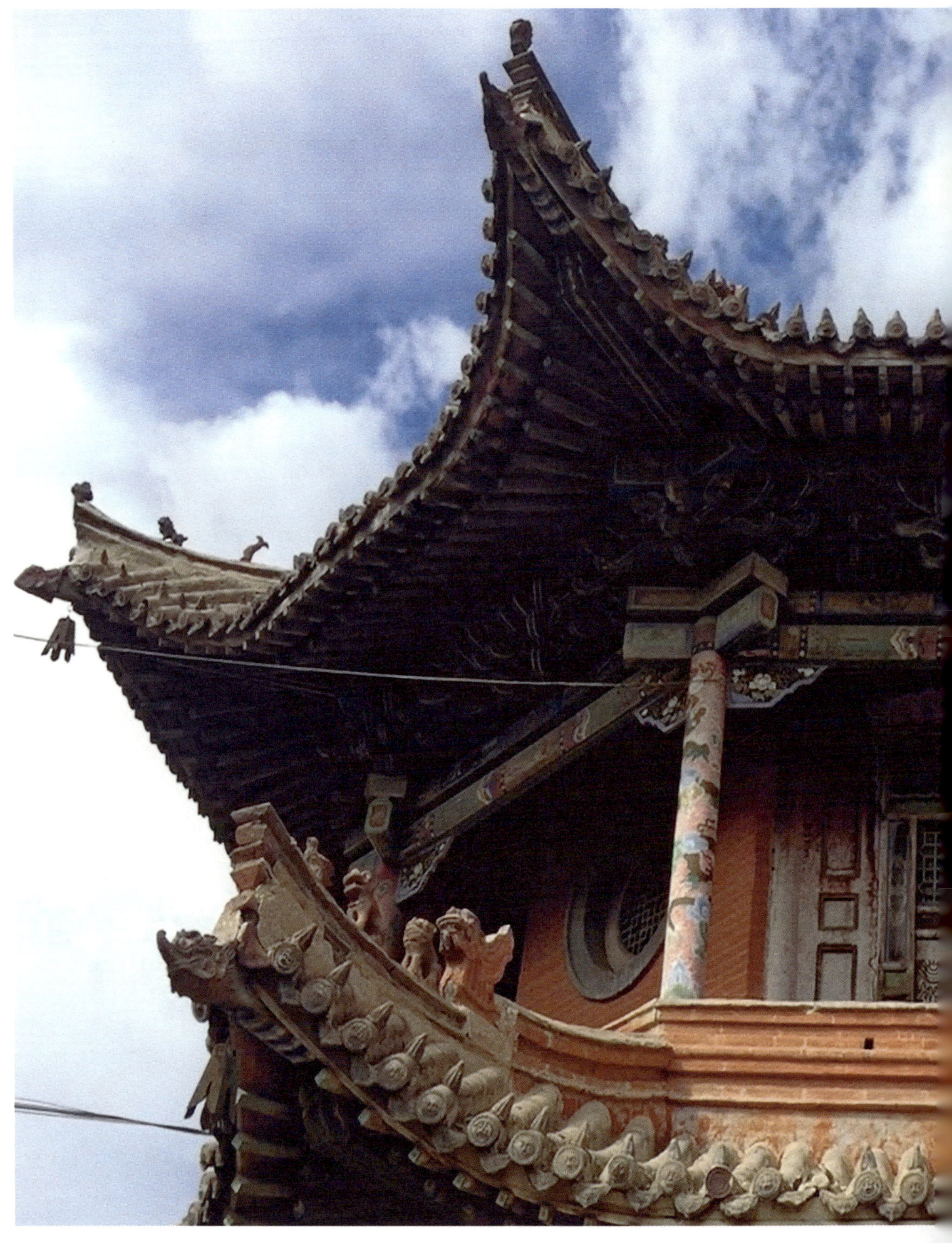

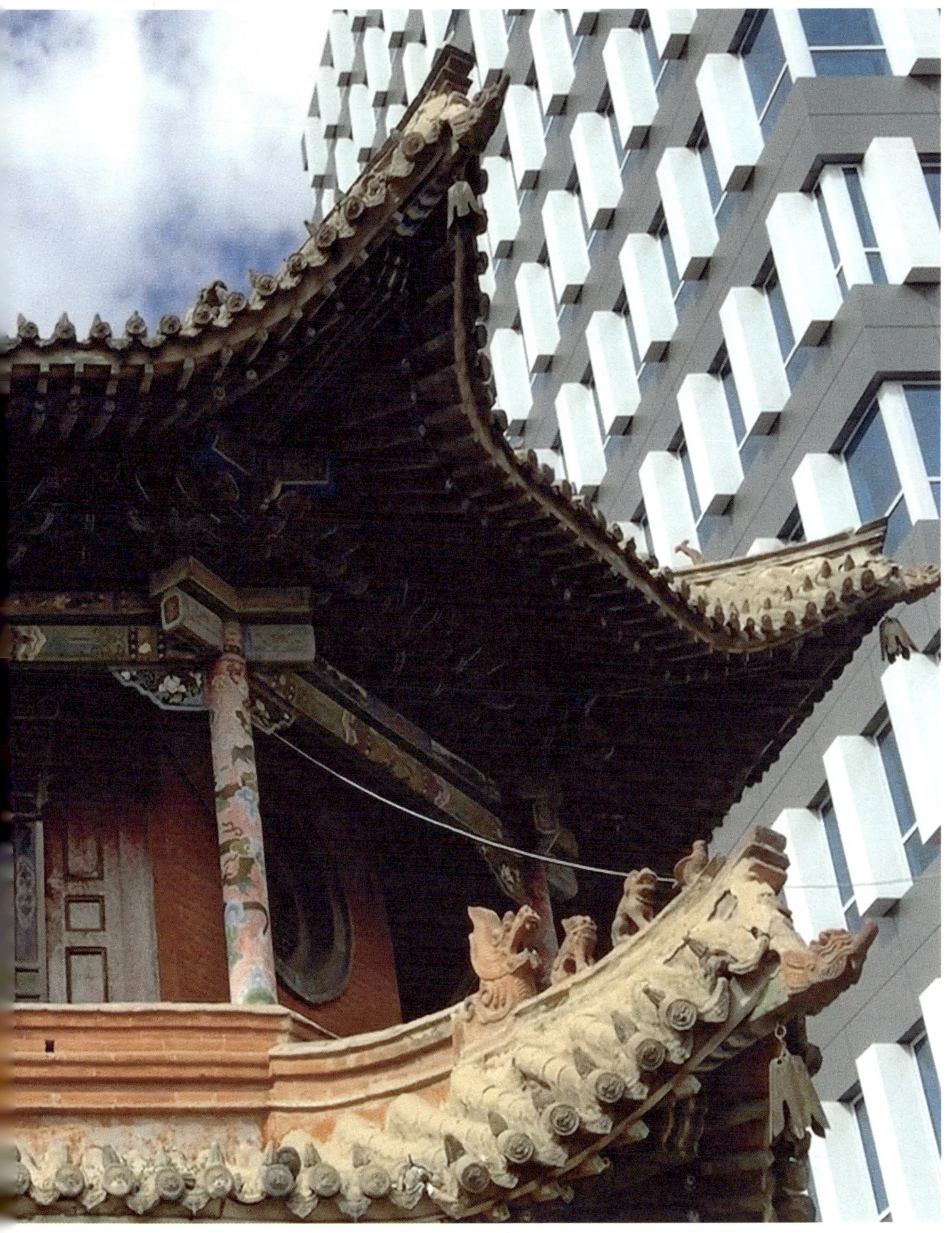

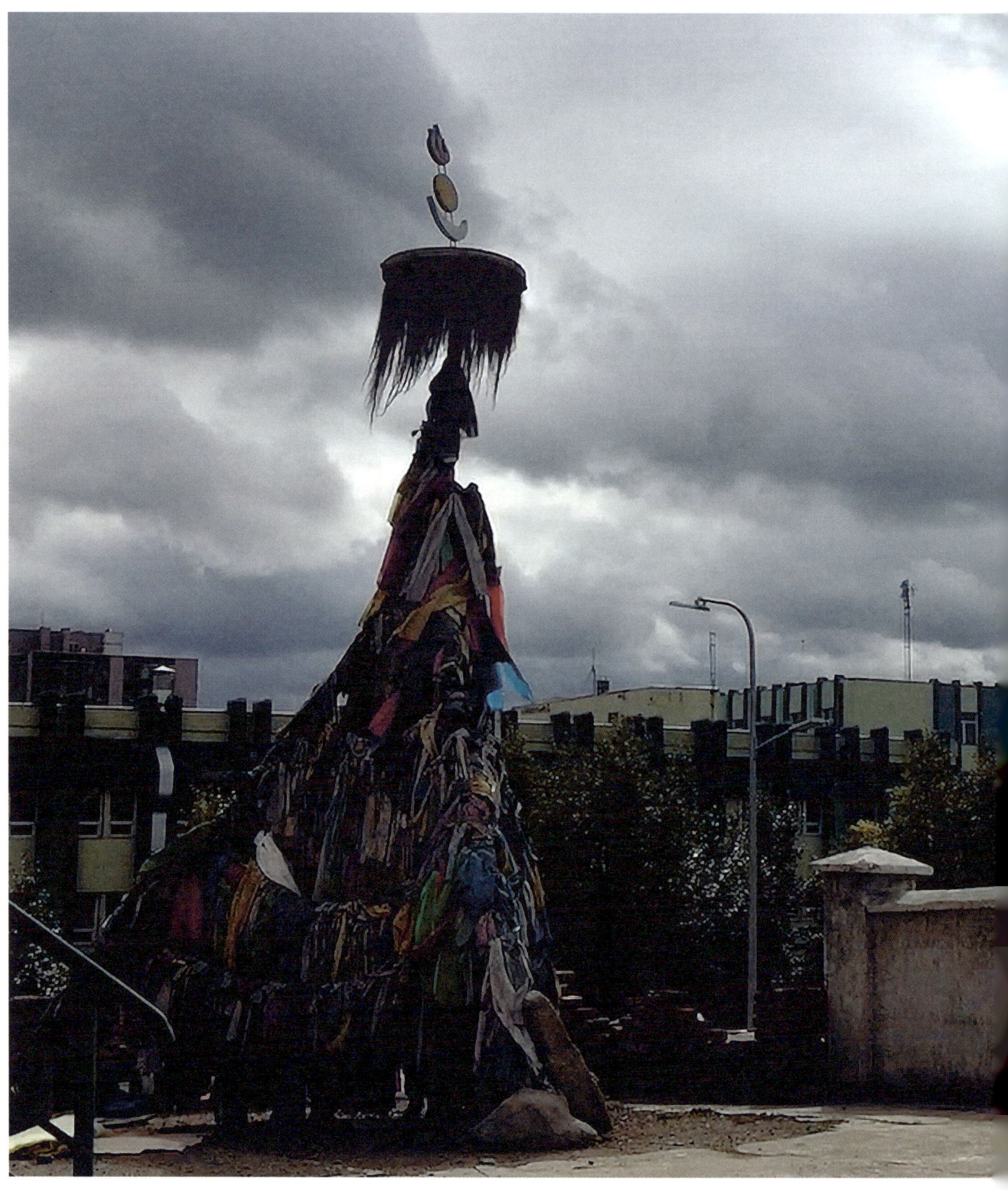

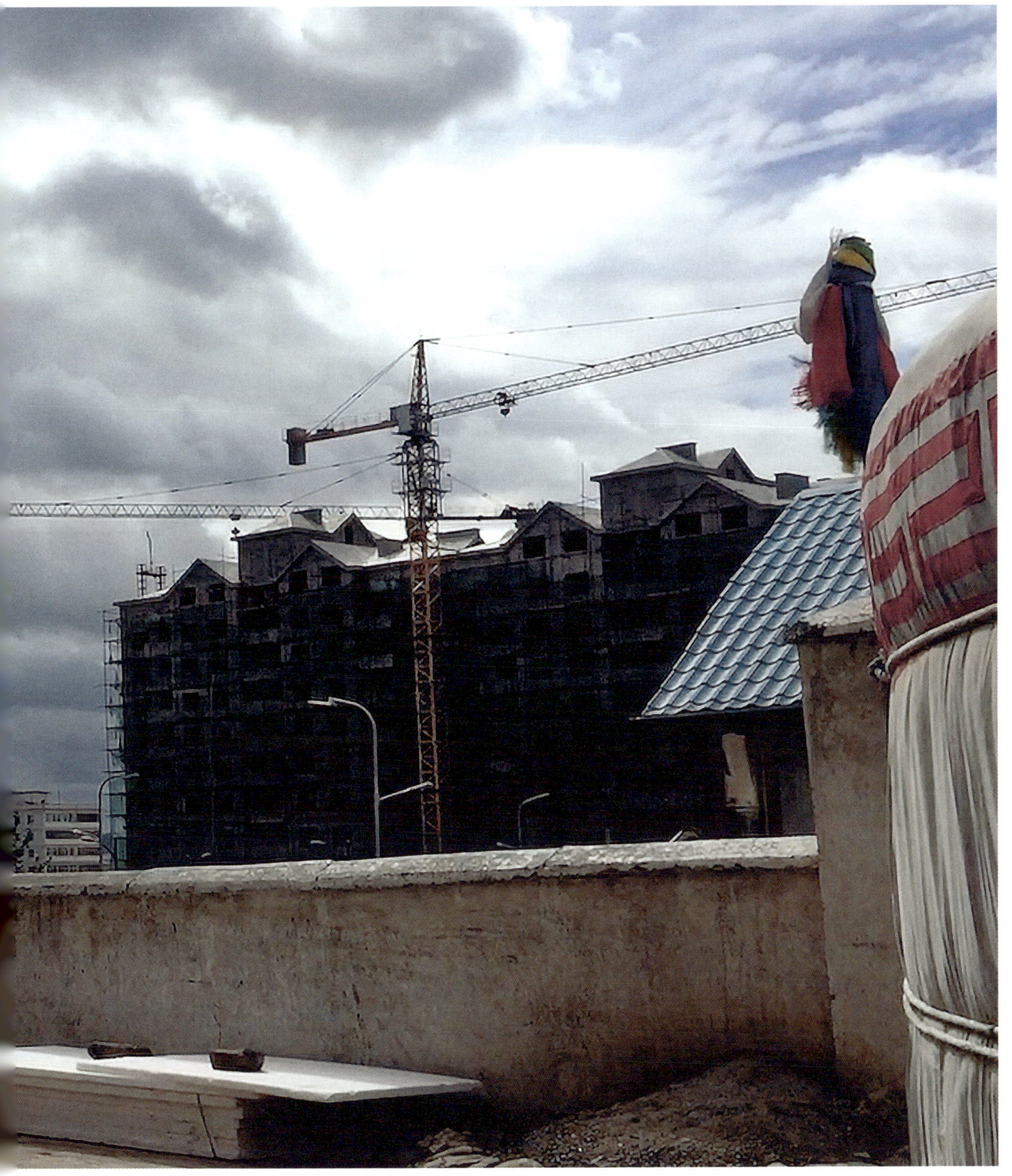

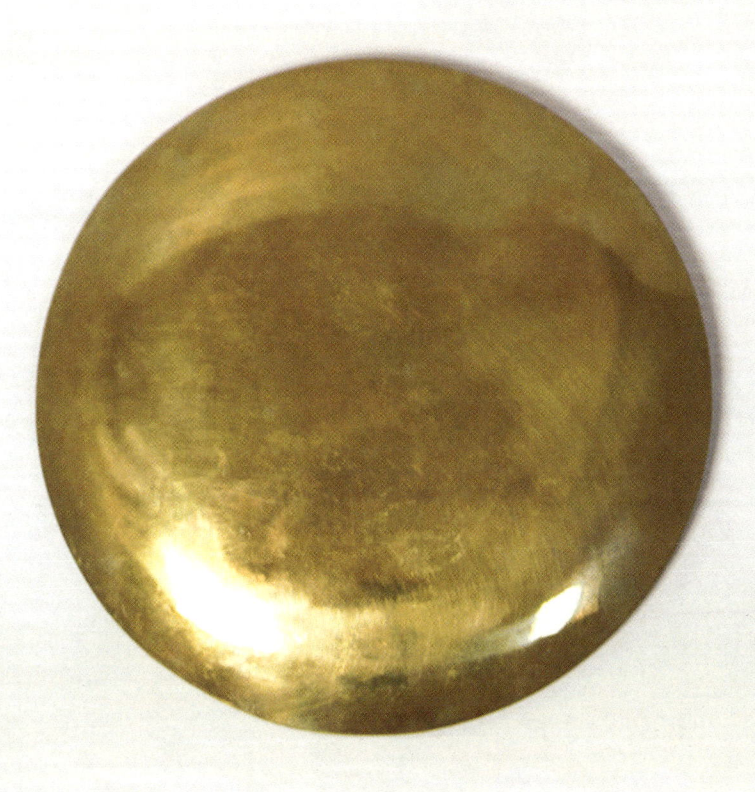

Miracles

Federico Campagna

★

Talking about Miracles

Like the centre of a labyrinth in a Renaissance garden[1], the topic of miracles can be approached only through a long, winding path. As in a labyrinth, where the first turn appears to move away from our desired destination, the first step to look at miracles is to consider them negatively, in reference to what they are not.

Miracles are events that can be defined only on the basis of their relationship with the field of the "speakable phenomenon", that is, with what is apparent to us humans in such a way that we can have clear and distinct ideas about it (ideas that we can at least potentially communicate exhaustively through language). Its relationship with the field of the "speakable phenomenon", however, is complex. On the one hand, a central element of the miraculous is the presence of a witness: a miracle is such not in itself, but in relation to a witness. Yet such witnessing can only take place as direct experience/apprehension, that is in a form that is not mediated by linguistic categories. Miracles are defined by the field of "speakable phenomena", only inasmuch as they exceed and rupture it. Impenetrable to descriptive language, miracles are immune to any attempt at capturing them into a set of exhaustive definitions. Rather, their recollection after experience is as difficult as that of a dream upon waking.

The impossibility of talking about miracles through descriptive language, however, is no reason to despair about the possibility of talking about them altogether. We can attempt to address the essence of miracles through a different kind of language (if indeed it is a language): that of symbols. Differently from the descriptive language of allegories, symbols merely hint or point towards their object, while not attempting to capture or exhaust it. As the great scholar of Iranian philosophy, Henry Corbin pointed out:

> Every allegorical interpretation is harmless; the allegory is [...] a disguising, of something that is already known or knowable otherwise, while the appearance of an Image having the quality of a symbol is a primary phenomenon (*Urphanomen*), unconditional and irreducible, the appearance of something that cannot manifest itself otherwise to the world where we are[2].

The Ineffable

What is there, that exceeds the "speakable phenomenon", while remaining open to experience? By definition, we can call this ontological "excess": the Ineffable.

Here the first aspect of the mystery of miracles emerges: although the ineffable can't be spoken of, yet it speaks. As explained in the *Upanishads*:

> He is never seen, but is the Seer; He is never heard, but is the Hearer; He is never thought of, but is the Thinker; He is never known, but is the Knower. There is no other seer than He, there is no other hearer than He, there is no other thinker than He, there is no other knower than He. He is the Inner Controller – your own Self[3].

If we think about it, in order to take place, language needs something outside of itself that is able to utter it and to produce it. How could it ever be *causa sui*? Likewise, how could the speakable phenomenon be self-sufficient? To exist as such, it requires something external to itself, something phenomenally unspeakable, that is able to relate to it phenomenally.

*

The *Upanishads* locate the prime example of this relationship, in the case of one's own self. As I utter my own name, it is not "I", but an "I" behind the "I" that does so. In uttering its own name, "I", this ineffable self begins its construction of reality by placing its first building block, its first name. After all, what is reality but the sum of the names of the existent? However, as it proceeds projecting a web of names and of language out of itself, and calls it reality, the self almost invariably starts to adopt exclusively the perspective of its own names. The self thus forgets itself, and identifies with its "I". The "suspension of disbelief" which is necessary to enter reality, often develops into an unending labyrinth. Yet, there are still moments in which the "I", that is the name of the self, suddenly looks back towards its original utterer, its own ineffable self.

"If I'm not this 'I' that I call 'I', then who am I?" – this is the archetypal question that can enable the experience of the miraculous. It is at once an experience of ecstasy and of return, in that one "steps out" of its identification with its own name, while "stepping back into" its own ineffable self. As the nineteenth-century Algerian thinker Ahmed Ben Mustafa Ben Alliwa said, it is the moment in which one ceases to see merely the letter of reality, and sees instead the ink of which it is made.

> Truly, letters are symbols of the ink, because there are no letters outside of the ink itself. [...] They are its determinations and its stages of actualisation, and there is nothing else apart from the ink. [...] And yet, the letters are different from the ink. [...] Because the ink was there before there were the letters, and it will remain there after the letters will be no more. [...] There is no existence outside of the existence of the ink. [...] Wherever there is a letter, the ink is not separate from it[4].

In its most fundamental form, the experience of the miraculous is the experience of existence in itself – behind and before its alienation through its names. For this reason, as in the *Vedas*, the fundamental experience of one's own ineffable self can function as a model for the experience of the ineffable in all aspects of reality: like ink on a page, existence runs through all names and letters and alphabets. This is the experience of the miraculous.

Knowing as Being

But what is a miracle for? As in most religious traditions, we can understand miracles as important and beneficial opportunities – but why?

On the surface, their effect is merely gnoseological: they allow their witness to expand their understanding of what the world is. While until the experience of the miraculous, they had fallen for the illusion that the world started and ended at arm's reach of language, they now know that much lies in the field of the ineffable. Also, they now know that descriptive language is an important but insufficient tool, since only symbolic language can function as a medium for the difficult sharing of a miraculous experience of the Ineffable.

Yet, the effects produced by witnessing a miracle, that is of directly apprehending it, are not limited to the gnoseological level. To appreciate their ontological effects, we should consider how direct apprehension works. Direct apprehension functions differently from that kind of understanding that relies on descriptive language. While linguistic understanding allows for the positions of the subject and object of knowledge as two separate entities, and thus promotes an acquisitive form of

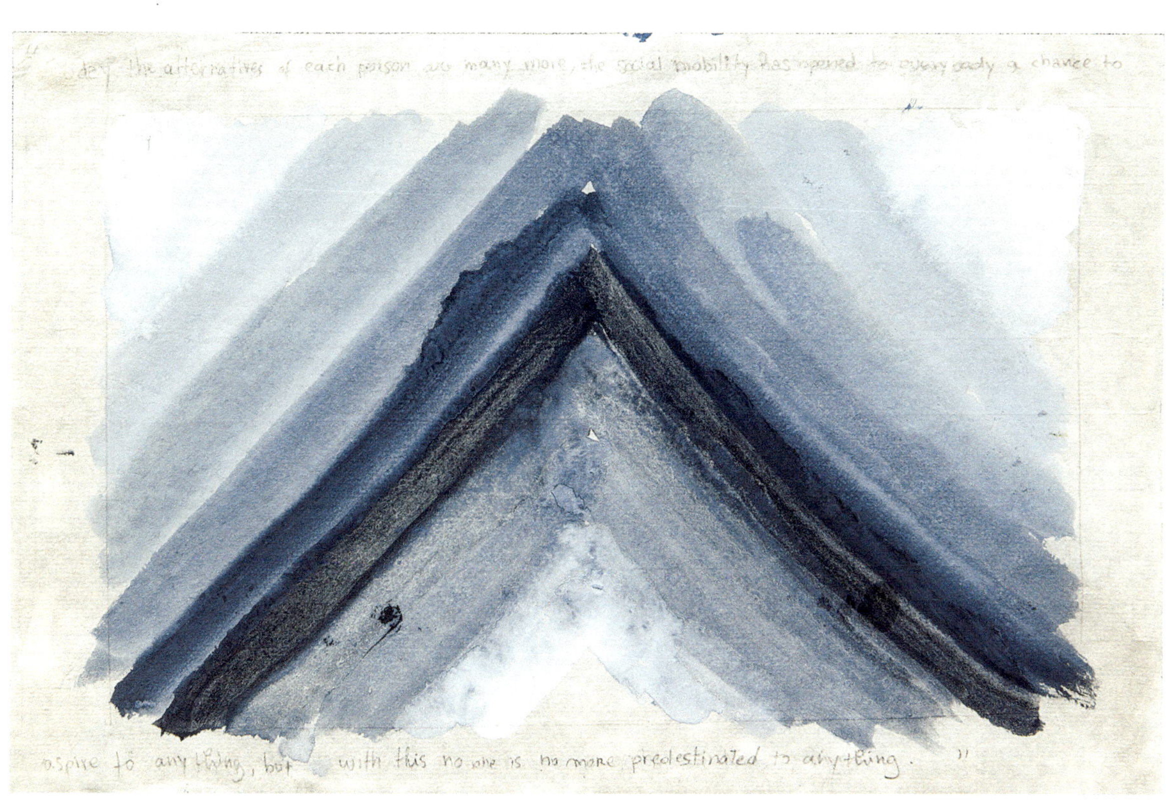
"...day the alternatives of each person are many more, the social mobility has opened to everybody a chance to
aspire to anything, but with this no one is no more predestinated to anything."

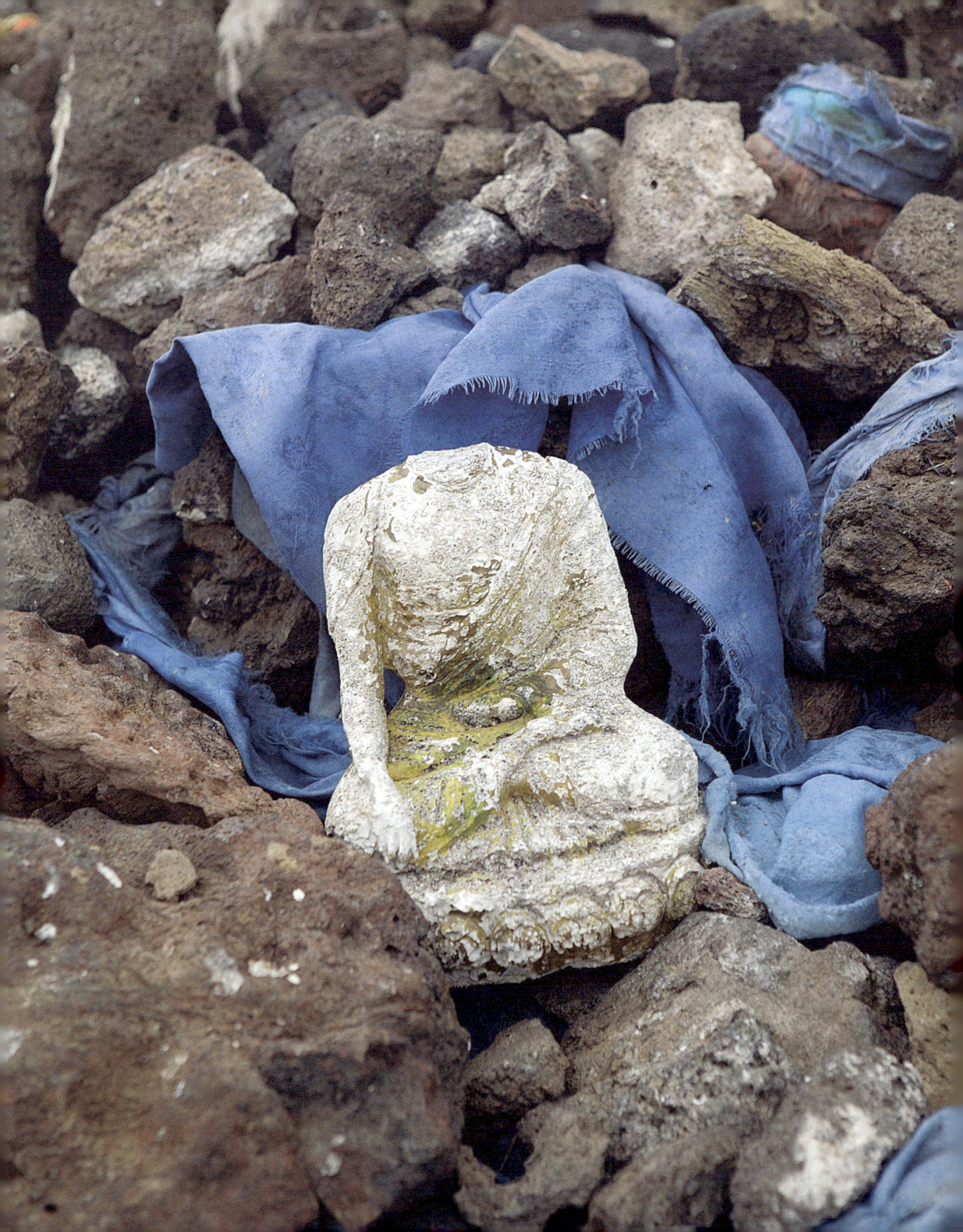

★

understanding (as the acquisition and stockpiling of information), direct apprehension functions on different ontological foundations. According to traditions spanning from the Persian theosophy of Sohrawardi and Mulla Sadra[5], to the Russian orthodox mysticism of Pavel Florenskij[6], it isn't possible to talk about knowledge if we consider the subject and the object of knowledge as two distinct entities, and knowledge itself as a third, mediating one. As long as "knowledge" and "truth" remain distinct entities, it won't be possible to talk about "true knowledge". If we wish to ground our knowledge on solid foundations, we need to refer back to the very basis of our act of knowing. Long before Descartes' "cogito", the eleventh-century Uzbek/Persian philosopher Avicenna had demonstrated through his "floating man" argument[7] that the most fundamental form of certain knowledge was the direct apprehension that one has of their own self. He claimed that one's knowledge of one's own existence is direct, unmediated and beyond doubt. On this basis, subsequent philosophers such as Sohrawardi and later Mulla Sadra developed what is known as the doctrine of "knowledge by presence". According to their view, the fundamental knowledge that one has of one's own existence, is based on the coincidence of the subject and the object of knowledge. You can only truly know what you are, you can only truly be what you know. While Parmenides claimed that "the same thing is to be thought of and to be"[8], for Mulla Sadra the same thing for knowing truly and truly being[9].

We can now appreciate why miracles have an effect that isn't merely gnoseological, but also ontological. If the authentic form of knowledge is the direct apprehension of oneself, and if miracles offer an unmediated apprehension of the same kind as the "knowledge by presence" that one has of one's own self, then the miraculous experience affects not only the field of the knowable, but also one's very existence. Thus, whenever the reality of the ineffable emerges miraculously in objects and situations and events and time, one reaches the realization that one already "is" (that one cannot say to be different from) that ineffable which made itself miraculously manifest. When the experience of the miraculous makes the ineffable manifest itself in a rock, for example, its witness realizes the identity of its own ineffable self and the ineffable dimension that inhabits the linguistic unit of "the rock". This is to say that while every single thing maintains a distinct existence as a linguistic unit, they all share exactly the same existence in the dimension of the uncategorizable (and thus unfragmentable) ineffable. While their names are different, their existence is one and the same.

The Paradox of Hierophanies

This miraculous understanding, however, should not lead us to completely discard language as mere illusion, awkwardly glued upon the undifferentiated "one" of existence. Although the names of things (i.e. the linguistic reality of the speakable phenomenon) do not exhaust the field of existence, nonetheless they do exist. Indeed, their existence is ultimately dependent on ineffable existence, but they nonetheless exist. This coexistence of language and ineffability, is the paradox at the centre of the experience of the miraculous. Mircea Eliade often described this paradox as a hierophany. A typical example of hierophany, suggests Eliade, is offered by the sacred stones of countless religious traditions[10]: as the place of a hierophany (or, if you wish, a miracle), the sacred stone is *at the same time* a normal stone and a sacred stone, it simultaneously partakes of historical time and of cosmic time, it is, in other words, at the same time merely a stone and the whole unity of existence.

The approach of most esoteric traditions invites the witness of a miracle to understand the world as the paradoxical combination of existence-in-reality, where ineffable existence and linguistic reality take place in a state of integration. One is at the same time exactly oneself (his/her name, identity, etc.), while also coinciding existentially with the ineffable existence which runs uninterrupted and undifferentiated through plants, rocks, concepts, and humans alike. To be one and many at the same time, to be both ineffably existent and linguistically real, is the position of the *coincidentia oppositorum* discussed by Renaissance neoplatonists all the way to Carl Gustav Jung[11].

This paradox expands to a renewed conception of the whole world (or existence-within-reality) as something at once profane and sacred, that is as a hierophany in itself. While it would be reductive to consider it wholly profane (that is, wholly reducible to a chain of linguistic units), it would be equally reductive to consider it exclusively under the blinding light of the ineffable. The challenge presented by the miraculous, is that of constantly re-connecting the experience of the linguistic and that of the ineffable, or, to borrow a metaphor dear to Islamic mysticism, to never allow the image in the mirror to obfuscate the mirror as such, or the surface of the mirror to obfuscate the image reflected in it. The experience of the miraculous demands that we take up the seemingly impossible challenge of being able to see at the same time the image and the mirror, or to consider at the same time the letter and the ink with which it is traced.

Death and Rebirth of the World

Thus, the experience of the miraculous invites to embrace not a static, but a dynamic relationship with the world as a paradox of existence-in-reality. Hence the importance of rituals, as dynamic practices that allow to reconnect symbolically the linguistic with the ineffable, and thus to replicate the miraculous in symbolic form.

The traditional importance of rituals of death and rebirth, for example, can be understood in the light of the role of the miraculous in shaping our relationship with/in the world. The experience of the miraculous produces death and rebirth, since it forces its witness to "die" to its exclusive identification with the names of reality, and to be reborn in the expanded ontology of the integration of the ineffable and the linguistic. It also indicates the importance of constantly re-creating the world as a paradoxical integration: without this constant creation, without this endless ritual of remembrance and replication of the miraculous experience, the world as existence-in-reality would once again dis-integrate into its constituent parts: an empty virtual reality on the one hand, and a deaf thunder of existence on the other. It is by the combination of these two elements that the world emerges, as Greek mythology teaches us.

It is important to notice how this necessity for regeneration and this awareness of a risk of dis-integration of the world, can be found in the mythologies usually associated with the element of water, and particularly with the myth of the flood. As the realm of all virtualities, water symbolizes the totality of all possible forms, but also a cosmic dimension that precedes and exists alongside the linguistic world of specific forms. As they emerge

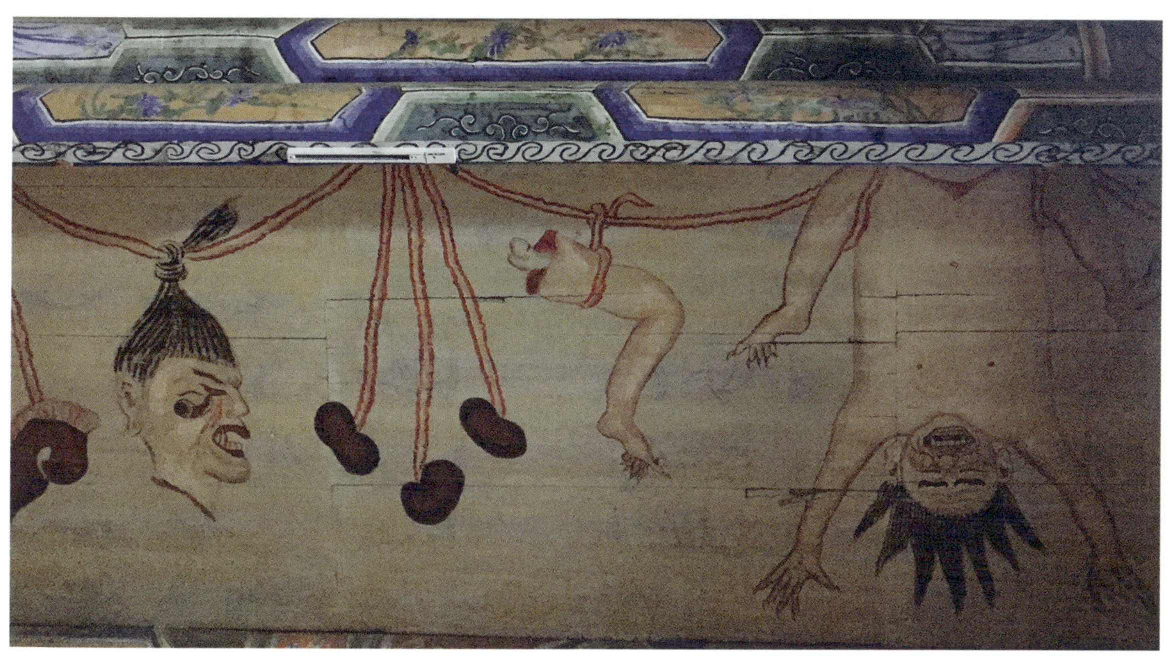

★

from the water, the forms (or names) that make up the world acquire their definite shape and autonomy, yet they also enter historical time, and thus become subject to degeneration, exhaustion and death. The ritual immersion in water, as with the ritual of baptism, refers to the symbolic burial by water, the cleansing flood which at once dissolves exhausted forms, thus reintegrating them into limitless virtuality, but also allows for the renewal of form-creation. This series of mythologies and rituals replicate the movement of the miraculous experience (the witness being "submerged" into the "water" of the Ineffable, to return renewed and expanded to linguistic reality), while also reminding us of the necessity to cyclically repeat the miraculous experience, to prevent the exhaustion of the linguistic forms (particularly, their simultaneous hypertrophy and emptying which we call metaphysical nihilism and that characterizes our current age).

The linguistic world needs to be cyclically "submerged" into the "water" of the Ineffable, so to be regenerated and to shed the "dead skin" of shallow, rigid and exhausted forms. This cyclical process amounts to the dynamic relationship with the world inspired by the experience of the miraculous, that is, with the very process that gives origin and grants the survival of reality and of the world. As the Italian anthropologist Ernesto De Martino[12] pointed out, neither the world or reality are a *datum*, something whose presence is stable and granted: both of them are the product of a constant re-creation, always vulnerable to crisis. In line with a long tradition of magic, the ultimate lesson of miracles lies exactly in this understanding of reality and the world as the product of a ritual weaving between ineffability and language – a tailor's work that is constantly threatened by destruction and vanishing. As we know all too well today.

[1] For an interesting discussion of the symbolism of Renaissance gardens, see Joscelyn Godwin, *The Pagan Dream of the Renaissance*, Boston, MA: Weiser Books, 2005, pp. 153–180.
[2] Henry Corbin, *Mundus Imaginalis or The Imaginary and the Imaginal*, Ipswich: Golgonooza Press, 1976, p. 10 (*Mundus Imaginalis ou l'imaginaire et l'imaginal*, Brussels: Cahiers Internationaux de Symbolisme 6, 1964).
[3] *Brihadaranyaka Upanishad* III.7.23.
[4] Sheikh Ahmed Ben Mustafa Ben Alliwa, "Il prototipo unico", in Titus Burckhardt, *Considerazioni sulla conoscenza sacra*, Milan: SE, 1997, p. 93. My translation from the Italian edition.
[5] See Henry Corbin's masterful discussion of the development of this theosophical tradition in Henry Corbin, *History of Islamic Philosophy*, London: Routledge, 2014 (*Histoire de la philosophie islamique*, Paris: Gallimard, 1964).
[6] See Pavel Florenskij's development of this theme in his discussion of icon painting, in Pavel Florenkskij, *Le porte regali*, Milan: Adelphi, 2012 (*Ikonostas*, Moscow: Bogoslovski Trudi, 1972).
[7] For a lively and succinct exposition of Avicenna's thought experiment of the floating man, see Peter Adamson, *Philosophy in the Islamic World*, Oxford: Oxford University Press, 2016, pp. 133–139.
[8] As reported in Fr. 3 Clement *Strom.* VI, 23; Plotinus V, 1, 8 in. This translation from Geoffrey Stephen Kirk et al. (eds.), *The Presocratic Philosophers*, Cambridge: Cambridge University Press, 2005, p. 246.
[9] For an interesting discussion of Mulla Sadra's epistemology and its relationship with contemporary existentialism, see Muhammad Kamal, *From Essence to Being: the Philosophy of Mulla Sadra and Martin Heidegger*, London: ICAS Press, 2010, pp. 157–178.
[10] See in particular Mircea Eliade, *Patterns in Comparative Religion*, Lincoln: University of Nebraska Press, 1996, pp. 216–238 (*Traité d'histoires des religions*, Paris: Payot, 1949).
[11] For an interesting discussion of Carl Gustav Jung's reception of Nicholas of Cusa's notion of *coincidentia opositorum*, see David Henderson, "The Coincidence of Opposites", *Studies in Spirituality* 20, (2010), pp. 101–113.
[12] See Ernesto de Martino, *Il mondo magico*, Turin: Bollati Boringhieri, 2010, pp. 70–168.

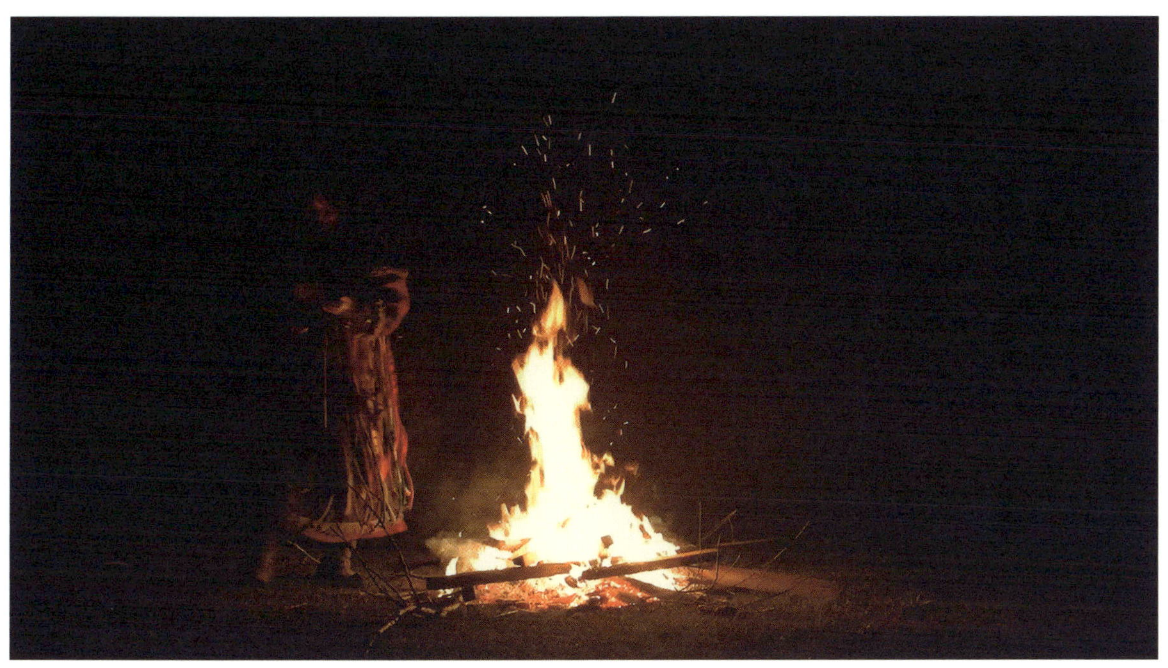

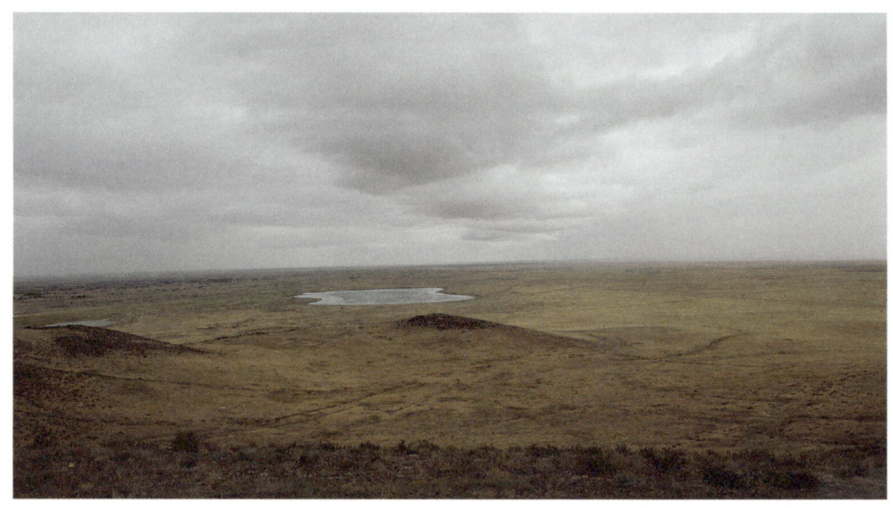

Altan Ovoo Sacred Mountain, Dariganga, south east edge of the Gobi Desert,
Mongolia, 24th August, 2016
photographic documentation

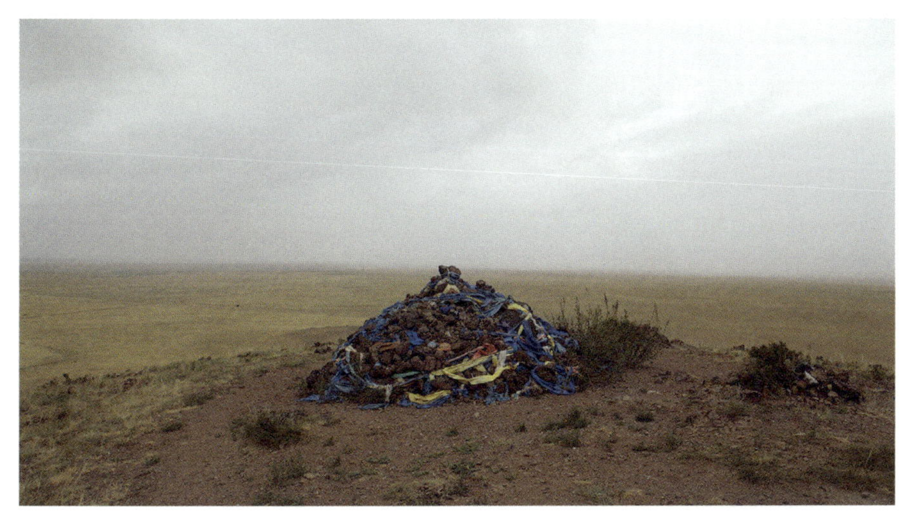

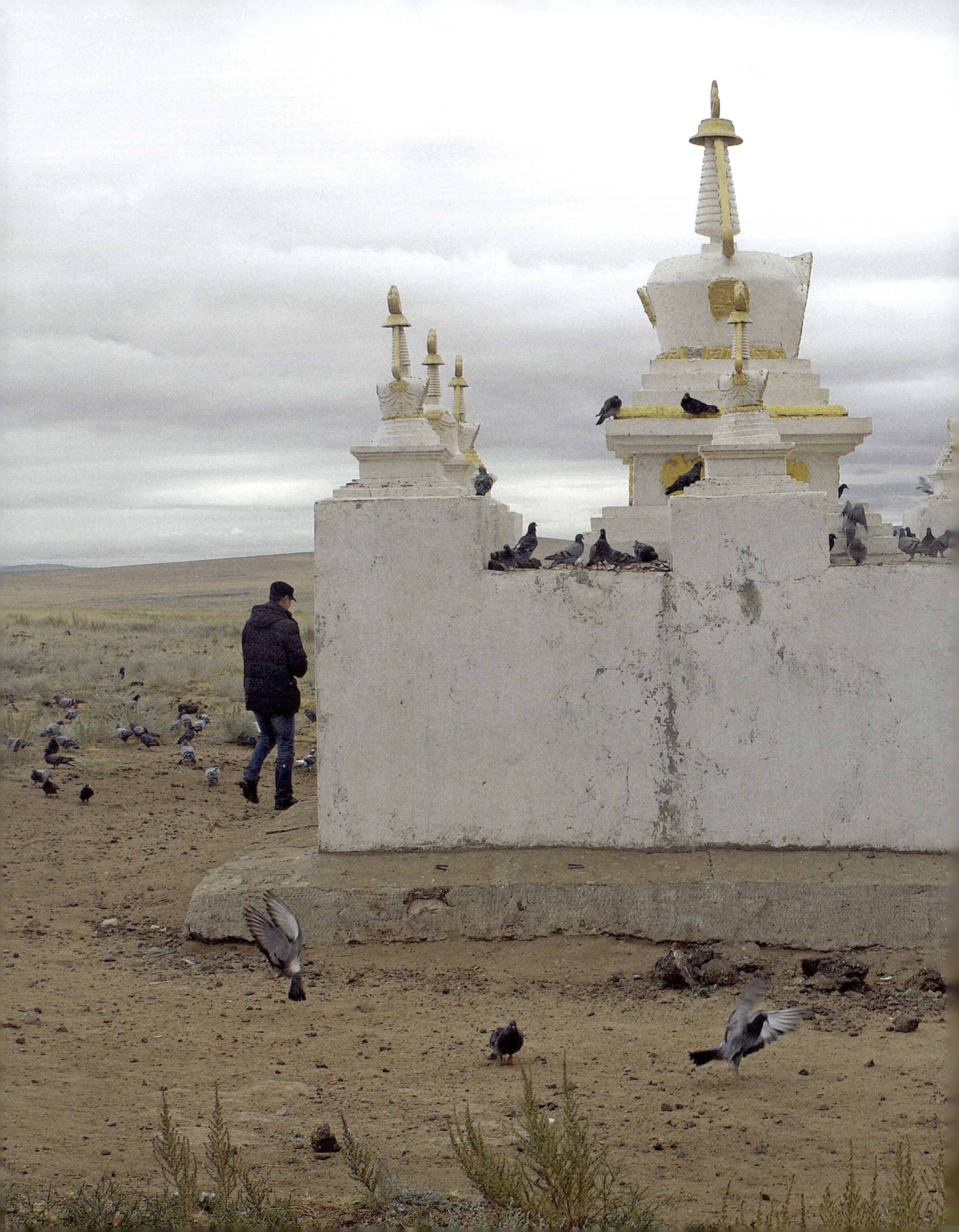

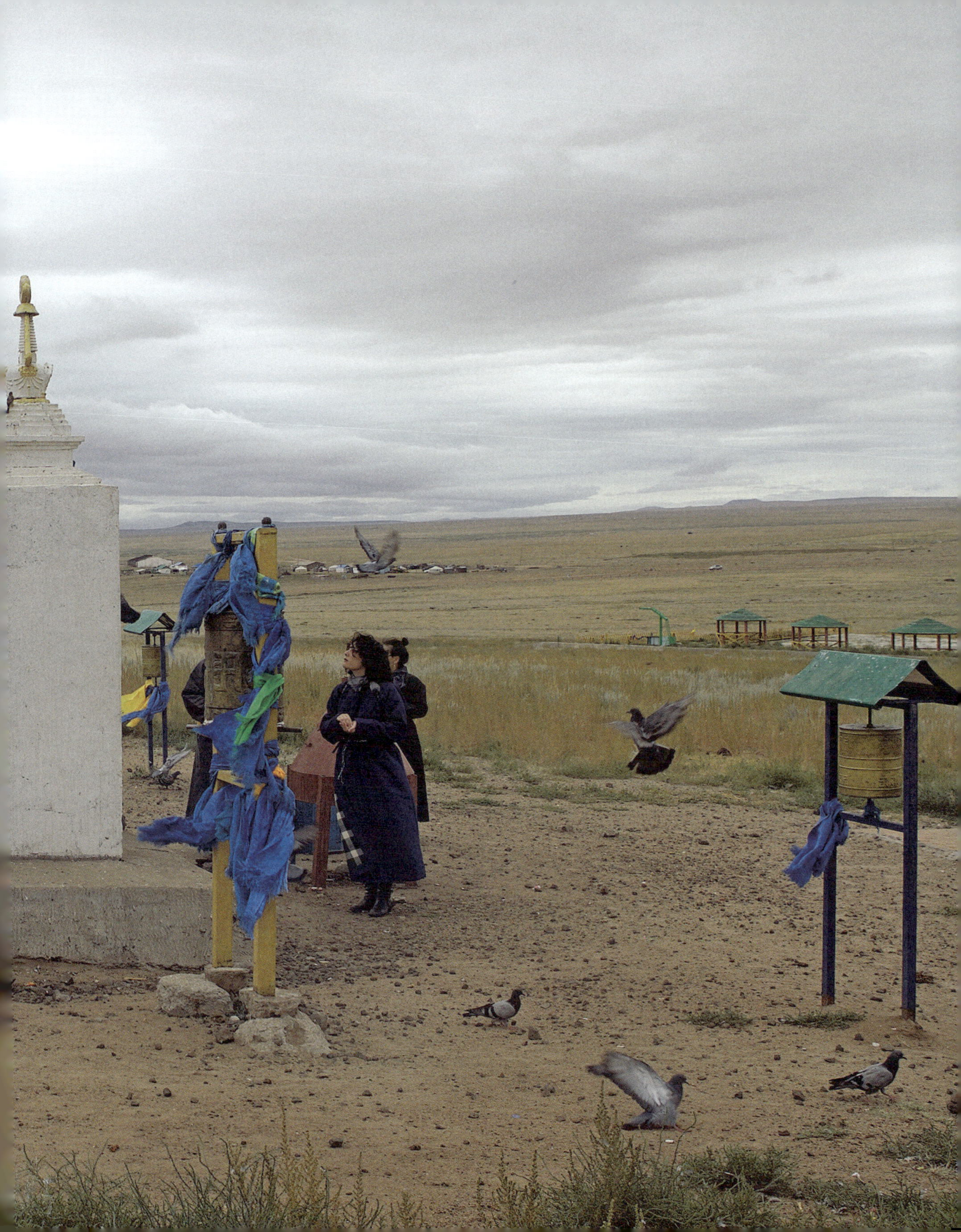

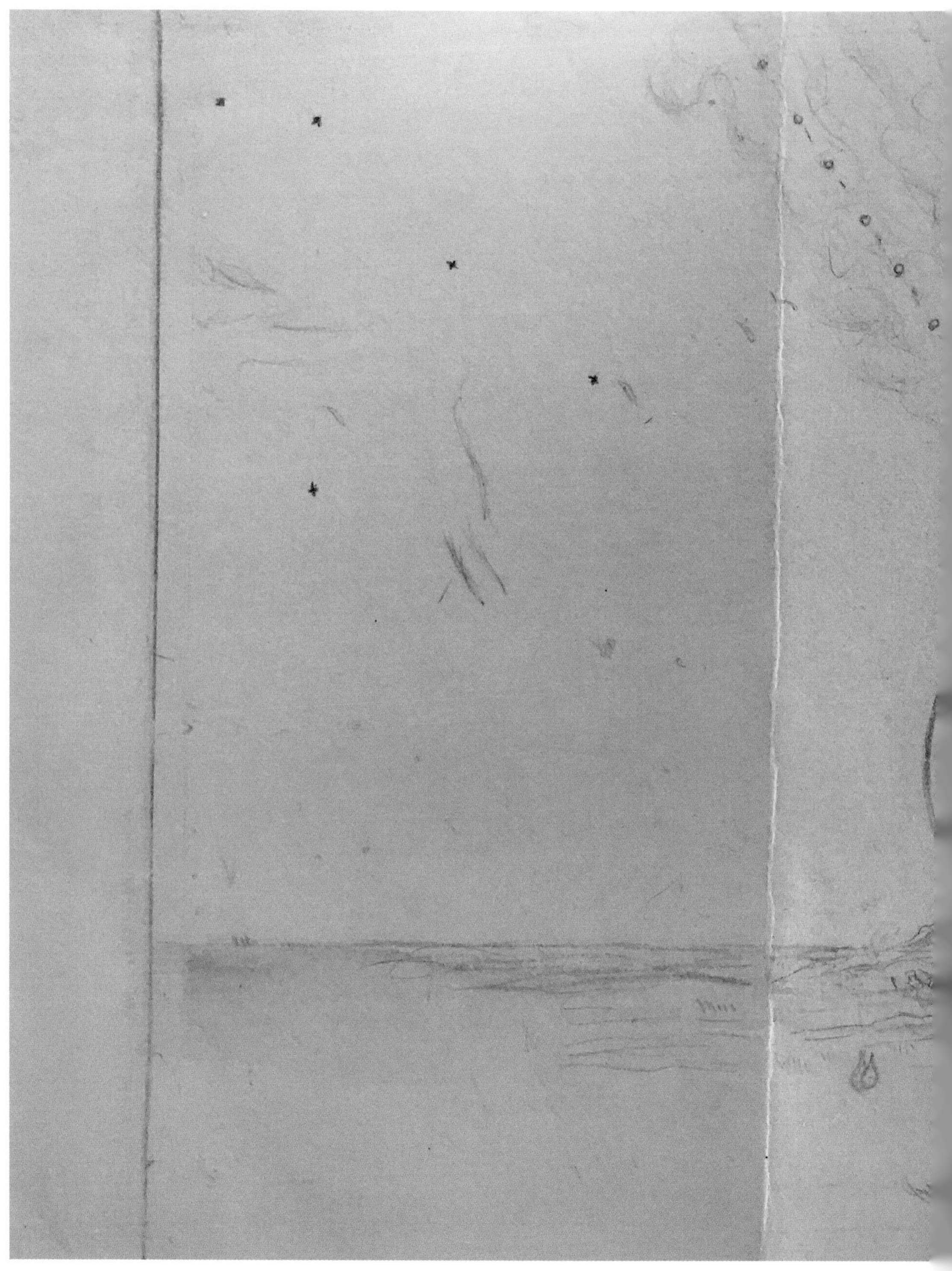

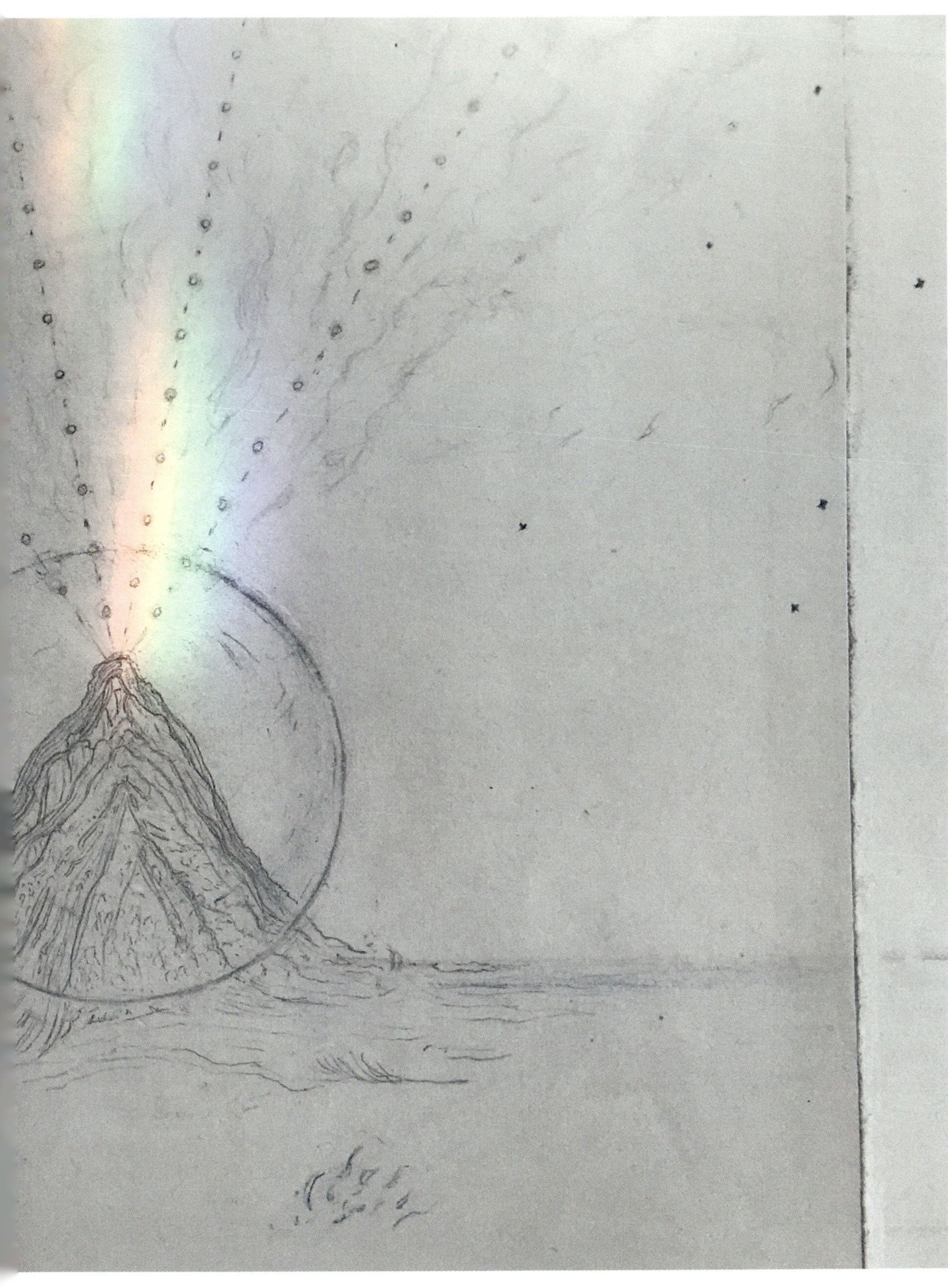

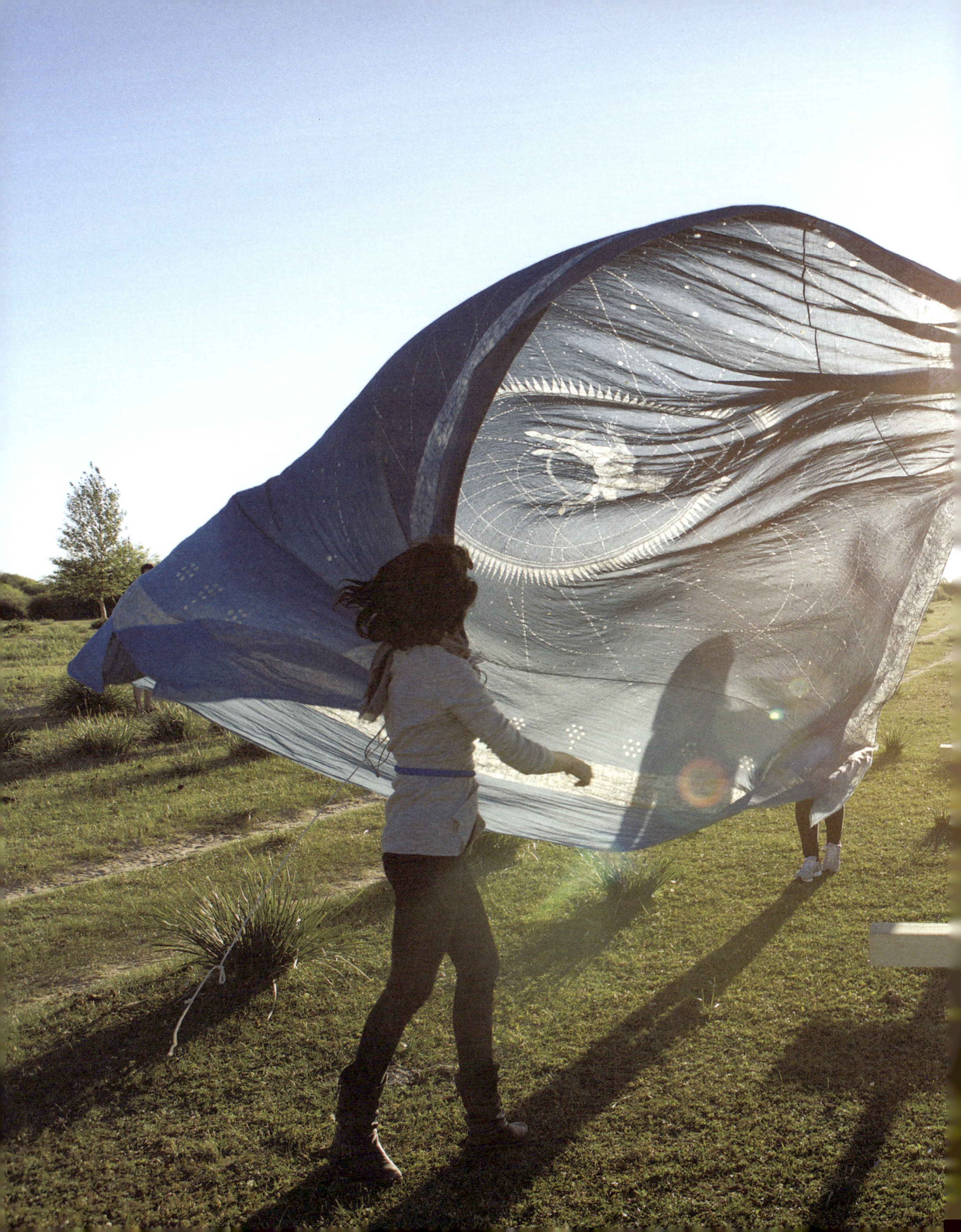

May I Travel with the Strength of Infinite Mind! An Introduction to Lisa Batacchi's Art

Valentina Gioia Levy

★

Like the rising of the white lantern of the moon,
In the depths of night, enfolding the world,
Heavenly lady, perfect in every way,
Please remain forever in my heart!
[...]
Crossing the borderless world in the mind,
Its pleasant form gives pleasure to pure eyes.
Roaming through different times, in far away lands,
May I travel with the strength of infinite mind!

A Poem of Homage to Yangchen Lhamo[1]

"A tree as wide as a man's embrace grows from a tiny shoot. A tower of nine stories starts with a pile of dirt. A climb of eight hundred feet starts where the foot stands [...]". This can be read in section LXIV ("Preponderance of the Small"), in the *Tao te Ching, The Book of the Way and its Virtue* attributed to the Taoist philosopher Lao Tzu (fourth century BC)[2].
An invitation to focus on the little things, but also almost praise of the expectation and those imperceptible temporal cadences which lead to the gradual unravelling of events. A step, a pile of dirt, a small branch can be the prelude to a future full of promises, or going back in time, they can represent, as in Lisa Batacchi's work, an artistic practice which is at the same time the trail of a passage, the testimony of a meeting, the residual matter produced by a ritual action, individual or collective. Therefore, not only an artistic object, but the tangible demonstration of a complex series of interactions among people, cultures, spaces and territories.
The Time of Discretion is a work, or rather, a series of works, which is impossible to define. Perhaps "project" is the most correct word to use to describe it, but "journey" is certainly the word closest to its essence. *The Time of Discretion* is a path which starts from the earth, from under your feet, to then develop in various directions, enriching itself with continuous layers of meanings, beyond geographic and temporal limits. A slow process, as is the time of discretion, requiring pauses, moments of assimilation and above all of thought.
Approaching Lisa Batacchi's work involves a certain amount of emotional involvement, but also the inclination to discover and learn, which is not just a cognitive effort but means placing oneself in front of the work with the same open-mindedness towards possibility and becoming which every journey implies. It is impossible to understand *The Time of Discretion* without allowing the necessary time for listening and self-analysis.

A Climb of Eight Hundred Feet Starts where the Foot Stands...

Looking back on Lisa Batacchi's past you can discover that since the time of her fashion-design studies, she has always been interested in the conceptual, and at the same time emotional, dimension of textiles. In fact, the artist herself revealed that even in this phase of her studies, her attention was often attracted by everyday objects which were part of an intimate dimension, private and also familiar like old aprons or scarves from farm-life linked to her paternal grandparents, but also napkins, rags, curtains which she would embroider or print on. Enriched with these new values and layered on to the old ones, these textile objects were in fact transformed into something which was completely new and yet not totally different. Speaking about her work in those years the artist affirms: "my research was always full of incitement, meaning and references to nature (fragile and strong at the same time) where I transferred my whole inner world, blending visions of places and cultures, even distant ones"[3]. So, even in this phase Lisa Batacchi's

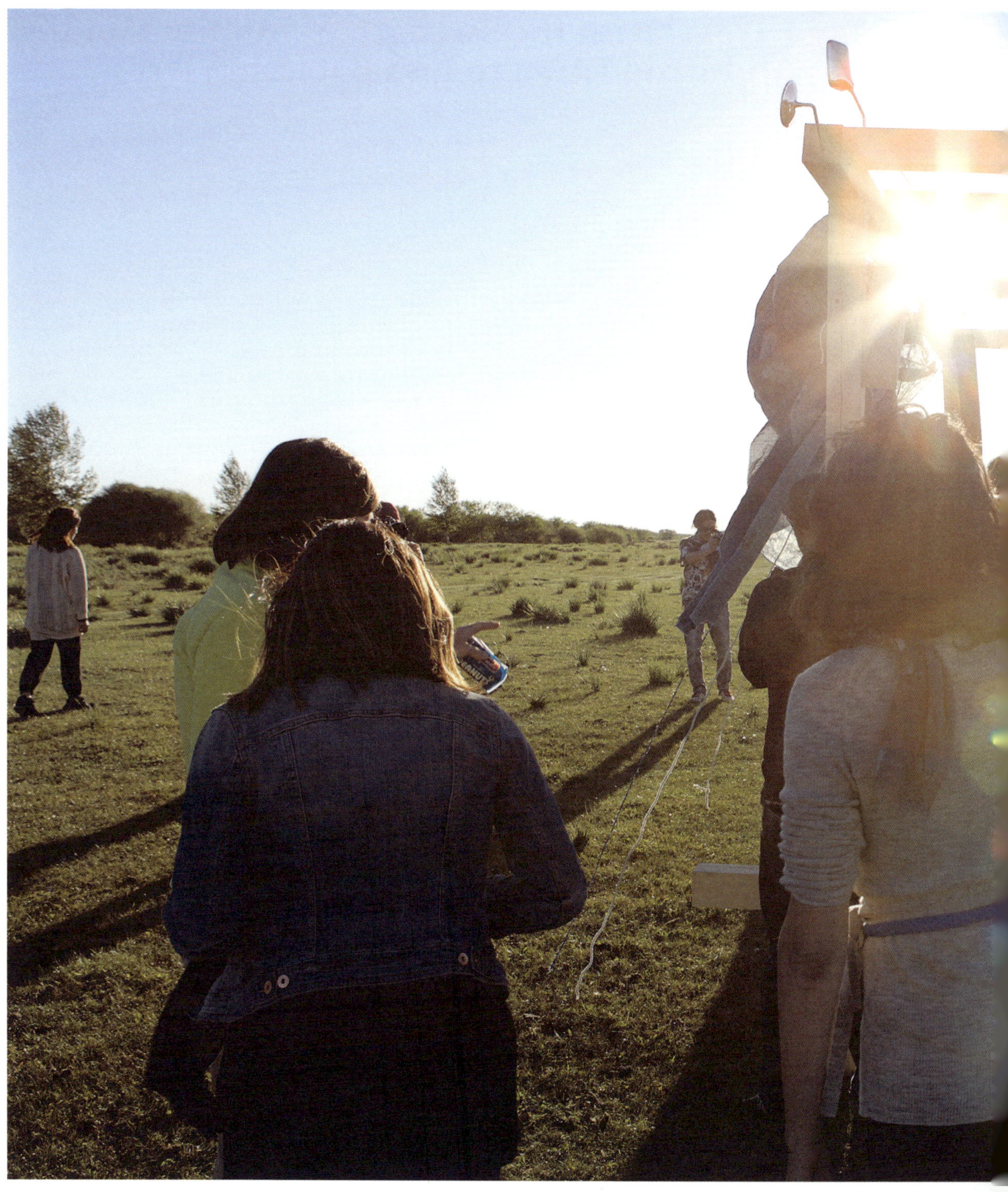

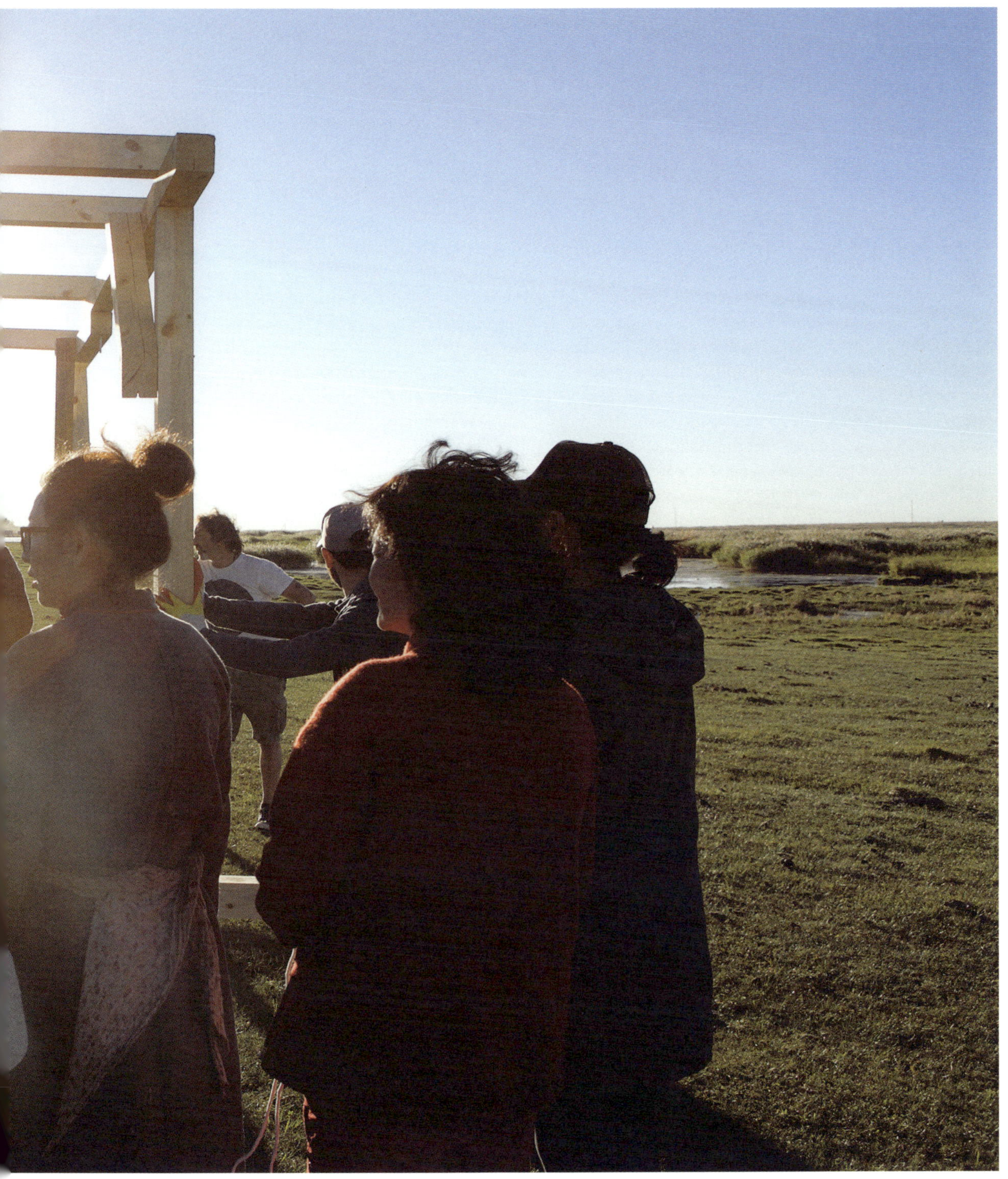

⋆

creative research possessed some essential characteristics which settled within her art. After her studies she started working for important fashion brands, including Vivienne Westwood in London, and began distributing her first collection in 2006, but when she was advised to move at least part of the production to China to lower the costs, she realized that those rhythms and methods imposed by the global market were not for her. Unwilling to follow the mechanisms of mass production and distribution, the procedures of mass consumption and the bulimia of the global markets, with her interest focused on the cultural, creative, social and anthropological aspects which are inherent in textile production, she realized that the natural evolution of her research was to take up an artistic career.

Her vision of a textile object was already close to the concept of habitus as defined by Pierre Bourdieu, in one of his most famous essays *Distinction: A Social Critique of the Judgement of Taste*. In this text the French philosopher described the habitus as the incarnation of a system of structures created during collective history and then transferred into the individual one, which work in a practical way for practical aims. For Bourdieu the dress-habitus is a mediation between the body, society and its conditioning, but above all, an interiorized system of meanings, that is, a device which holds a variety of information and sociocultural values[4].

Lisa Batacchi's artistic practice immediately concentrated on the complex ties which are created between the individual and the objects surrounding her between the person and those everyday materials like clothes, but also pillowcases as in the site-specific installation on Palmaria Island, *In silenzio il silenzio* (2008) and in *Isabella Color* (2010) or in the parchment paper series *Heated Oracles. While Waiting for Something to Change*, which carry within them traces of life and interaction between the individual and society. The object is often a pretext to explore coincidences and connecting points, the experiences and the lives of those who participate in her projects, a tool for building relationships between the artist and people, sometimes a whole community.

If at first the artist's research tended towards horizons which she knew and were nearby, from the banks of the Arno river, with the public art project *Reduction from River to Stream* (2014) to the work produced together with some Tuscan knitters with *Soulmates (Within Time)*, very soon she had the idea of exploring other horizons. Besides her interest in clothes and textiles, the artist began considering the idea of integrating travelling and ethnological research within her artistic practice. This kind of consideration led her to India, trying to get in touch with some embroiderers from the Banjara Gormati tribe. The project which resulted from this meeting, part of a residence at the Clark House Initiative art centre in Bombay, directed by Sumesh Sharma and Zasha Colah, can be considered a sort of prelude to *The Time of Discretion*. Also with this work, the artist concentrated on the study of ancient techniques connected to textiles which are now dying out due to the pressure of global capitalism which cannibalizes local energies and resources to divert them to the service of the consumerism of world markets.

The Time of Discretion came to life as a silent scream of protest against the speed and bulimia of the fashion market and global consumerism, to then be transformed, along the way, into a path of initiation in the heart of some of the most fascinating cultures of central-eastern Asia. The opportunity to start this new journey was presented with the fourth edition of the art biennale LAM 360°, a unique artistic event of its kind which started about ten years ago, between the Gobi Desert and the Mongolian

*

capital, Ulaanbaatar. The main characteristic of this event is that it takes place outside the walls of a museum, or what is usually defined as a white cube, to be transformed into an experience of full immersion in nature. The artists, curators and organizers have the chance to stay for some days in a camp set up in one of the semidesert areas of the Gobi Desert. In this context the artists carry out performances, interventions and environmental installations made with organic materials which remain in the chosen place until they waste away. The fourth edition, which I had the pleasure of co-curating, took place at Dariganga where the Altan Ovoo mountain rises. This is a sacred area, a place of pilgrimage, where for centuries the Mongolians have gone to make offerings and ask for pardon, traditionally considered as the eternal artery of time where human beings can temporarily reunite with the celestial dimensions.

The title of the fourth edition of the biennale *Catching the Axis. Between the Sky and the Earth* was a real invitation to explore the invisible tie which connects the sky and the earth and as a result all the parts of creation. This thought is inspired by the ancient Mongolian and central-Asian conception of the cosmos, for which the universe is formed by various dimensional layers, overlapped and crossed by a single central axis. According to this vision, the sky covers and closes all the other layers of the dimensional layers of the cosmos, like a tent, while a pillar keeps them together and in order. Therefore, the title of the Biennale was above all an invitation to relate with the sacred through art, in lands where sacredness is represented by the earth itself and its present, past and future elements, where the living, the dead and those who still have to be born live together under the same sky.

Replying to this invitation, Lisa Batacchi began thinking about realizing a large indigo-blue colored curtain, a mystic-symbolic representation of this union between the sky and the earth. A live and not synthetic color, as the artist personally specified, but rather, sacred and above all far from the use and consumption which is present today in the fashion industry. The interest in this natural color with its strong mystic-cultural meaning and in the ancient techniques of producing it, was, for the artist, dictated by the fact that their existence is endangered today due to the changes in production imposed by the global fashion market. In fact, the spreading of aniline in China, has produced a gradual abandonment of the cultivation of indigo, the plant which gave the natural blue color to clothes, which survives today only in a few and limited areas of the country. The artist decided to head towards these regions to carry out her project.

The journey which followed led her first to southern China, where she stayed in a village of Miao ethnicity. Here she learnt the natural technique of indigo tincture and with the help of a small community of local women she produced a batik fabric decorated with the image of an animal, half cow and half horse. The choice of this pattern was not by chance. Before her departure the artist had consulted the *I Ching*, a sort of ancient Chinese form of fortune-telling which goes back to the western Zhou era (1000–750 BC) and which later, in the era of the Warring States (500–200 BC), became a fundamental text of Chinese tradition, included in the Five Classics of Confucianism.

During the consultation the artist had questioned the oracle about the future of the world at the beginning of this century, asking if humans would be able to slow down the spread of materialism on a planetary scale, freeing themselves from the chains of global capitalism. The oracle's response was interpreted by the artist as an

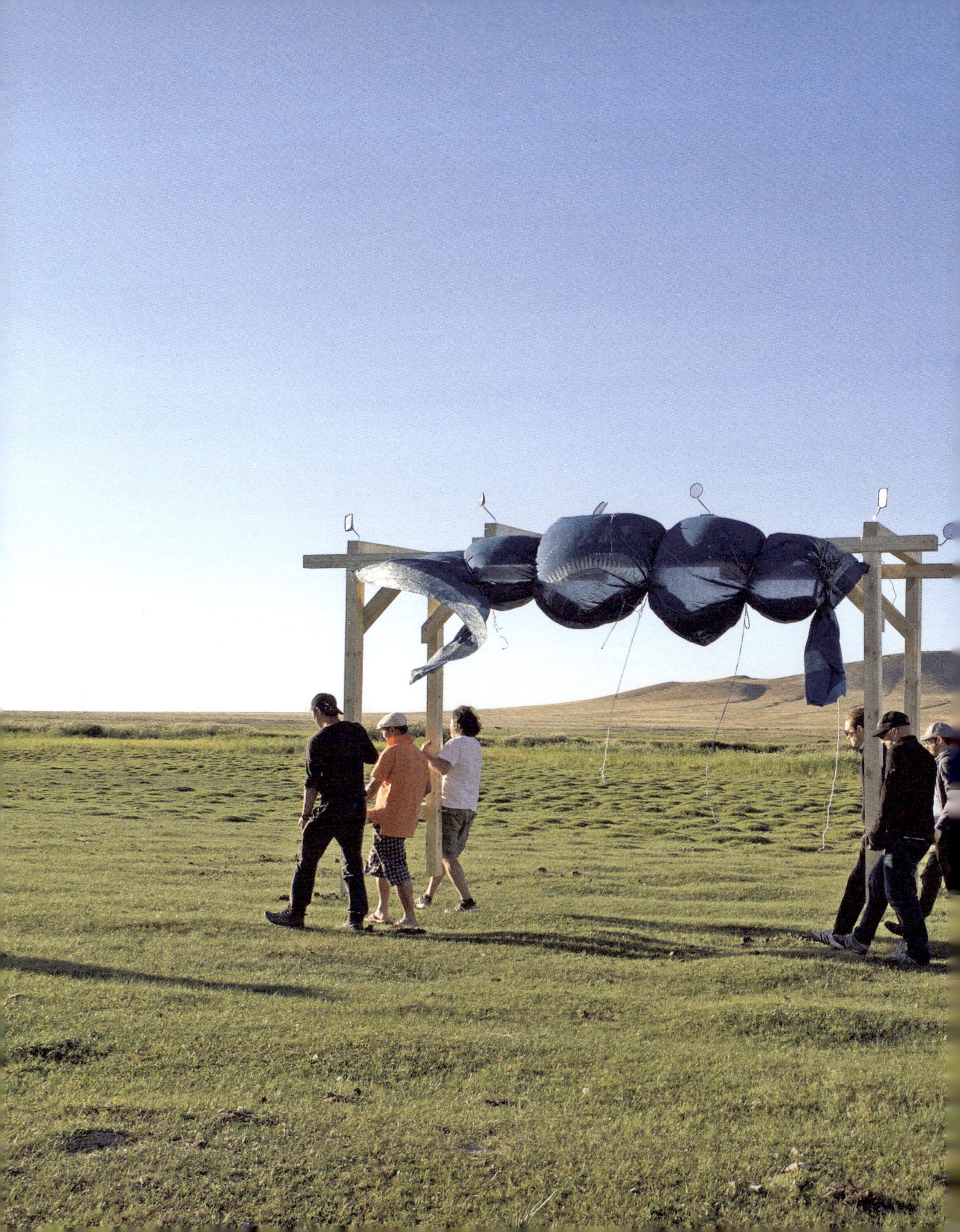

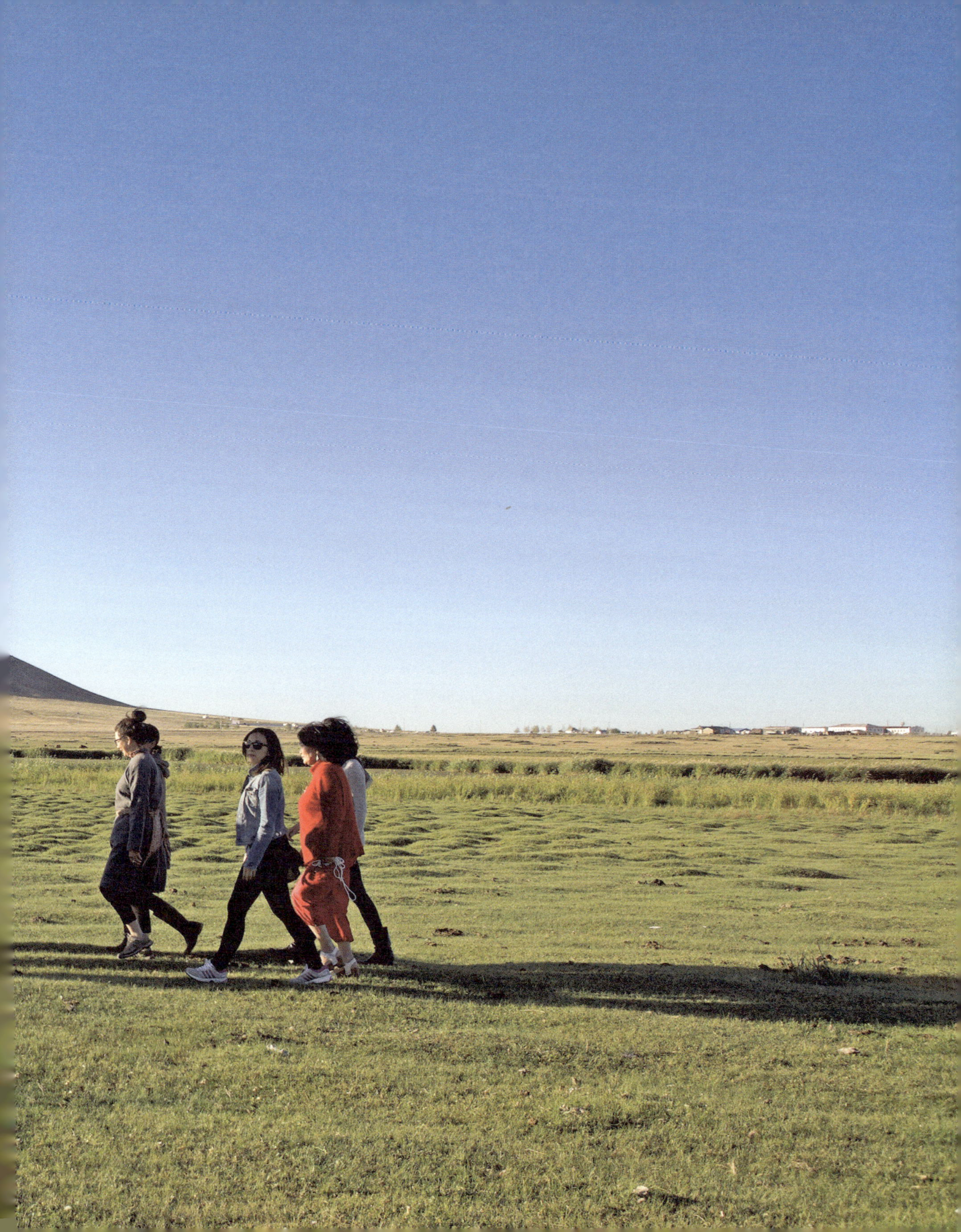

*

opening towards the possibility. If at this moment great changes do not seem attainable it is however possible to sow new seeds which will sprout in the future. A change of direction will only be possible if there is an effort to find a new equilibrium which can happen if human beings are able to balance creative spiritual energy, also considered as aggressive and masculine, represented by the image of a horse, with female energy, passive but which gives serenity and nourishment, represented by the cow. This is where the image of the horse-cow comes from, which the artist represents on the batik produced with the women of Miao ethnicity who still have that artisan knowledge, which is disappearing, that is the indigo tincture. Once she arrived at the foot of the Altan Ovoo, the artist mounted the cloth on a wooden structure where she had applied some motorcycle mirrors. Traditionally held sacred in various far-eastern cultures to reflect evil spirits, in Mongolia the higher symbolic representation of the mirror is found in a polished brass disc, a Toli (Toyl), used by a shaman to deflect the spirit's attack, and also to absorb energy from the universe to increase shamanic power[5]. The motorcycle mirror was chosen by the artist also as a symbol of the new Mongolian means of transport which has today partly substituted the horse.

A Tower of Nine Stories Starts with a Pile of Dirt...

To reach the artists and the other organizers, from Ulaanbaatar I crossed the Mongolian Steppe and a great part of the Gobi Desert by bus, on a journey of over sixteen hours, among arid dunes and very little vegetation. Along this route without any roads and lights to get your bearings, where internet access is limited to just a few minutes while stopping at some tiny village which is nothing but a handful of small houses lost in the midst of nowhere, you can often see piles of dirt and colored rags. In fact, these are burials which mark the presence on this earth of who came before us to then move to the other dimension.

Death represents the moment of passing towards another level of existence and the shamans are the ones who enable communication with those who have crossed that frontier, just like with the forces which enliven nature. These intermediaries may be men, but they are mainly women, according to sources which testify to the presence of a socio-political and religious organization of a matriarchal nature in the Mongolian-Siberian areas since third century BC. The role of these figures in pre-modern societies was not only religious but mainly social. The shamans, as holistic healers, had the task of mediating, resolving individual and social tensions, solving conflicts and harmonising the relationships among the various elements of creation. The Mongolian historian and researcher Otgony Purev wrote about this:

> It can be affirmed that Mongolian shamanism was founded and developed around the concepts of "totem" and "Holy sky". This includes the cult of various beings and natural phenomena like animals, plants, stones, wind and other beings and powers. This was clearly born during a period when the relationship between man and his natural environment was still very close [...]. In this sense, the shamans, as heads of the religion, were those who could penetrate the mysteries of space and time and reach high levels of awareness. They carried on with their rites and habits, helping others to overcome pain and sufferance, the difficulties and losses, giving the basis for social order and the reciprocal understanding among people[6].

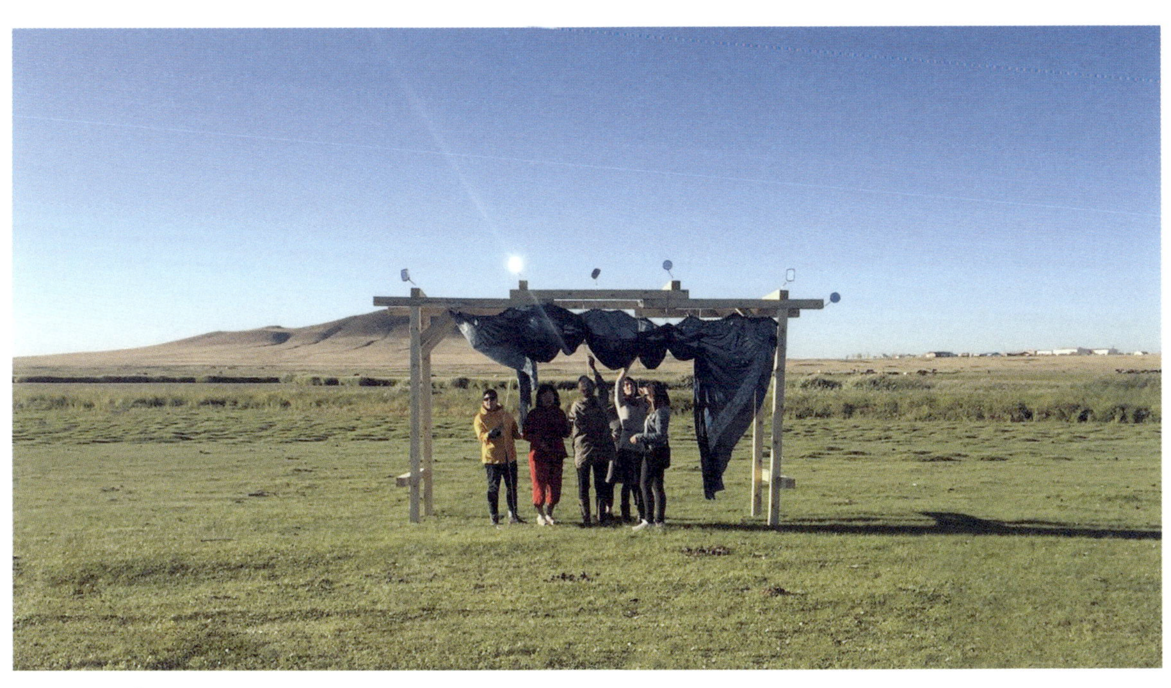

⋆

Mediators and creators of relationships between man, society and nature, the shamans held the knowledge and power, but they were also those who set the pace of the rhythms of community life through their rituals. Therefore, if in pre-modern societies it was the rites which ordered social rhythms, in the era of hyper-modernity time appears like an accelerated and "increased" flow. The presence at the same time of multiple time lines, which overlap in the maze of virtual reality on the web, condemns humanity to remain blocked in an *eternal present,* immediate and expanded, where consumerism becomes compulsive and continuous.

The Time of Discretion does not follow the accelerated rhythms of hyper-modernity, but it ideally reconnects with that of the ritual. Orchestrating small actions, both individual and collective, which bud with their cadenced and slow rhythm, Lisa Batacchi creates a break in reality, transforming her artistic practice into a practice of mediation which we could define as almost magic-shamanic. *A disappearing act*, as the artist defines it, where the term disappearance means a sort of distancing or exit from ordinary reality towards an extraordinary dimension. In this procession a group of men carried the blue curtain, produced in the Miao village, and its wooden structure, while a group of women, led by the artist, followed the procession in the desert, silently expressing their desires for their land. Once they arrived in the place indicated by the artist at the foot of the Altan Ovoo, the procession stopped. Only then the women unfolded the curtain completely, leaving it free to blow in the wind and sun while the light reflected off the mirrors, leading to the completion of a performance where the value of the experience can barely be understood with a purely cognitive effort.

In this performance, which the artist structures as a real contemporary rite, the blue curtain, is not only an artistic work but it is also a ritual object. It appears to our eyes like a tangible trace of the initiation journey taken up by the artist, a silent testimony of the passage to distant places, in a narration *outside of and beyond* time, space and history, where reality and imagination blend, in a message of hope suspended in the limited time of the performance which, using the artist's words *sediments with intensity, thanks to the female gesture, like a cosmic rain which falls from the sky to nourish our planet.*

[1] Gombojav Mend-Ooyo, *Altan Ovoo: The Golden Hill*, En. tr. Simon Wickham-Smith, Ulaanbaatar: self published, 2007.

[2] Lao Tzu (attributed to), *The Book of the Way and its Virtues*, tr. J.J. Duyvendak, London: J. Murray, 1954 (*Daodejing*, 4th century BC).

[3] Lisa Batacchi during a private conversation with the author (2019).

[4] Pierre Bourdieu, *Distinction: A Social Critique of the Judgement of Taste*, London: Routledge & Kegan Paul, 1984 (*La Distinction. Critique social du jugement*, Paris: Editions de Minuit, 1979).

[5] Sarangerel, *Riding Windhorses: A Journey into the Heart of Mongolian Shamanism*, Rochester: Destiny Books, 2000.

[6] Otgony Purev, Gurbadaryn Purvee, *Mongolian Shamanism*, Ulaanbaatar: Admon, 2010.

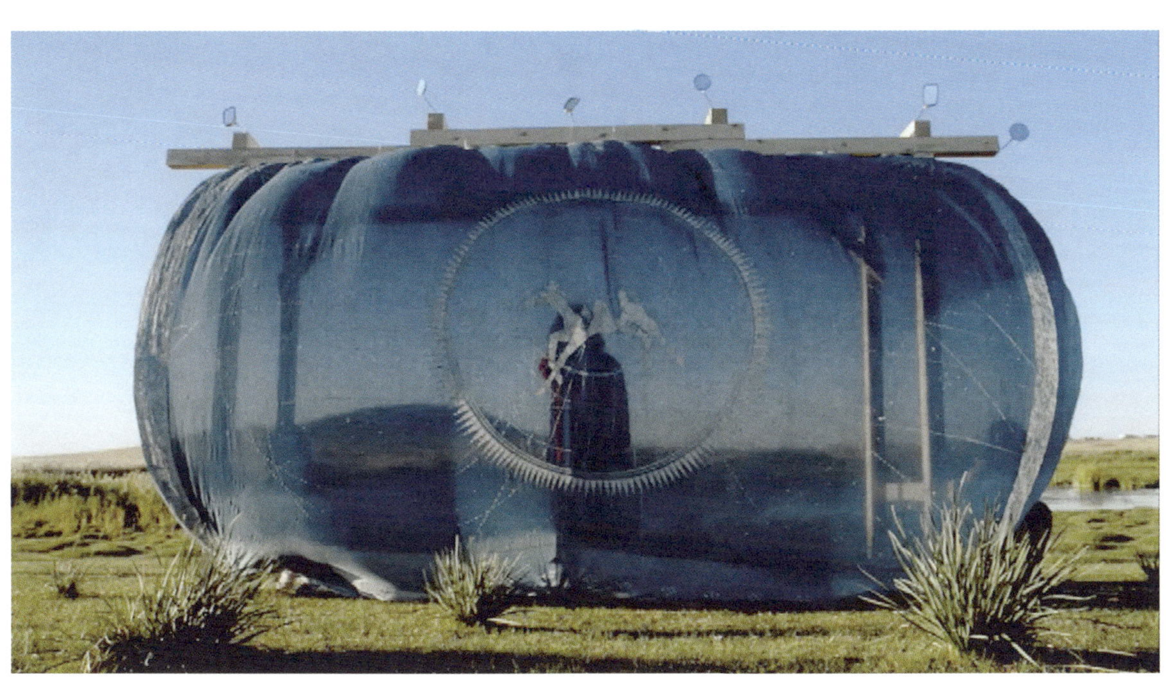

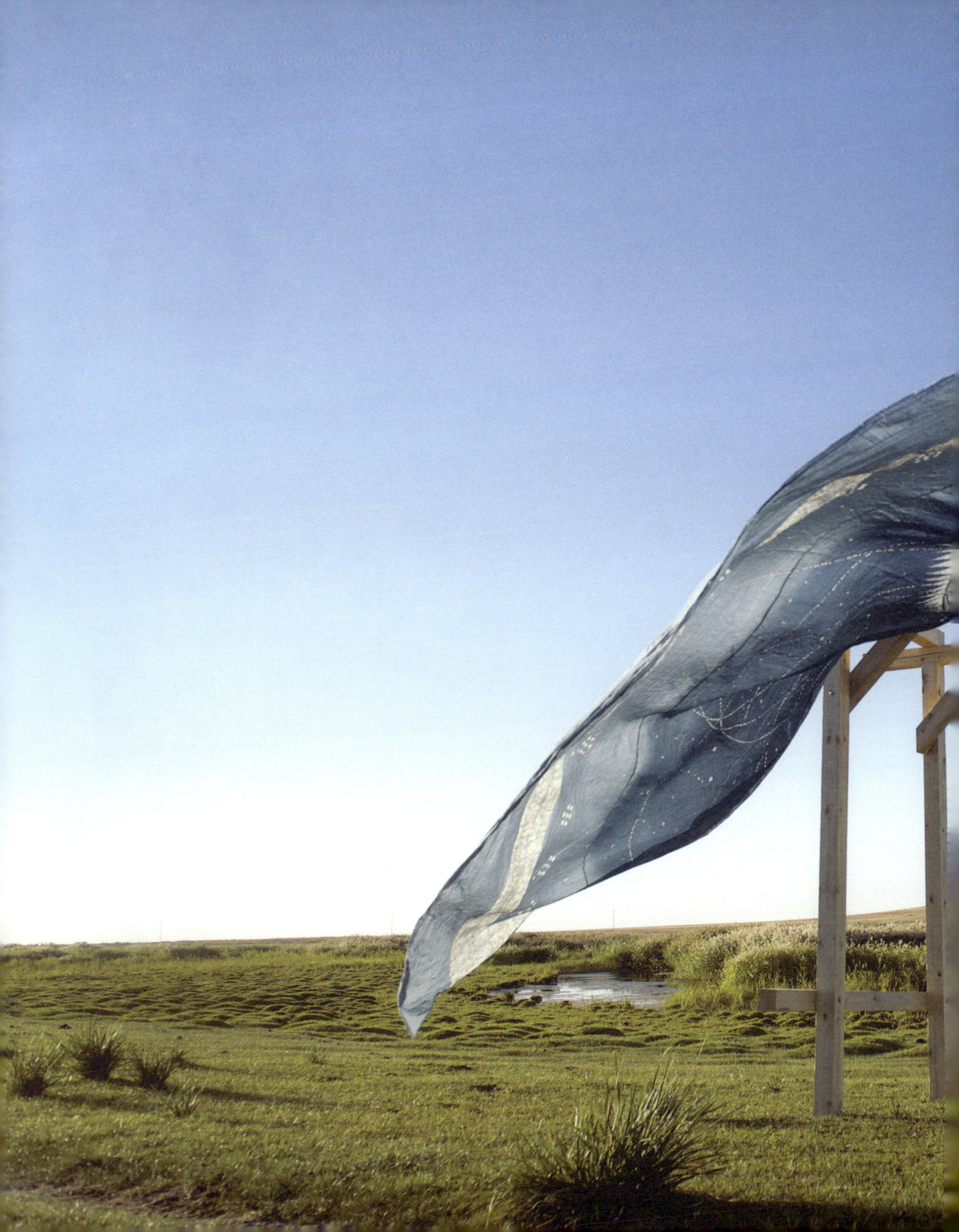

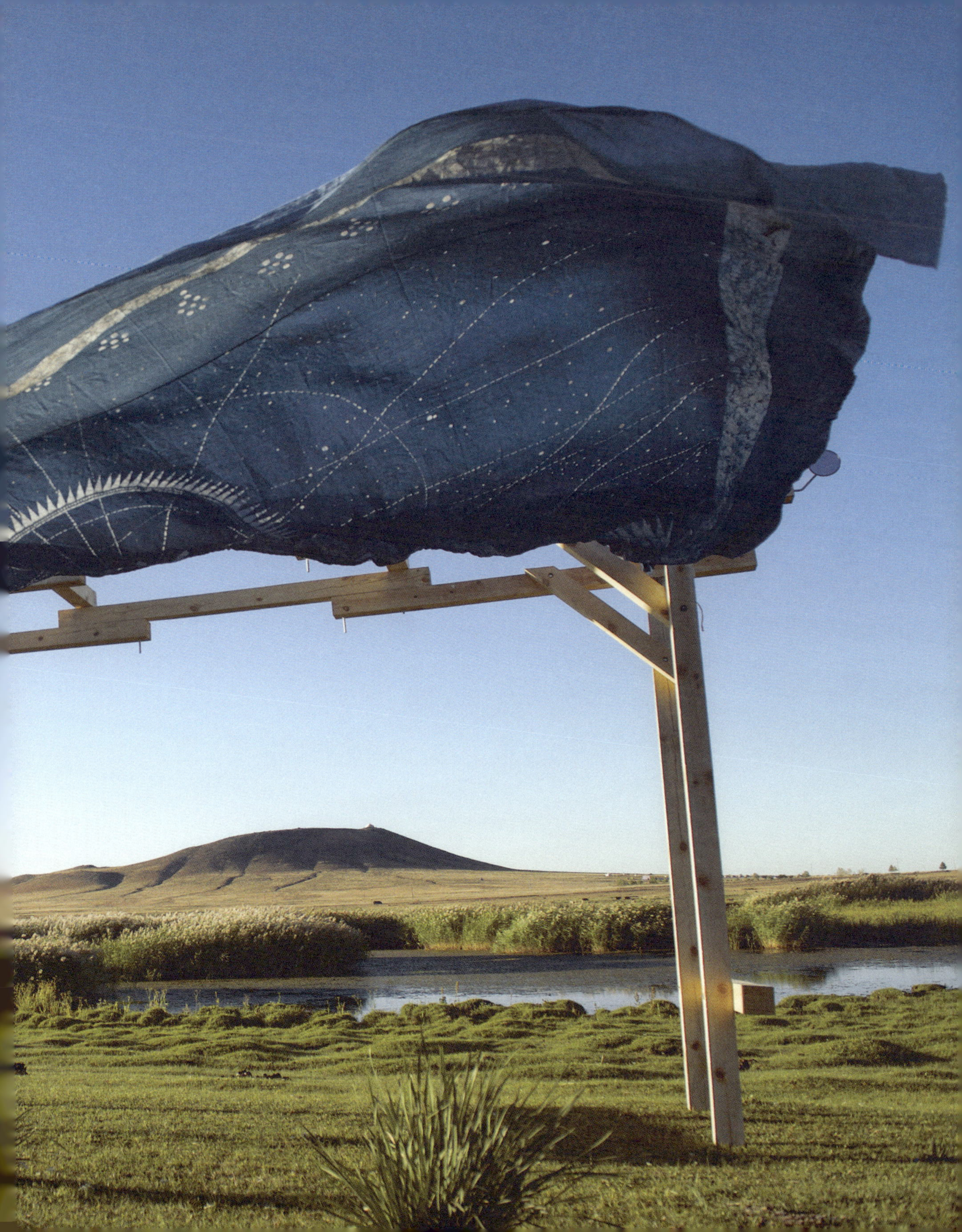

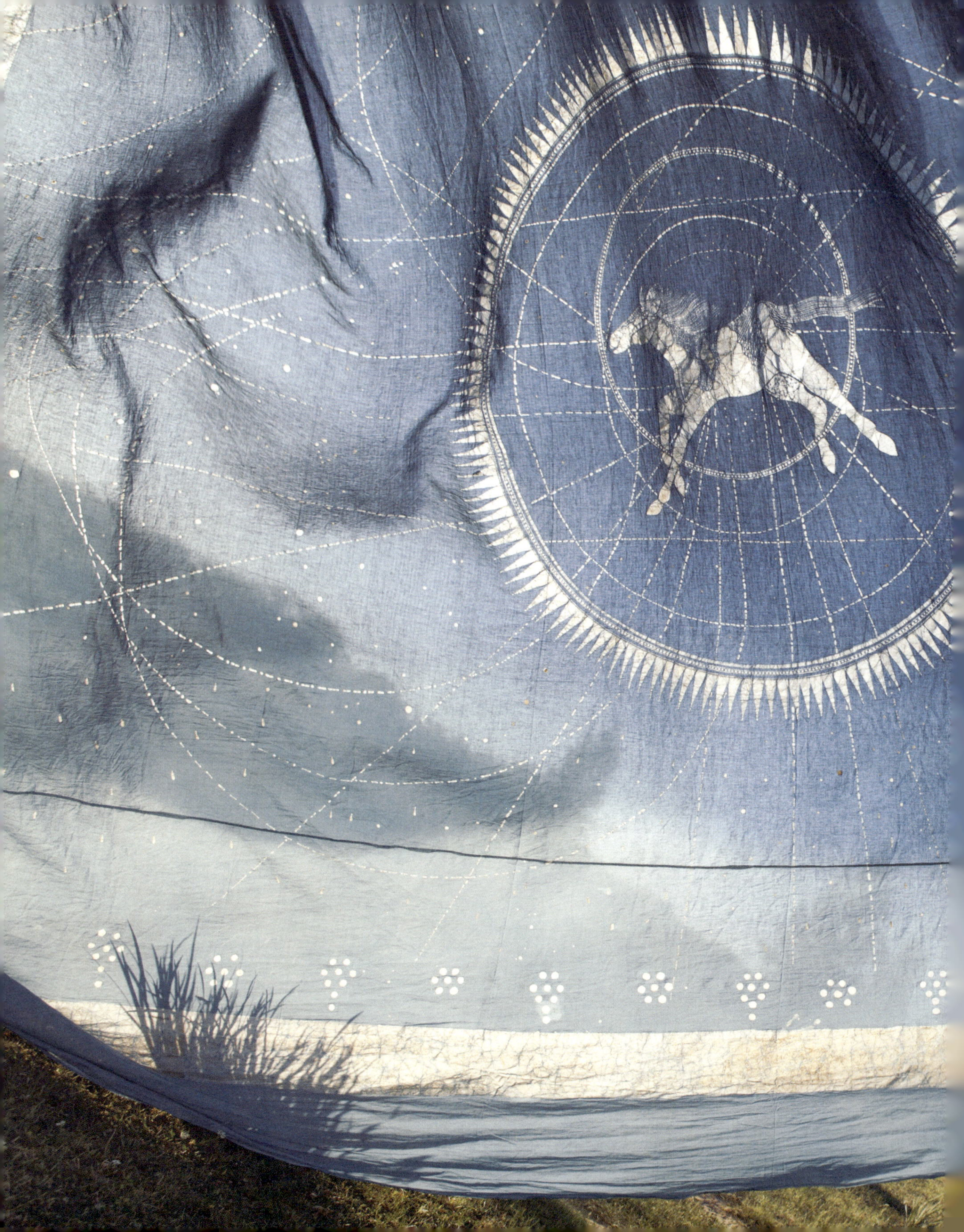

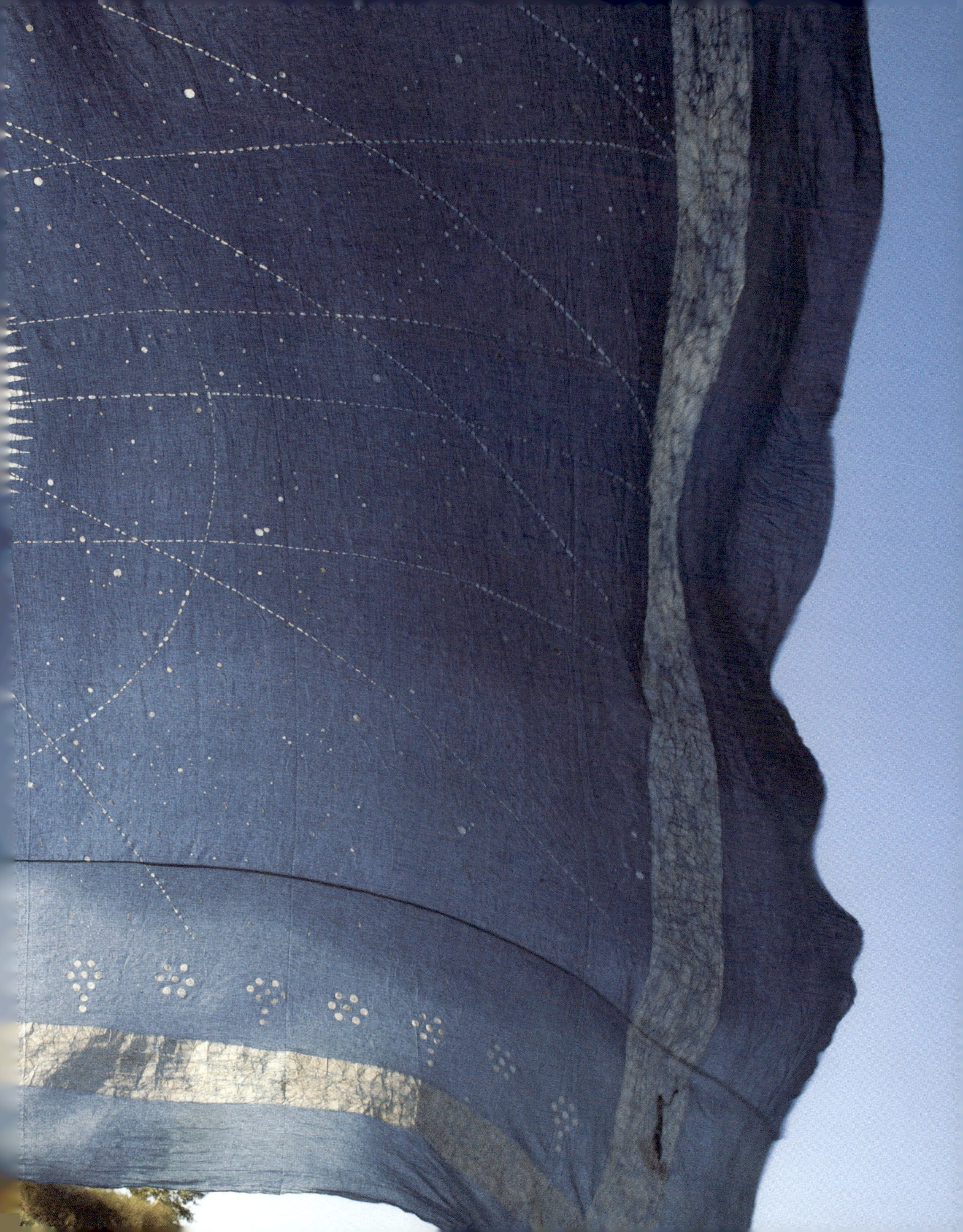

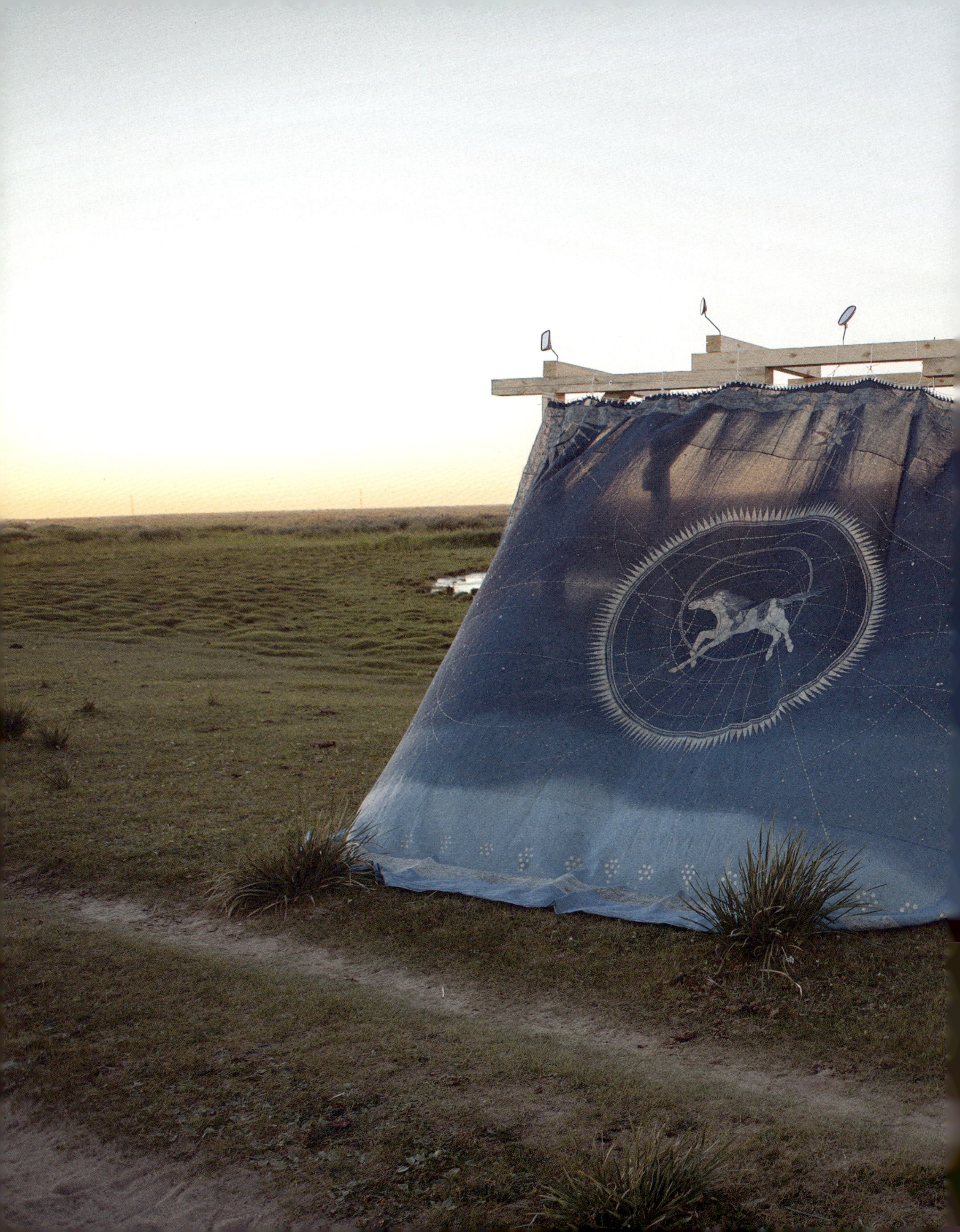

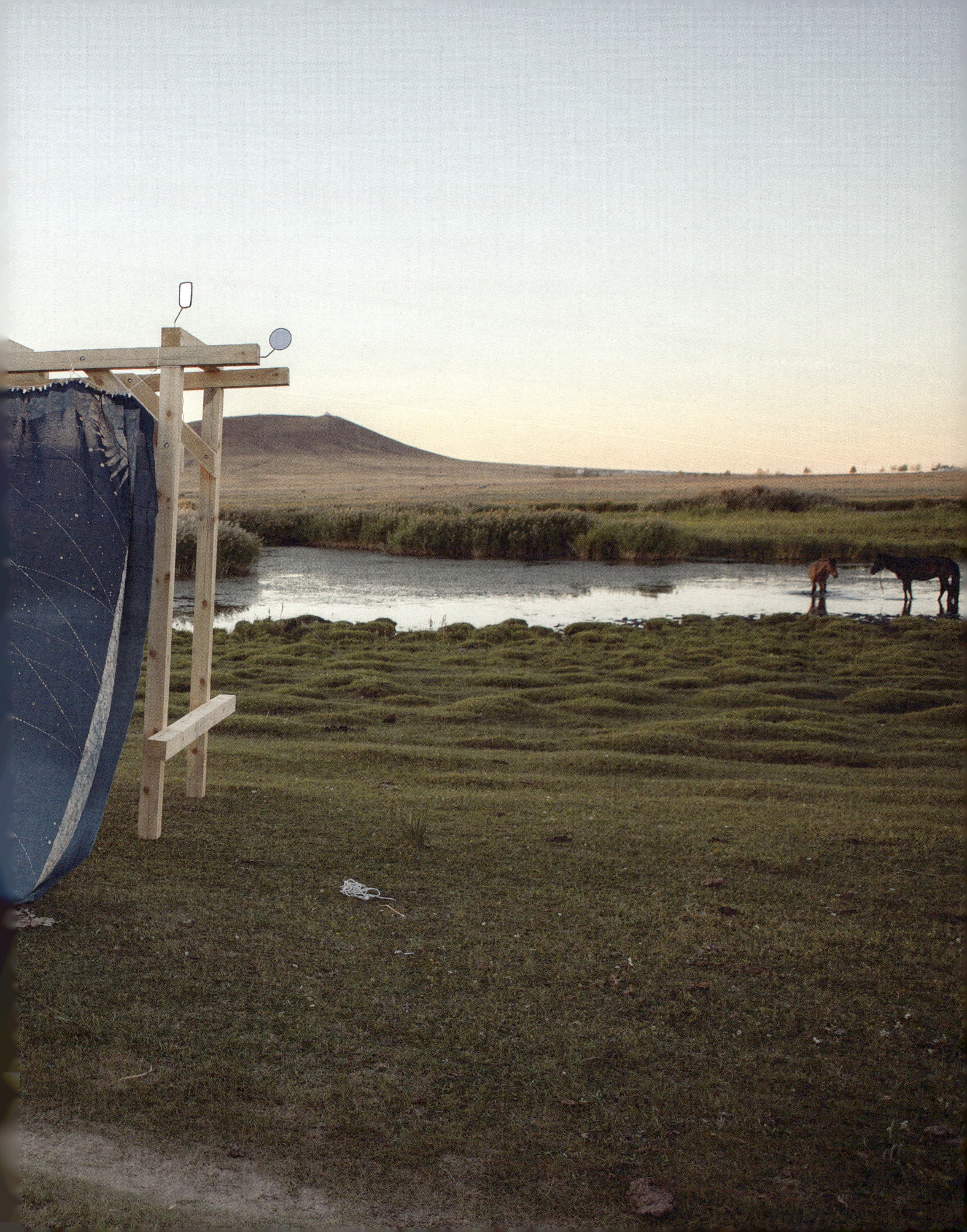

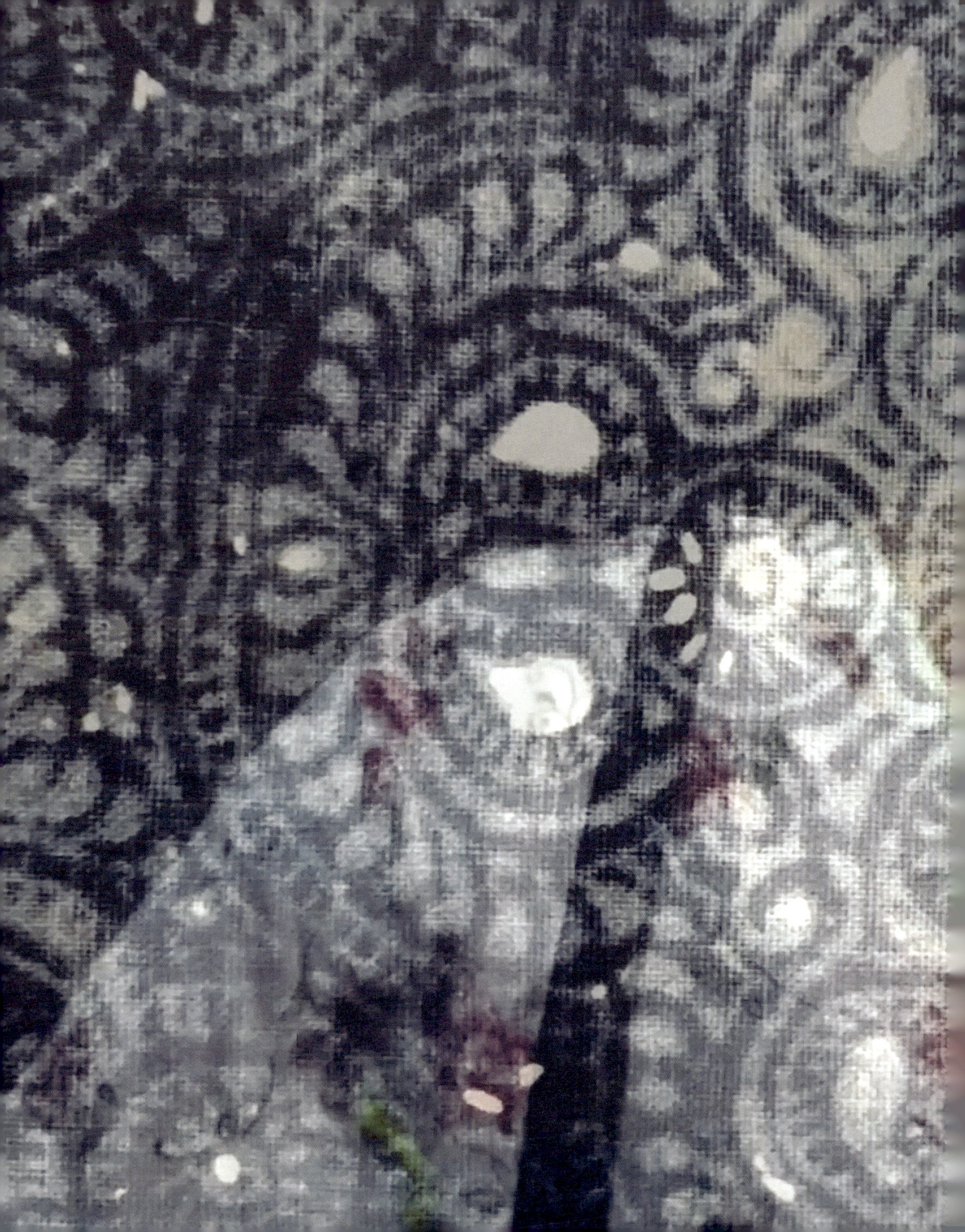

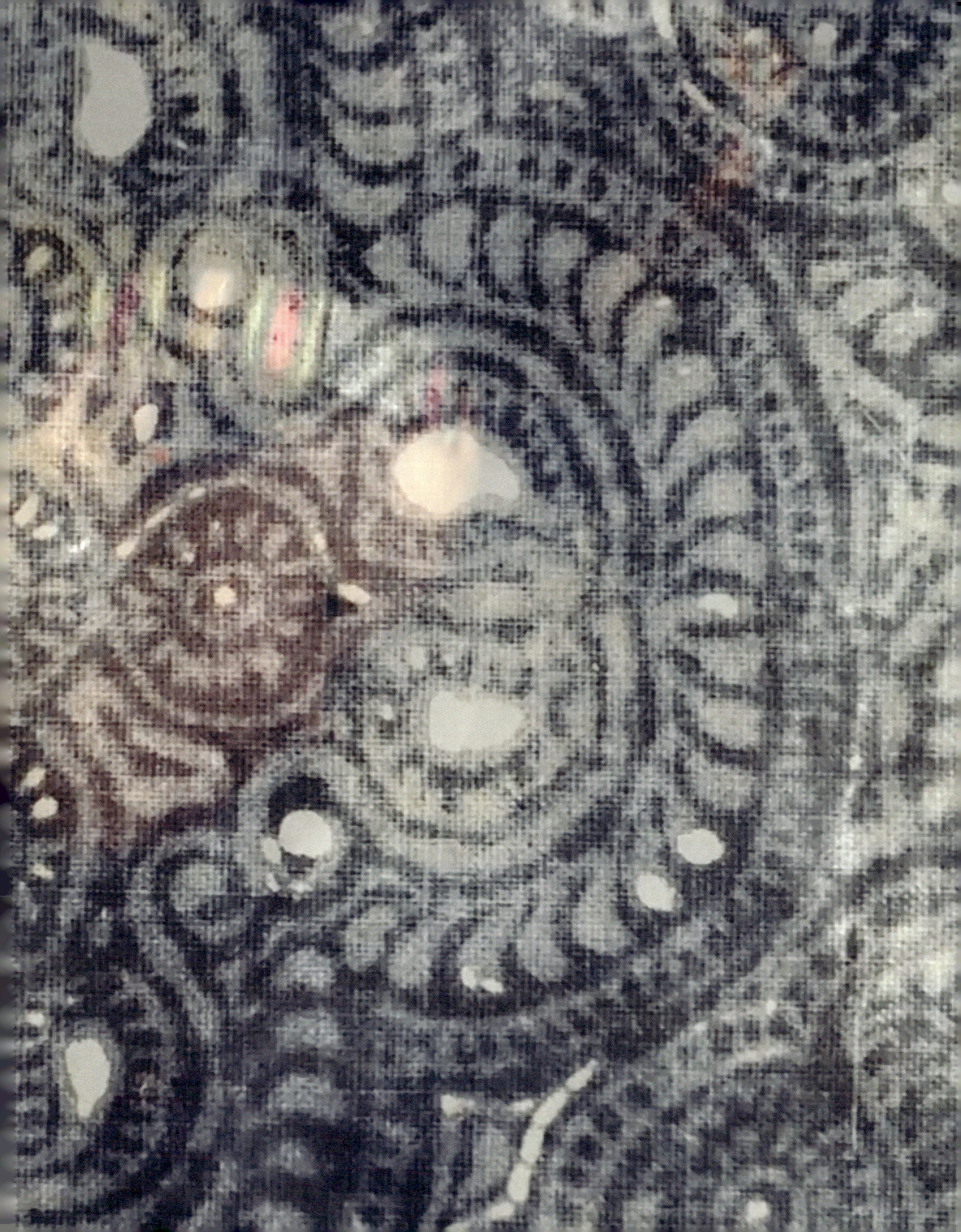

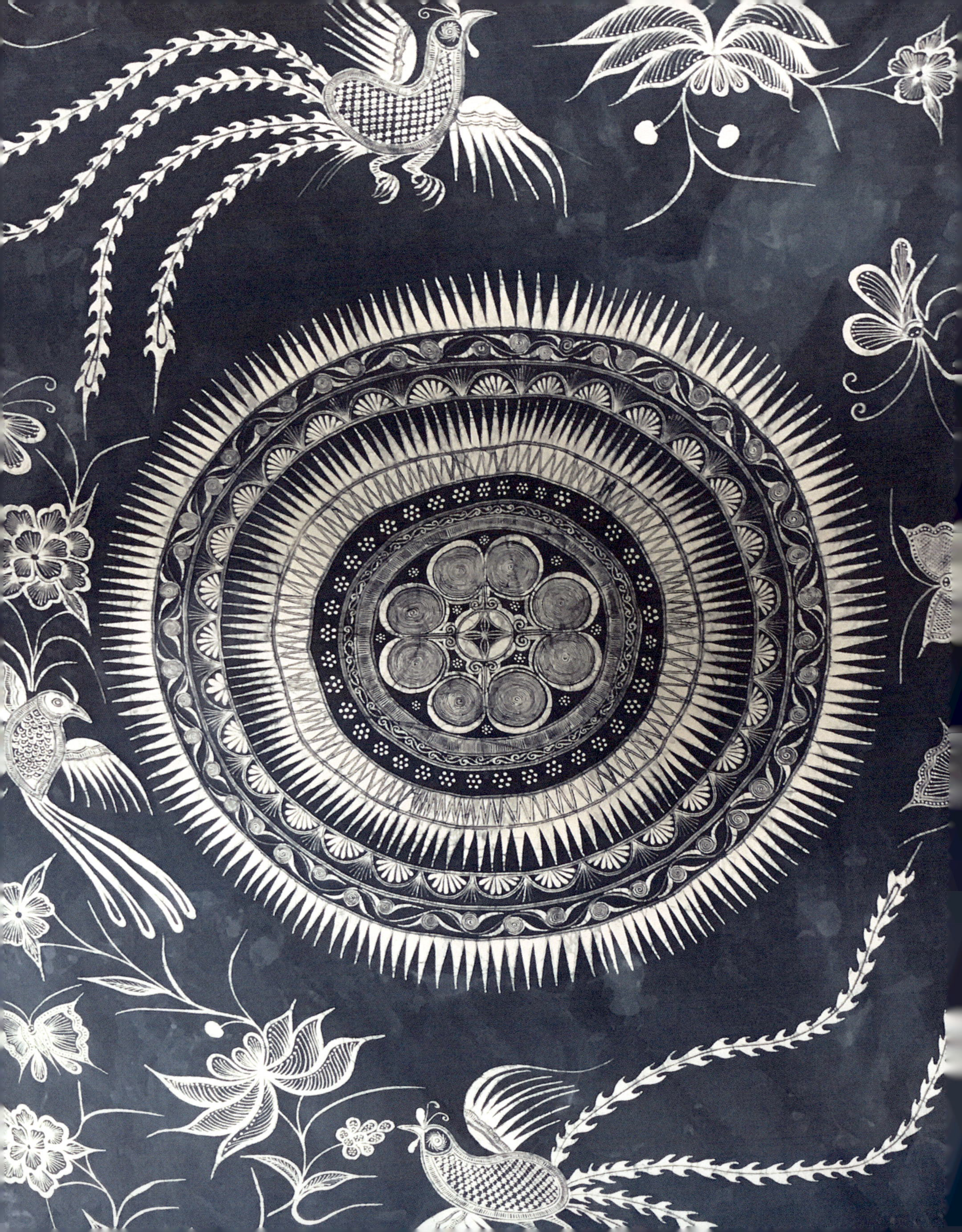

Memory on Hands. The Life Stories of Sister Yang and Sister Li

Xiaomei Wang

★

Introduction[1]

In 2010, China was undergoing rapid development. The outlook for the country was stable. Economy and society continued to evolve at an unprecedented pace. The triumphalism, individualism, and stratification associated with these "modernization" efforts put material pursuit at its core. More and more Chinese, including villagers, were motivated by, occupied with, and changed by dreams of success and riches in the city. Just like millions of farmers awoken by the new market economy, Sister Yang and Sister Li, two ordinary Miao[2] women from the mountain area of Guizhou Province, left their homes to find work in the city. However, unlike most migrant laborers, they were making a living in the city by handicraft – namely, batik – an art they had inherited from their ancestors. Sister Yang and Sister Li were working in a minority people's handicraft company and performing batik demonstrations for visitors at the Guizhou Provincial Museum.

Painting

There is an ancient Miao folk song, the "Batik Song", which explains the origins of batik: once, there was a group of old men who tried, in vain, to push up the heavens. But the sky kept falling down. Finally, they came up with an idea. They asked a girl, Meishuang, to sew a giant umbrella to prop up the sky. Meishuang wove the clouds and mist into a white cloth, and placed it under a pear-blossom tree to dry. While drying, flowers fell onto the cloth. These flowers were covered in wax residue left behind by honeybees feeding from their nectar. The wax-covered flowers left flower-shaped imprints on the cloth. Meishuang then dyed the cloth blue using an indigo plant, before rinsing it in the river and letting the sun melt the beeswax off. Flower shapes in white were where the wax had been, while the rest of the cloth remained blue. She made an umbrella using this cloth, which she then used to prop up the heavens. The blue cloth became the color of the sky, and the white flowers became the sun, the moon, and the stars.

This folk legend appears in a number of reference materials about Miao batik. Although the "true" origins of batik have been lost, this legend provides a window into the cultural beliefs of the ancient Miao people. The origin of the blue flowers is remembered through oral tradition.

Dye

A colorful batik dress found by archaeologists in a coffin excavated near Taohua Villahe, Pingba County, Guizhou Province, has been dated back to the Tang (618–917 A.D.) and Song (960–1279 A.D.) dynasties. It proves that the batik craft has been in Guizhou for at least 1,400 years. Almost two thousand years have passed, yet the ancient craft is still kept alive today among the Miao, Gejia, Buyi, Raojia, Yao, and Shui local ethnic groups. Young girls who wish to marry would draw all of their favourite patterns on two pieces of nine meters long batik cloth. On festival days, boys and girls would stand on either side of the batik cloth, singing antiphonally. If the boy won, the girl would send him home with a piece of her batik so that he could

★

then bring it to her house and propose. If the boy lost, the batik would be burnt immediately. Before Sister Yang and Sister Li married, they made a whole batik dowry set. The long pieces of batik are cherished family treasures, and will never be sold. When they pass away, the batik will be placed under their heads and buried with them. Today, younger generations no longer make these pieces and do not believe that the batik will guard their love.

Ripples

Although the market economy encourages many villagers to leave the mountains, work in the cities, and wear Han clothing, we were pleasantly surprised to find that throughout Rongjiang, many women still make batik. It is still used widely in their daily lives and for weddings, funerals, and other major festivals and ceremonies.

More than one hundred years ago, when the Han culture was considered fashionable, ethic minority groups were trying to learn from and imitate it. Now, the tides have turned. Government-led initiatives to promote cultural heritage conservation and self awareness are bringing ethnic minority cultures back into the mainstream. As a preserved resource, ethnic handicrafts are now viewed as important tools for local sustainable development. In the larger context of China's development, restoring and recovering traditional culture has received increasing attention. The cultural campaign "Colorful Guizhou" is a prominent example of how traditional and minority cultures are being capitalized on to promote economic development.

Awakened to the Truth

Sister Yang and Sister Li had been living in big cities since 2005, yet they still represent rural culture. Traditional cultural products, such as batik, incorporate and reflect the pressures of a modern market economy. Sister Yang and Sister Li no longer use the traditional patterns in their batik, nor can they represent the ideas of their entire ethnic group. However, from their individual transformations we can gain insight into what is happening to others in rural ethnic minority groups.

From Sister Yang and Sister Li's experiences, we can see that interactions between rural and urban areas play a very significant role in cultural heritage protection.

Indigo

Early one morning, with hoes on their shoulders, Sister Yang and Sister Li took us to the fields to pick indigo. The tung oil trees had already burst into blossom, light pink flowers scattered along their branches. To pick indigo we needed to walk along the road on the top of the mountain opposite us. Growing indigo is an important step of making the natural dye for batik. During the harvest season, women collect the branches and leaves of the indigo plant, and soak them in water. After a period of time, the water is poured off, and the indigo solution is put on a fire to be boiled. The mixture is then strained and mixed with lime (calcium oxide), producing the dark blue color of

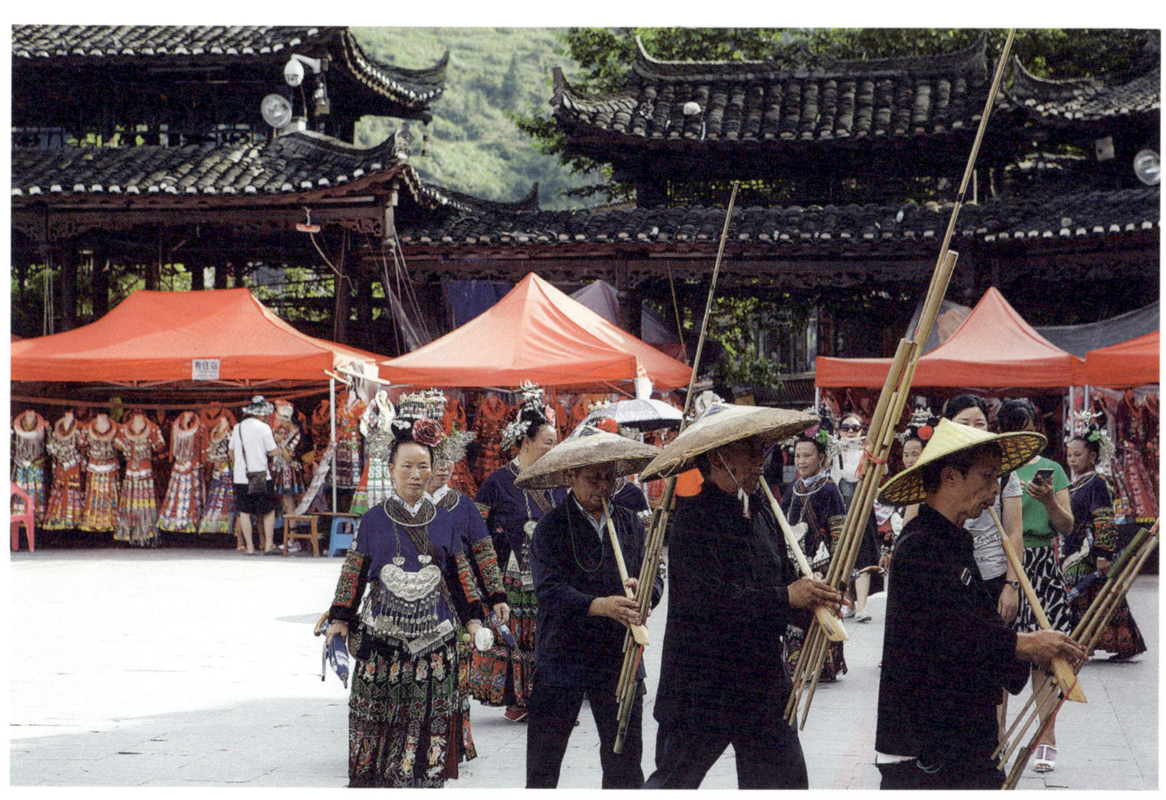

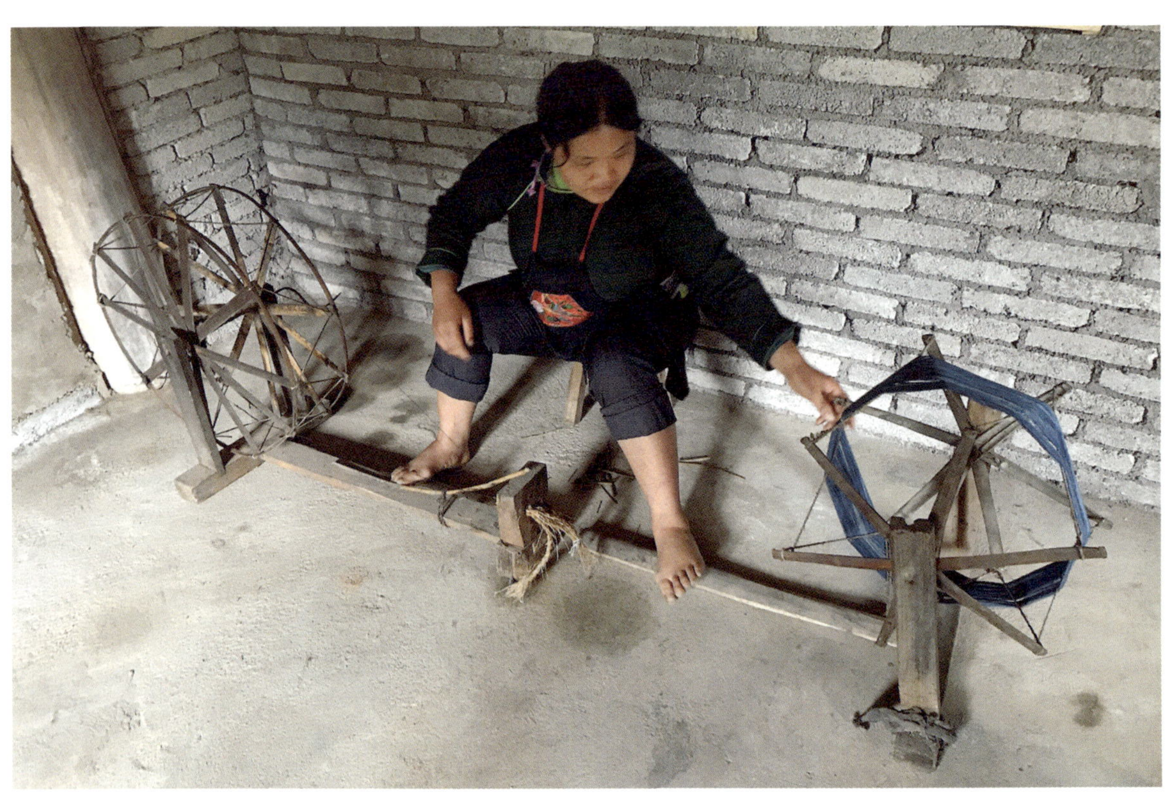

★

the dye. Dyeing dates are chosen very carefully. It is said that only the date of the dragon or ox in the lunar calendar is good for dyeing. On top of that, it has to be sunny and warm. Cold days are avoided. Pregnant women aren't to get close to the dye because there is a saying among locals that pregnant women will contaminate the indigo and take away its "strength". Also, women who have given birth in the last month should not take part in the dying process. The work should be done by senior members of families. If one wants to make high-quality dye, Sister Li said, good wine should be added. They usually use rice wine made from sticky rice.

Gewo and Other Patterns

Many of the patterns used in Miao handicrafts reflect their indigenous beliefs and religion. Across several different Miao branches there is a pattern that looks like a sun or a bronze drum, called "gewo". It is a symbol of the mysterious world where the ancestors of all Miao tribes and branches are believed to originate from. Although global capitalism has already brought many changes to remote areas of Guizhou, Miao women continue to use this traditional spiral pattern for items used in major events like weddings, funerals, festivals and sacrificial offerings to ancestors. When the Bailing Miao people make batik, they cannot specifically tell you the meaning of the patterns. But that does not mean that the patterns are meaningless. Take the butterfly pattern, for example. There is an ancient Miao song about a butterfly who was born in the heart of a giant maple tree and then turned into the mother of the Miao people. Of course the patterns and their meanings have likely transformed over time, particularly in light of increasing exchange with the outside world. They have largerly lost their ritual functions, and instead, have become the women's way of making a living. Besides God of Sun and Butterflies, we can find Centipede-Bird Dragons, Centipede Dragons, Dragons with Lady's Head, Man's Head, Buffalo's Head, Buffalo Dragons with Sharp Teeth, Long Beard and Big Eyes, Cows, Snake Fish, Giant Salamanders, Insects, Shrimps, Spiders, Frogs, Birds, Monkeys and Tortoises.

Indigo Dye

According to the original religious beliefs inherited from ancestors, indigo dyeing is a special skill only inherited by women. Most of the women learn the skill in sacred ritual ceremonies. Through repeated observation, the techniques are transferred from grandmothers and mothers. Speaking and talking during these rituals is strictly forbidden. The quietness is an expression of respect towards the sacred. Those who are running ceremonies can speak out loud to communicate with the spirits. Unlike the demonstrations for tourists, this ritual cannot be held at any time; just once a year. Many ethnic groups in Guizhou Province believe that only by wearing the oldest and most splendid traditional dress embroidered in ancient patterns, they can be seen by their ancestors in the ritual ceremonies. If they cannot be recognized by the spirits of their ancestors, when they are dead, their souls will not find the way to the world where they live.

★

Gu

Witchcraft is still a widespread belief among ethnic groups in Guizhou Province. It is integral to Sister Yang and Sister Li's community. The local people call it *fanggu* ("fang" means "use"). Pan Nianying believes that in the local belief system, *gu* is a kind of poisonous micro-organism produced through a special technique. One makes it by collecting poisonous insects or animals like snakes, centipedes and snails. People catch these animals alive, and then they dry them under the sun and let them ferment. Finally, these materials are grounded into a powder and put into a jar. After a certain amount of time in the jar, the powder becomes *gu* and can be used to poison people. Sister Yang and Sister Li repeatedly warned me about *gu*. When a person is poisoned by *gu*, centipedes grow inside of them. Once the centipedes mature, they crawl out of the person and then kill them. The people who use *gu* start by poisoning their own families first, and then they poison other people. *Gu* users are considered very vicious and do not feel any guilt about killing people.

[1] Xiaomei Wang is the chief correspondent of the Guizhou Daily Newpaper Group, as well as executive partner of the Citibank Guizhou Handicraft Development Program and founder of the Guizhou Anthropology Association. She was born in a village in Guizhou Province and received her M.A. in International Development and Social Transformation from Clark University (USA). She has published three books on Miao batik. As both a ritual symbol and a cultural artifact, the "blue flower" offers a unique perspective through which to understand the tensions and opportunities of integrating traditional culture with modernity in the context of China's rapid development. Over ten years of interviews and field research across the Guizhou countryside, Xiaomei Wang documented the cultural traditions, oral histories, production techniques and market influences of the "blue flowers" (including batik dyeing, tie dyeing and print dyeing). *Memory on Hands* examines the batik of Wuji Miao Natural Village in Zhaiyong Administrative Village, Tashi Township, Rongjiang County and Guizhou Province. The book is also a narrative account of the lives and traditional batik handicrafts of two Miao women in Guizhou Province. Although there is some literature on Guizhou batik crafts, limited research has been done by academics or artists on batik as a ritual symbol as it relates to the life narratives of village people. The following chapters have been selected from her book *Memory on Hands. The Life Stories of Sister Yang and Sister Li*, Guizhou: Guizhou University Press, 2015.

[2] Miao is the Mandarin term for "Hmong", an ethnic group with branches in China, Vietnam, Laos, Thailand, and an immigrant population in the USA.

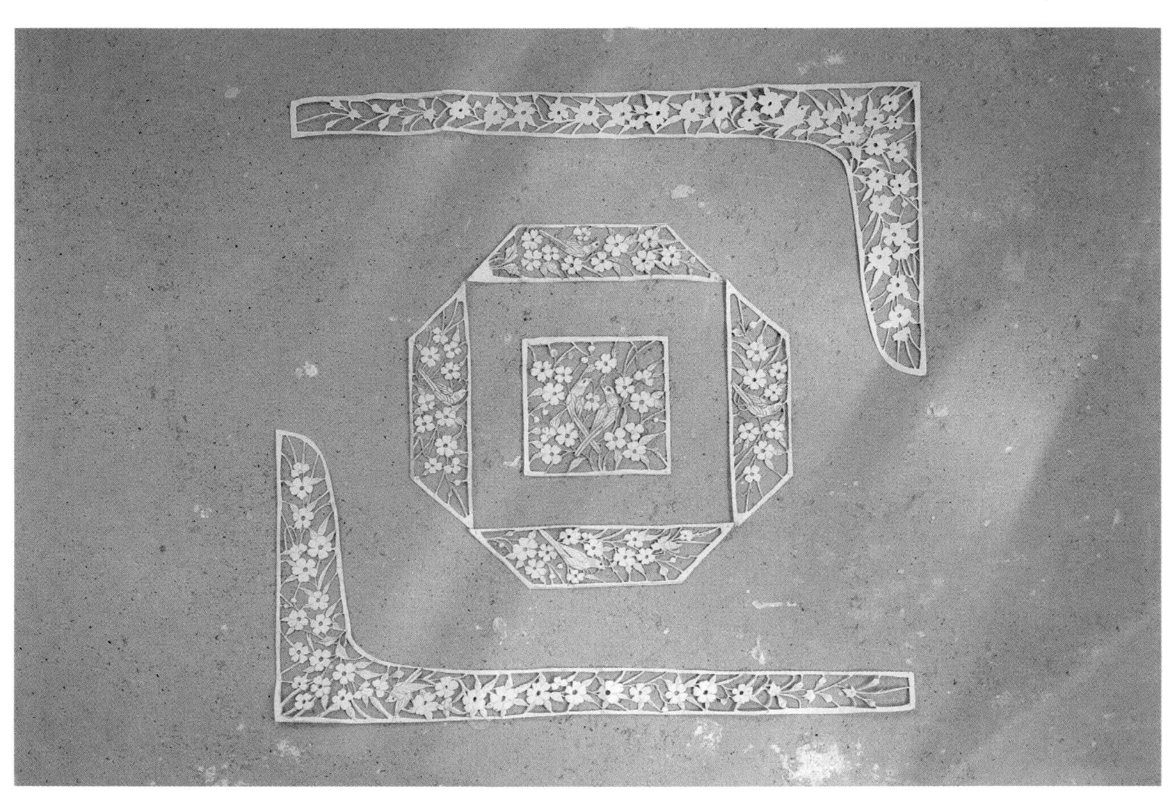

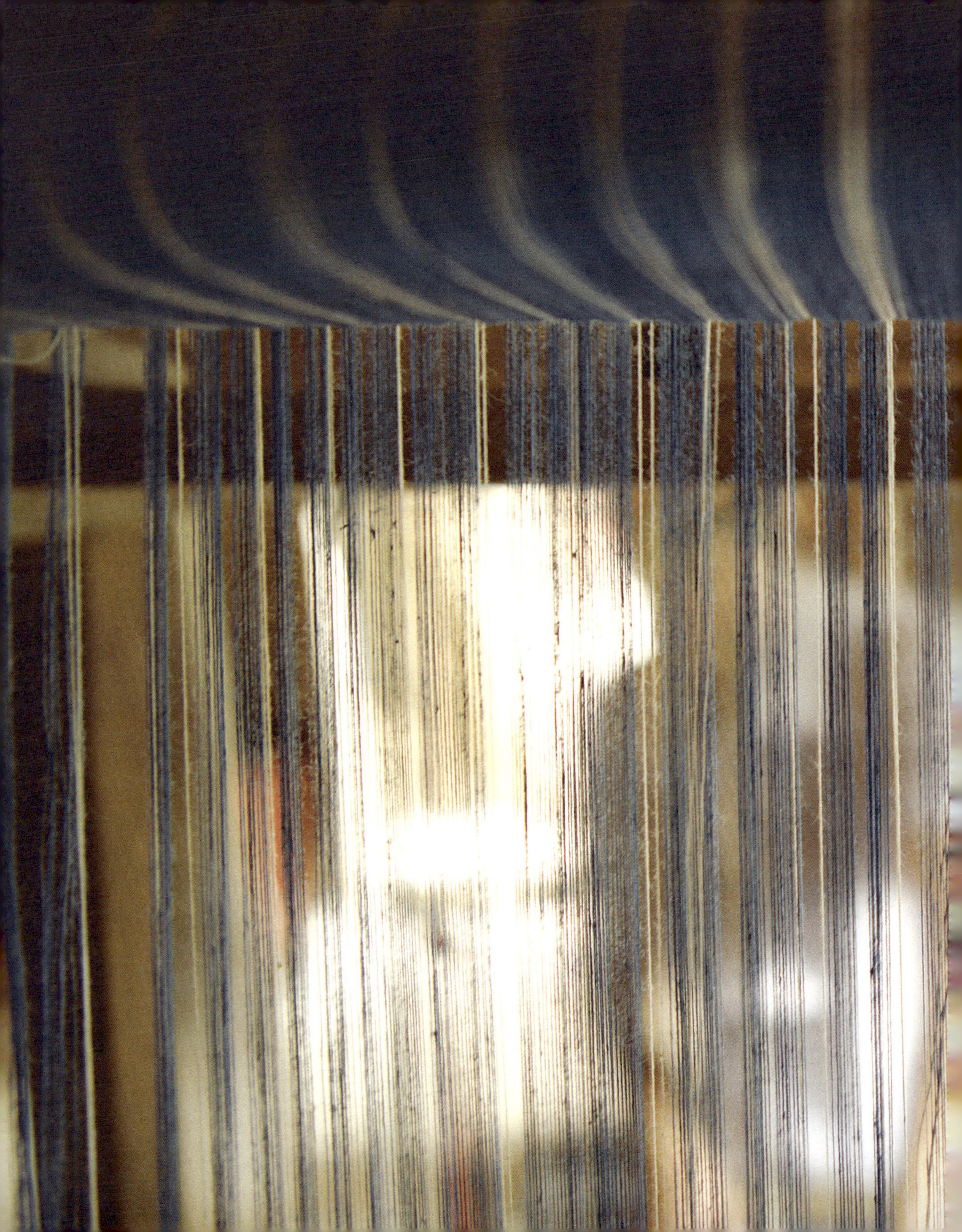

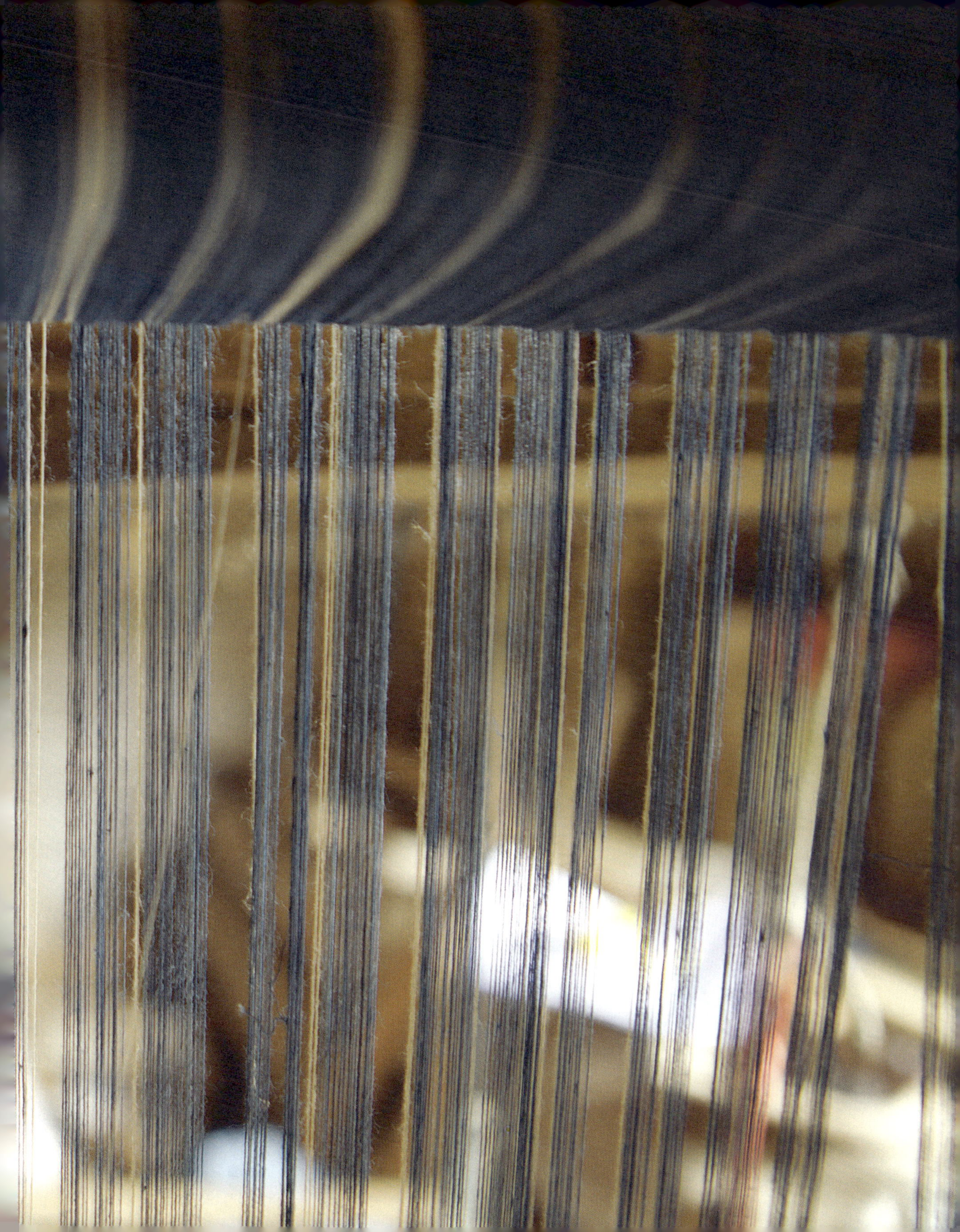

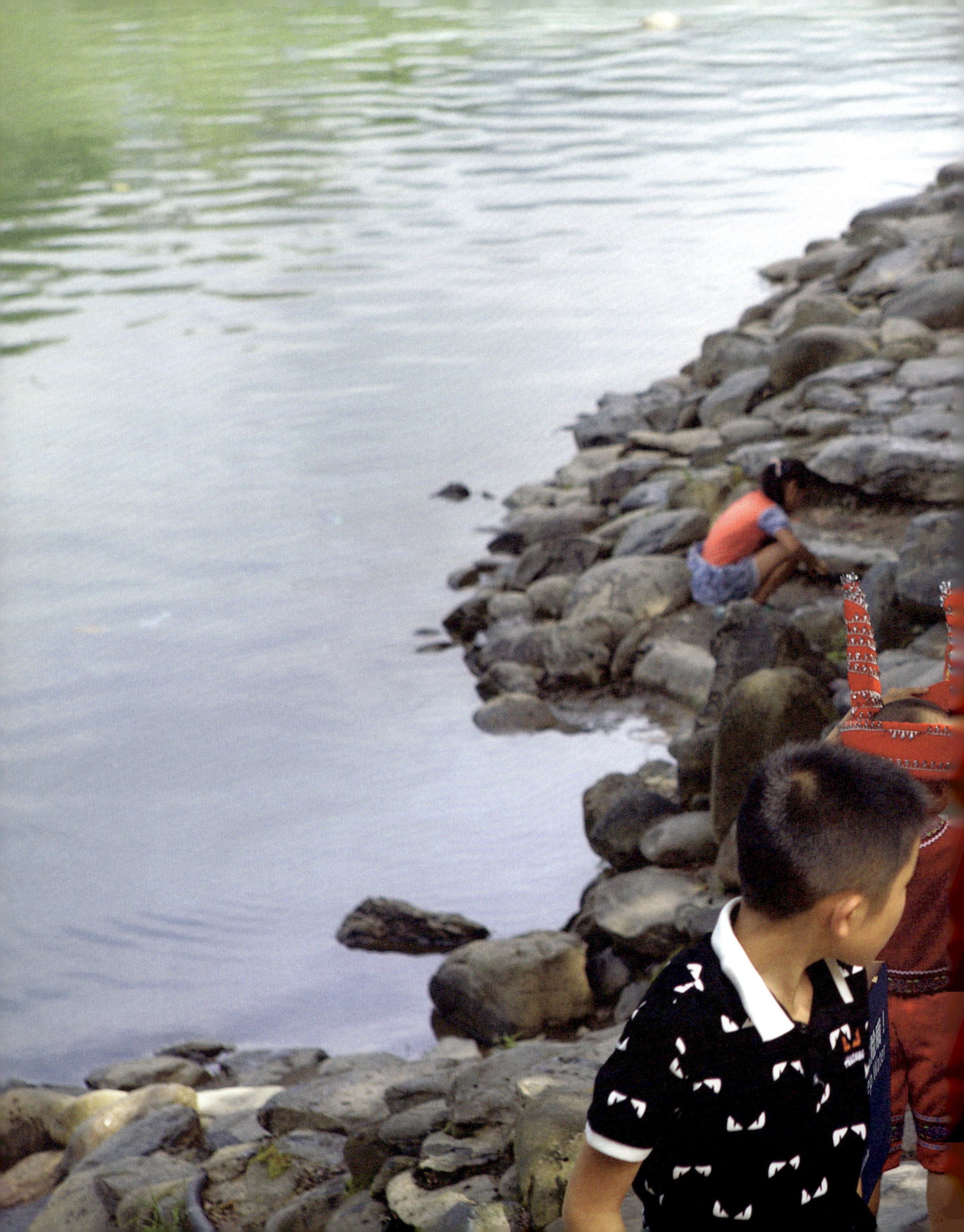

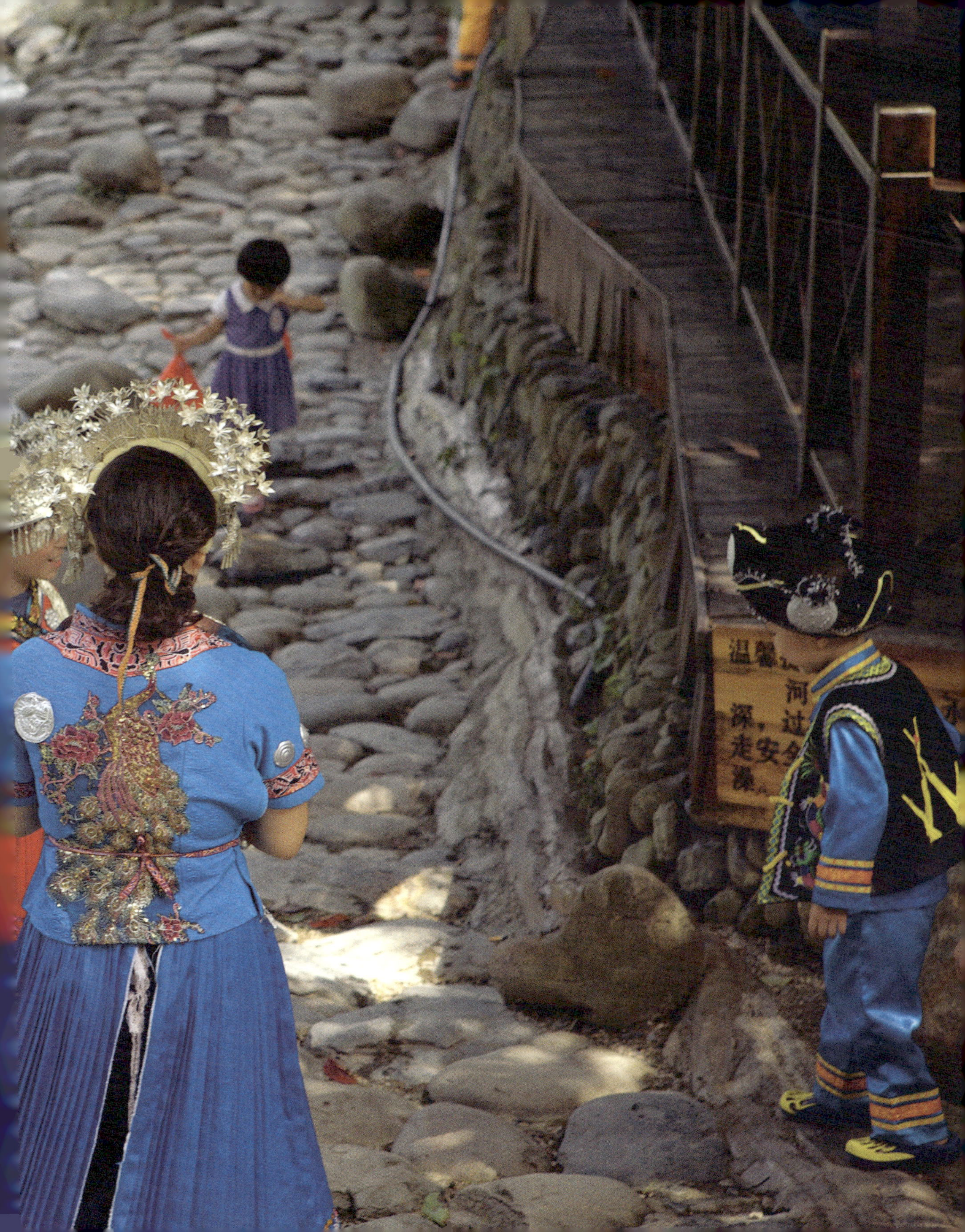
温馨
河
深，过
走安

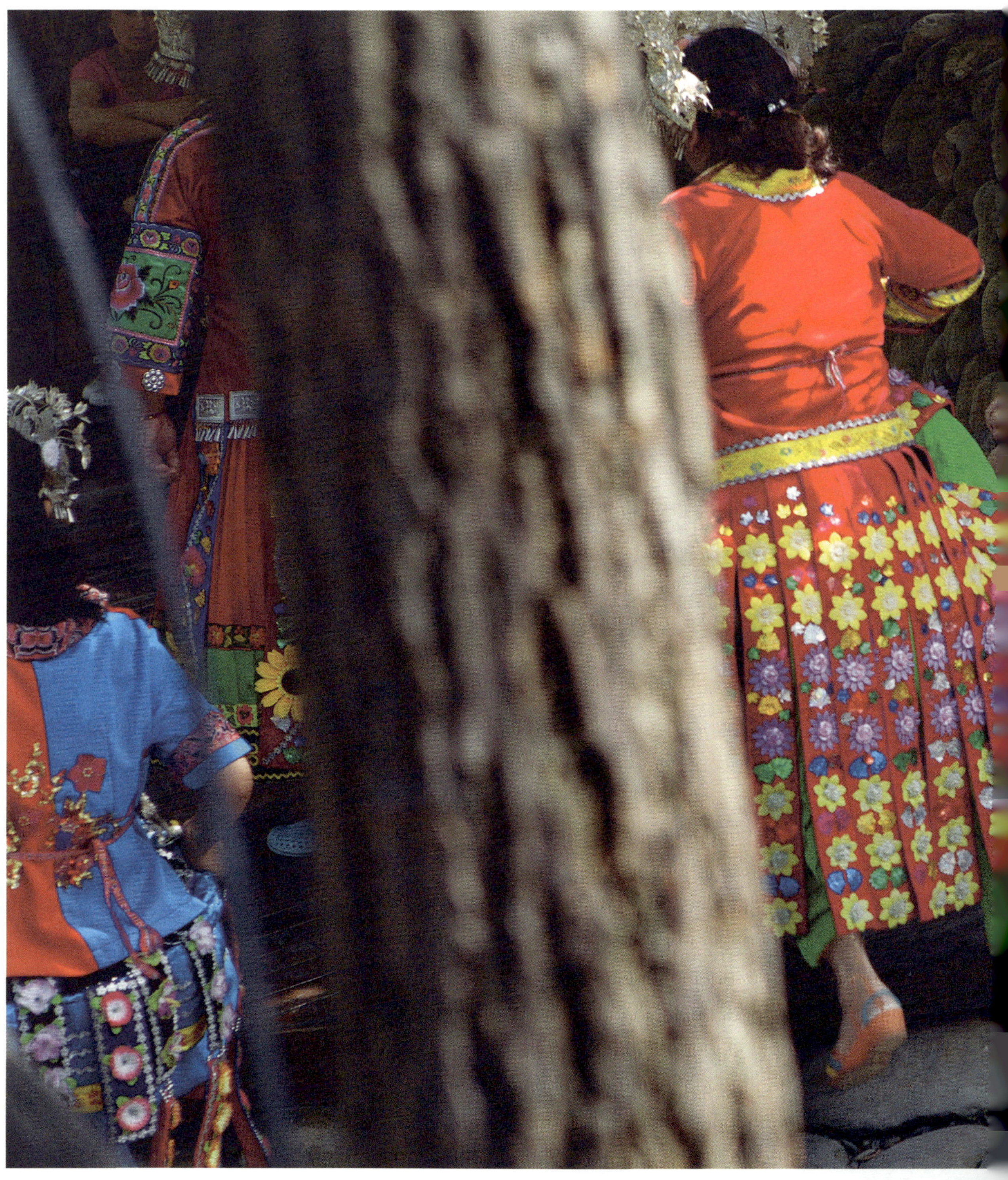

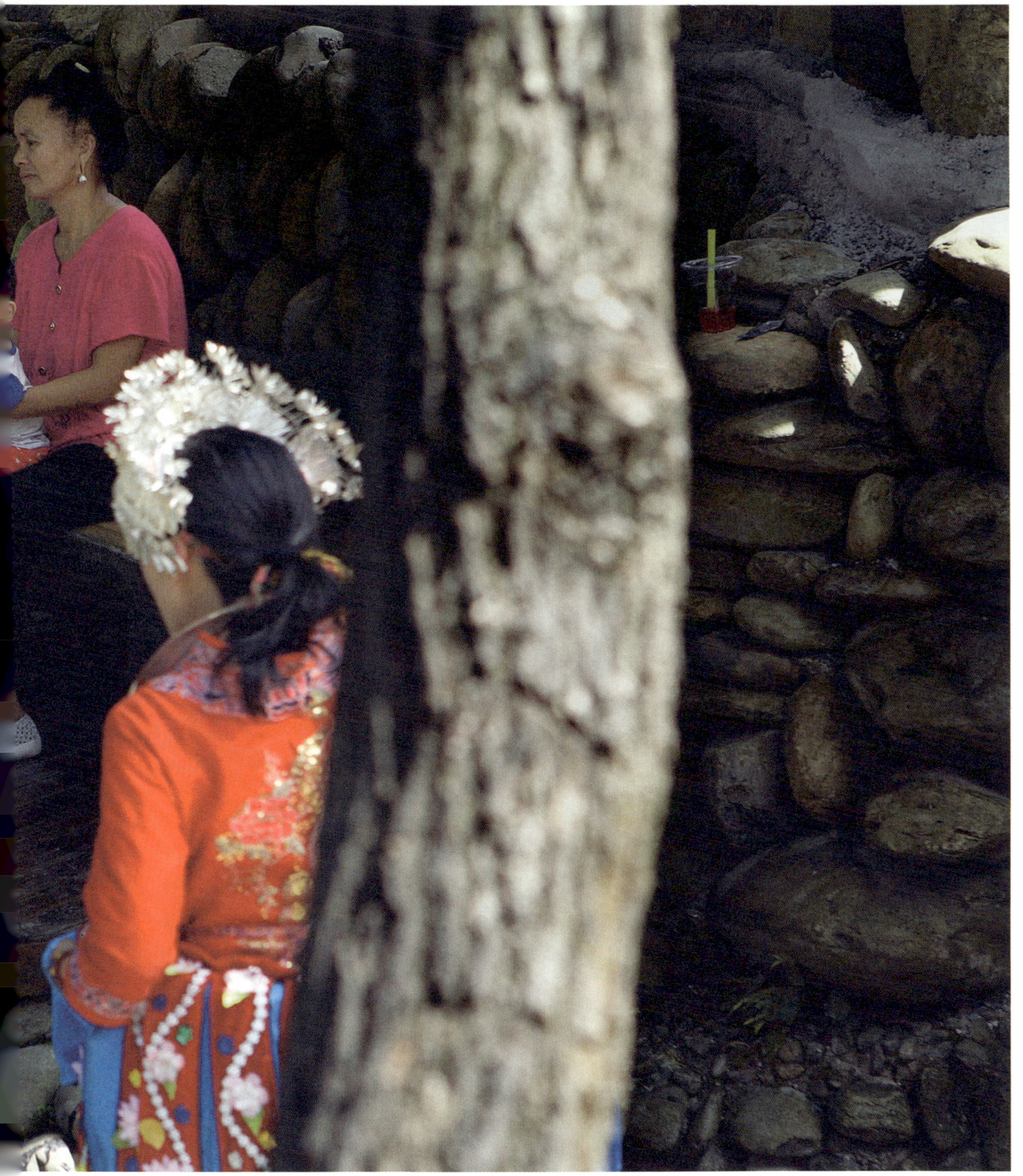

The Worlds of Others

Veronica Caciolli

★

From there, mountains will be divinities or rocky objects, forests will eat children, animals will have the right to speak but only on the night of the Epiphany, and the changeable syntax, which will serve as a relation between what the taxonomic West calls the division into kingdoms – vegetable, animal, mineral – will allow the emergence of the unexpected variation of possible worlds. Among these, the one we presume to be ours, of means and ends, of the industrious labour with certain tools that include the materiality of an abstraction called money, is certainly not the best one and is undoubtedly the most problematic. But it is the one that, for the moment, seems to have won against the worlds of others, leaving the majority of us to live amid the ruins, its own ones included.

Ilaria Bussoni, *ilmondoinfine: vivere tra le rovine*

"We are in a constant panic code"[1].
Though, among the less oppressed of "what we presume to be our world", our reactions of tiredness[2], of escape into a "magical world"[3], the search for "exit routes"[4], or the possible practice of an *epoché*[5], instead of capitulations, seem to be acts of resistance:

> What lies between destructions and survivals? The acts of *resistance*. An everyday struggle to oppose injustice, or, at least, so that justice may be done. Pasolini names *light* as the vital element of such resistance acts: a *poetic* element because "poetry is in life", a *political* element because life itself expands, breathes, changes – even dies – politically[6].

Opposing further kinds of expansion/development, our existence may find its ways of survival through specific acts *à rebours*, between a political movement of degrowth[7] and a poetic research of the "Great Time"[8]:

> *Past is synonymous with archaic* (=what remains). In its most radical expression, the Plunge into the past happens referring not to the Ancient, but to the Archaic. The Ancient is, quite simply, what there was *once upon a time*. The Ancient is easily found – the Archaic has to be searched for. The Archaic is what society deliberately *wanted to forget or hide*: it is what was present in the experience of the Origins (of the infinite Origins which have been there from the beginning), and which society has had to reckon with, by removing it.
> *The Archaic has been removed by society.*
> It is what lies at the bottom, and which, if brought to light, would reveal the character of mere Appearance of the social institutions. It would reveal their *ideological nature*.
> The Ancient is represented by *objects*.
> The Archaic by "questions".
> The Archaic is represented by the myth and the persuasion that the myth can happen also today. In fact: the myth doesn't gather every problem, but only *essential* problems. [...] Essential problem does not only mean something which happened once, but *which happened forever*[9].

But there is certainly more. The unsolvable centrality of the identity-making problem, the search for the archetypes, the prevailing of irrationality, the conception of the myth as a form of knowledge. [...] To a "chronological primitivism" which western culture had possessed since the times of Homer, to give substance to the search for the Golden Age, a "cultural primitivism" was added, expressing the dissatisfaction of civilised man towards civilisation, urging him to believe that the most genuine and spontaneous values could lead to a spiritual life in all the most desirable respects[10].

★

If the archaic was present in the experience of the origins and it is what persists, as it is able to grasp *essential* problems, having been hidden by society, it is now impelling *to bring it back to light.*

Like dowers and "ethnographic modernists who search for the universal in the local, the whole in the part"[11] we anxiously follow the "*pure,* hierophanic, collective"[12] and archetypical footprints of that (eternal) time which elapsed beyond the dystopic deviance of ours. Because its urgent and idealistic recovery would show both its and our *resistance*.
Wavering though between the terror of a world destined in the best scenario towards monoculture[13], but travelling towards *Utopia,* suddenly the traces of that time presumably appear and unfold into one of *the other possible worlds.*

Resident in a place which is not by chance *remote,* in the Guizhou Province (southern China), some Miao people[14] live isolated in the mountains. They are the daily practitioners of an animist and shrewd oral culture. Resisting the industrial production[15] by now spread nearly everywhere, their original manual and natural indigo dye claims their tradition and identity, as well as their destiny. It is considered of course a sacred process, guarded only by women: from the sowing to the gathering of the flowers, from the phases of fermentation to dyeing, until its *divining* interpretation[16].

Recognizing "the axis between the sky and the earth"[17] in a peculiar shade of blue (indigo) color, our artist decided to reach both these mountain people as well as the Danzhai *sisters'*[18] community.

Through these experiences of mobility and inter-relations, like other female artists, Lisa Batacchi has been able to produce specific "heterotopias and heterochronies":

> Theirs is an art which "takes places into consideration" as well as the relationships which mark them, which often take a political position, which turn into cultural studies, by using forms and tools which frequently touch on anthropological research. [...] With their artistic odysseys, both spatial and conceptual, these artists seem [...] to continuously doubt or put into discussion their own observation point, and therefore our observation point, by creating heterotopias where art becomes a contact zone. In the definition of Marie Louise Pratt (1992: 7) the contact zones are spaces of cultural relations which are often asymmetric, which evoke "the spatial and temporal co-existence of subjects who were previously separated" by history and geography[19].

Along this *contact zone* which is mainly human, then collaborative, feminine and transnational, the artist has developed the local indigo dye technique but instead of following the rich abstract or zoomorphic symbolism of the Miao people[20], she has inserted her own one, producing a complicated series of cultural *collages*[21]. In *Curtain* (2016), the hybrid figure of the horse-cow derives from her interpretation of two *I Ching*'s hexagrams. This ancient – Chinese – oracle's attribution is further complicated by probable Taoist / Confucian[22] origins and developments. The horse in itself, a now "worn-out" symbol but traditionally central in the Mongolian system of representation[23], recalls the past of the companions with whom she shared her procession in the Gobi Desert. The final liberation of collective prayers embraces besides one

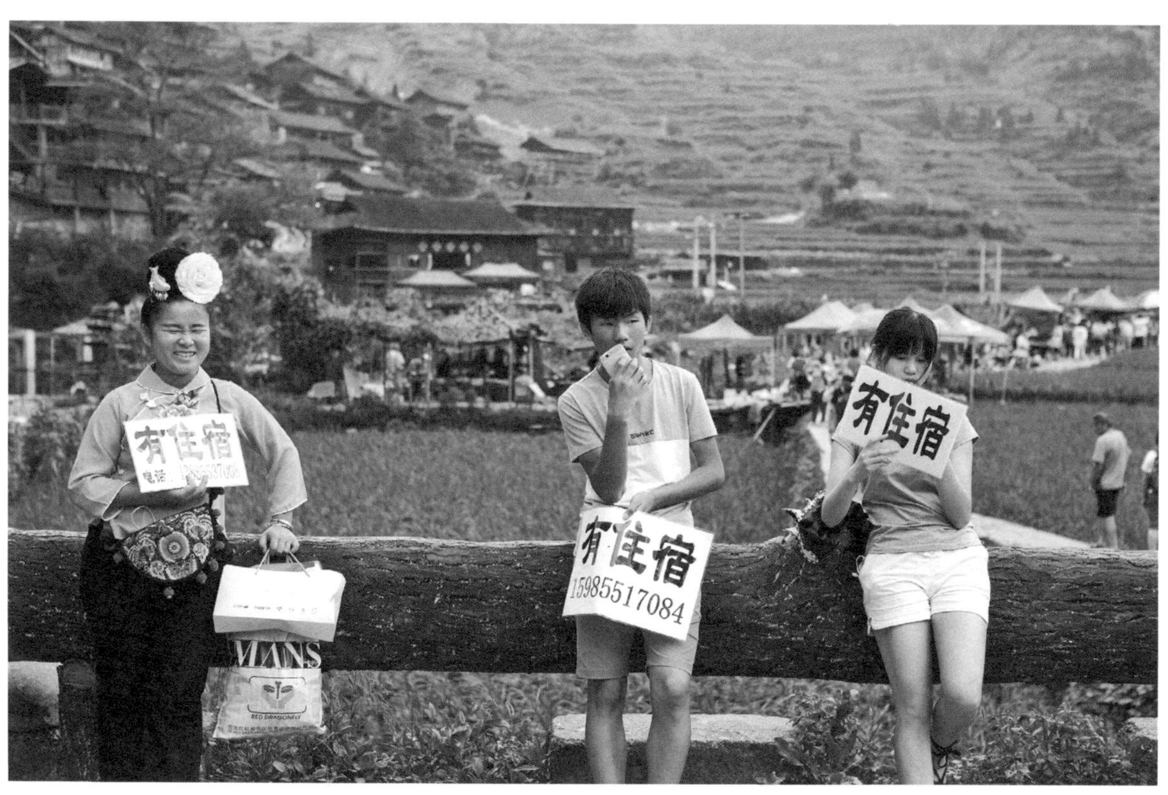
有住宿
有住宿
15985517084
有住宿

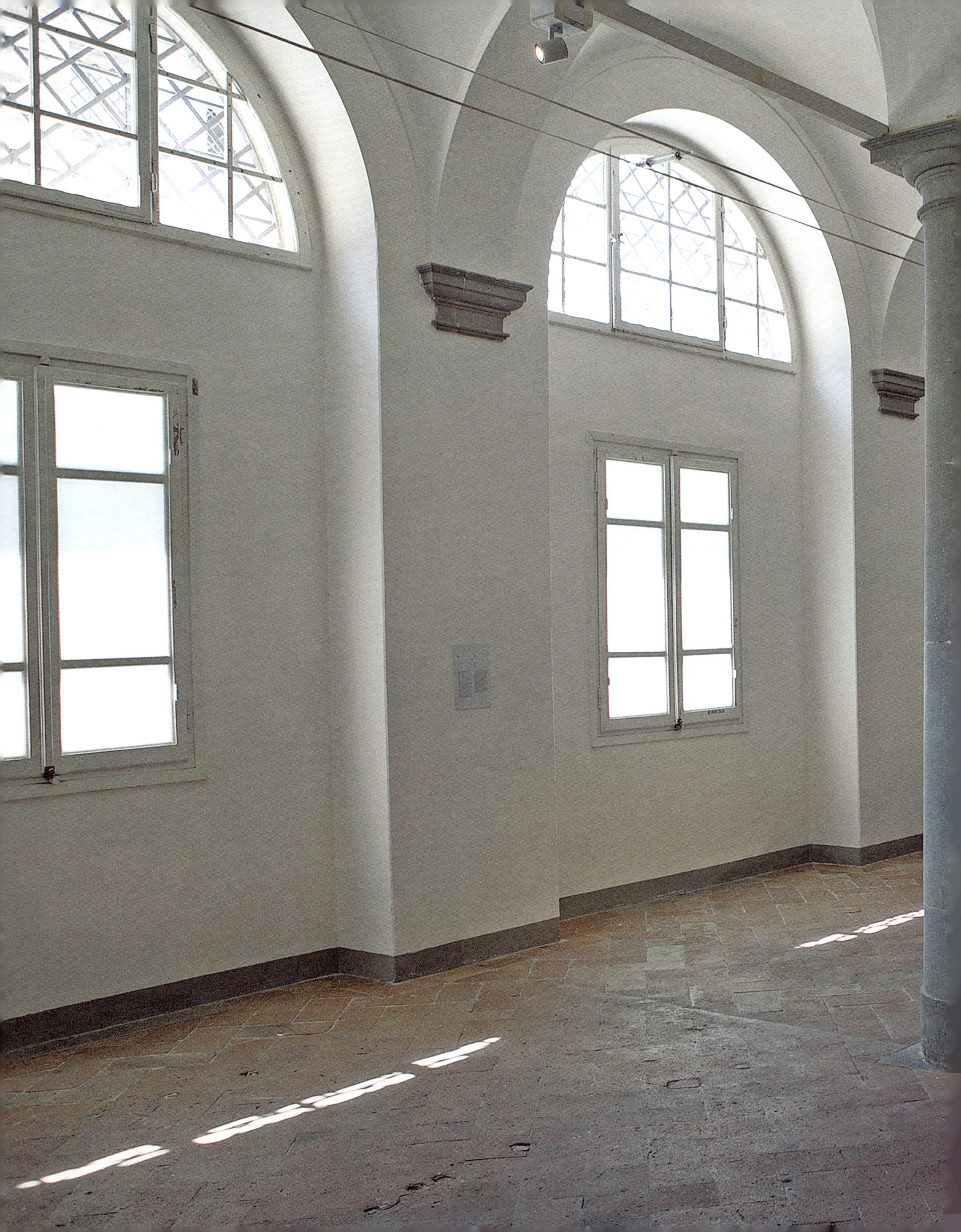

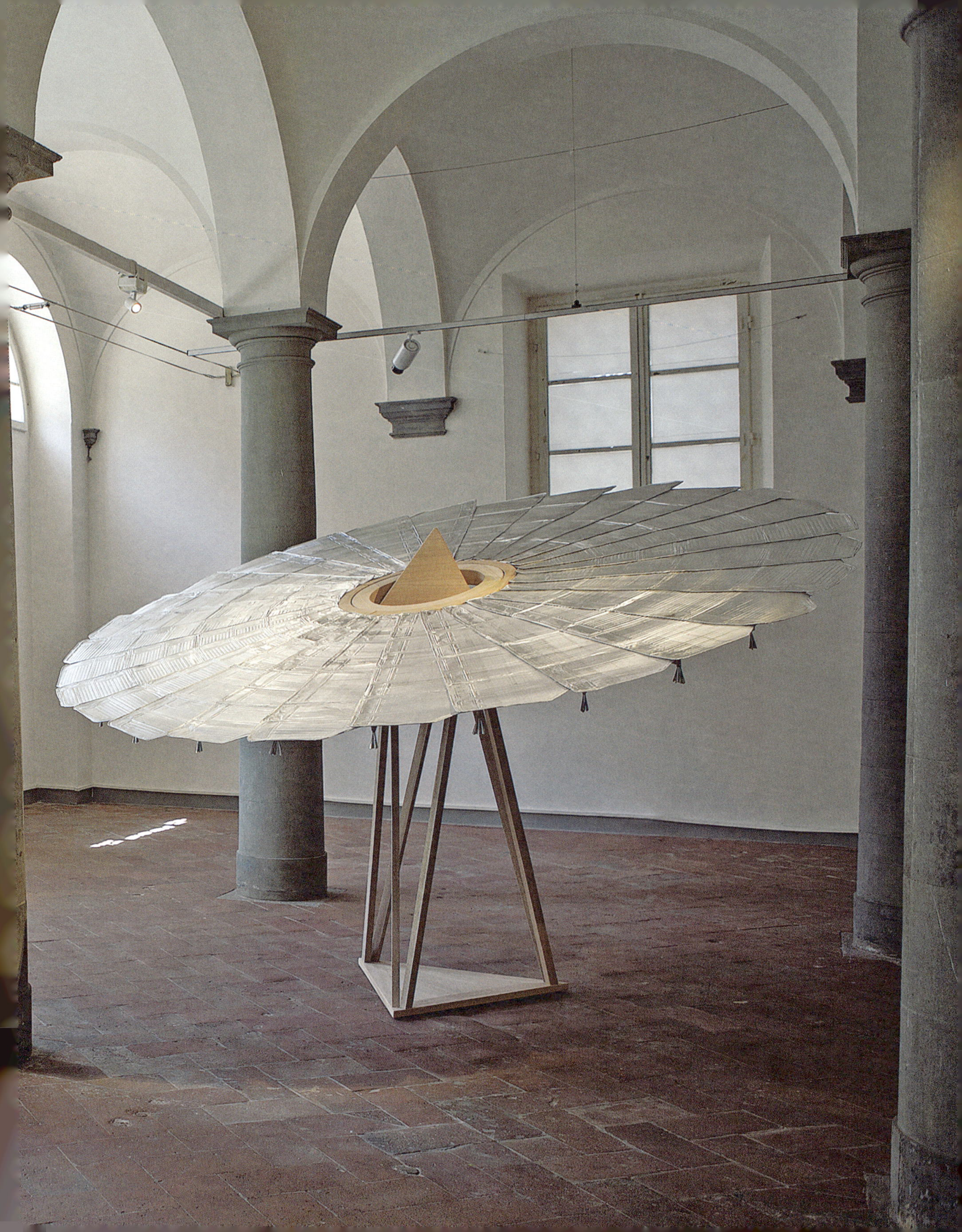

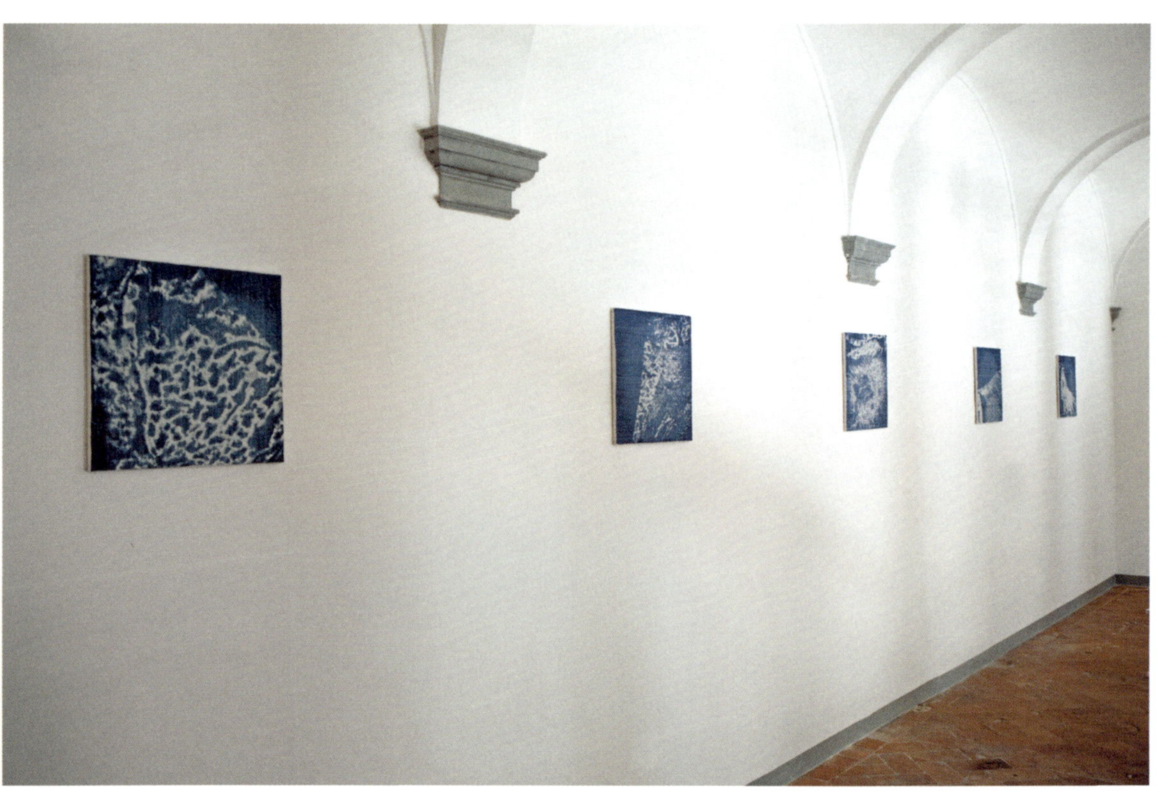

★

of their beliefs about the sacredness of mount Altan Ovoo, a place of pilgrimage[24] which was the backdrop for the action of this performance[25].
Similarly *Preface* (2017), through the verbal-visual transcription of the dialogue held with the oracle, has taken the form of a cosmological map.

The double experience in Guizhou produced a later release in 2018, through a series of further evocations.
"What I can do is to help people to change the position of the light and so, with a free choice, to change the shadows. I really believe in this: shadows can be changed". The words of the fortune-teller Norman in a passage by Tiziano Terzani[26], a figure who, through the conceptualization of his travels in Asia, acted in the background during the whole project, resonate in the big shamanic mirror of Mongolian origin, the *Toli*[27].
Crossing Destinies instead, represents the manifestation of the mediumistic power of the Miao indigo: "After the indigo solution sits untouched, a brilliant blue froth builds on the surface. Miao women believe that this is a sign that their ancestors are protecting them. Ancestors' worship rituals are an important part of the dyeing process"[28]. The result is a series of five tapestries interwoven with Miao yarns, still carried out manually and in a female context[29]. They recall celestial universes, as reflected by an earthly microcosm.
However, *Elisir of Return*[30] does not fail to show the sharp incursion of what "we presume to be *our*" world. The first photographic series captures a process of economic and cultural exploitation practiced by the Miao people from Xijiang towards tourists, through the explicit invitation to the fast and cheap hiring of their traditional clothes and ornaments; having checked their enthusiasm in wandering for a few hours through the little town dressed up like the residents for their most important ceremonies...: "Authentic traditions, the pure products, are everywhere yielding to promiscuity and aimlessness"[31]. Nevertheless, the other series shows the cohabitation within the same province, of a lifestyle still rooted in agricultural rhythms and superstitious customs, as for example, specific embroidery for the apotropaic use of textiles which swaddle new-borns[32].
The short film *The Time of Discretion* is a travel diary which in the same way, alternates fading worlds[33]: not just *ours* as we could guess, but not even only *that of the others*.

These last works as the whole project overall, seem to show more Lévi-Strauss melancholic despondency than the faith in survival of the indigenous cultures through their hybrid reinvention[34].
However, not submitting to surrender but indulging in the attempt, utopic in itself, of reaching "the removed and the hidden by society" and being able to allude to it through the representation (of one of its possible *symptoms*, as the Miao culture), it conveys a double act of *resistance*, both subjective and collective.

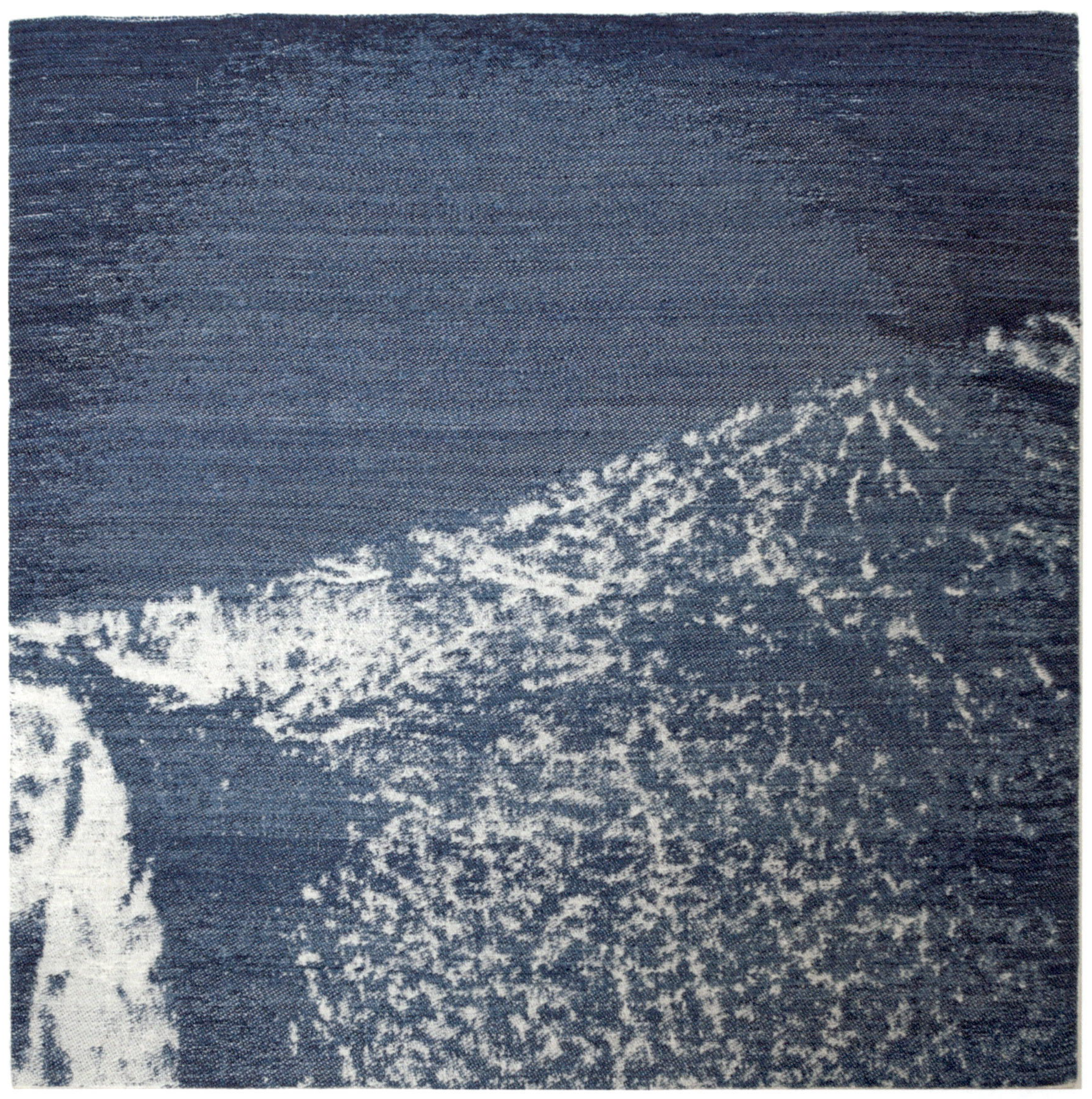

★

[1] Interview with Laurie Anderson led by the Louisiana Museum in Copenhagen on the theme of migration, 18 February, 2019: https://www.artribune.com/television/2019/02/video-viviamo-nel-panico-costante-video-intervista-a-laurie-anderson/?utm_source=Newsletter%20Artribune&utm_campaign=dccbba5d12-&utm_medium=email&utm_term=0_dc515150dd-dccbba5d12-153771481&ct=t%28%29&goal=0_dc515150dd-dccbba5d12-1537714811.

[2] According to Byung-Chul Han our society is dominated by the excess of positivity for which nothing is impossible, leading to a breakdown. "The tiredness of exhaustion is the tiredness of positive potency. It makes one incapable of doing *something*. Tiredness that inspires is tiredness of negative potency, namely of *not-to*". See Byung-Chul Han, *The Burnout Society*, Stanford: Stanford University Press, 2015, p. 33 (*Müdigkeitsgesellschaft*, Berlin: Matthes & Seitz, 2010).

[3] In my essay "Eternal Return to the Origins" (see *Global Identities. Postcolonial and Cross-Cultural Narratives*, Milan: Mousse Publishing, 2019) I introduced the current spiritualistic return with an exit from the history for the redefinition of the present through magic (Ernesto De Martino: 1948): "not like an escape route into the depths of the irrational, but as a cognitive means to face and reconstruct reality" (see Cecilia Alemani, *Il mondo magico*, Venice: Marsilio, 2017).

[4] Elémire Zolla suggests the possibility of an expanded experience of the space through specific "exit routes from the world", in *Uscite dal mondo*, Milan: Adelphi, 1992, an idea which inspired Lisa Batacchi's life/work.

[5] Francesco Remotti speaks about an *epoché* (suspension and emptying) of culture carried out voluntarily by specific groups with the aim of not only keeping their own culture alive, but life itself. See Francesco Remotti, *Cultura. Dalla complessità all'impoverimento*, Bari-Rome: Laterza, 2011, pp. 247–280.

[6] Georges Didi-Huberman, "Lumière contre lumière", in *La disparition des lucioles. Exposition à la prison Sainte-Anne*, exhibition catalogue (Avignon, Collection Lambert, May 17 – November 25, 2014), Arles: Actes Sud, 2014 (italics in the original), my translation. Didi-Huberman refers to the article "Il vuoto del potere in Italia" by Pier Paolo Pasolini published in *Corriere della sera*, February 1, 1975. The quoted part refers instead to the radio interview with Pier Paolo Pasolini by Achille Millo (1967) later published as: "La Poesia secondo Pier Paolo", *La Repubblica*, February 24, 1990.

[7] Proclaimed by philosophers/economists and environmentalists. See among others Serge Latouche, *Farewell to Growth*, Cambridge: Polity Press, 2009 (*Petit traité sur la décroissance sereine*, Paris: Mille et une nuit, 2007); Guido Dalla Casa, *L'ecologia profonda. Lineamenti per una nuova visione del mondo*, Milan: Mimesis, 2008.

[8] For Mircea Eliade sacred or Great Time is opposed to the profane duration of it and can be repeated through rituals. See among others "Sacred Time and the Myth of Eternal Renewal", in *Patterns in Comparative Religion*, London: Sheed and Ward, 1958, pp. 388–409 (*Traité d'histoires des religions*, Paris: Payot, 1949).

[9] Gian Antonio Gilli, *Arcaici specialisti. I testi di Solid Void 2011*, Turin: Diogene Edizioni, 2013, pp. 95–97.

[10] Francesco Paolo Campione, "Introduzione" and "L'armamentario primitivista", in Francesco Paolo Campione, Maria Grazia Messina (eds.), *Je suis l'autre. Giacometti, Picasso e gli altri. Il Primitivismo nella scultura del Novecento*, exhibition catalogue (Rome, Terme di Diocleziano, 28 September 2018 – 20 January 2019), Milan: Electa, 2018, pp. 17, 209. In the mentioned part (p. 209) Francesco Paolo Campione quotes Arthur O. Lovejoy and George Boas (1935) and George Boas (1948) on Primitivism in ancient times and in the Middle Ages.

[11] See James Clifford, *The Predicament of Culture. Twentieth-Century Ethnography, Literature and Art*, Cambridge, MA: Harvard University Press, 1988, p. 4.

[12] "A space-time synchronism synthetized by the so-called primitive art [...] is today returning as a vital and expanded *Orientalistic* trend, one that is ritual, spiritual, ancestral, *autre*, mixing with an archival-archaeological impulse that 'ignites the fuse of explosive material placed in the Already-been' (Benjamin 1982), sometimes revealing underlying psychological and social needs, ones that are post-Messianic, directed toward resurrection, if not to the construction of 'pure', hierophanic, collective roots", in my essay "Eternal Return to the Origins", op. cit., p. 65.

[13] See Claude Lévi-Strauss, *Race and History*, Paris: UNESCO, 1952.

[14] In the exhibition catalogue *One Needle, One Thread: Miao (Hmong) Embroidery and Fabric Piecework from Guizhou, China* (21 September – 30 November 2008), Honolulu: University of Hawai'i Art Gallery, 2008, p. 7, Tomoko Torimaru claims that the Miao began their migration about two-thousand years ago and that they mainly settled in Guizhou, involving a population of more than four million people; in smaller quantities, they reside also in Vietnam, Thailand, Laos and Burma. This thesis is shared by Xiaomei Wang, who adds the United States as another country of their residence.

★

With the impossibility of giving voice to the native, I have found it necessary to insert at least the one of their closest, current and constant local interpreters, who also met Lisa Batacchi in 2017. Therefore, as well as the following citations, some extracts from her monography *Memory on Hands* (2015) have been published in this book.

[15] For a detailed history of indigo see: *Sublime Indigo,* exhibition catalogue (Marseilles, Centre de la Vieille Charité, 22 March – 31 May 1987), Marseilles-Paris: Musées de Marseille/Editions Vilo, 1987.

[16] See Xiaomei Wang, *Memory on Hands. The Life Stories of Sister Yang and Sister Li,* Guizhou: Guizhou Educational Press, 2015, p. 278.

[17] *Catching the Axis. Between the Sky and the Earth* is the title and the theme of the 2016 Land Art Mongolia Biennial which sparked *The Time of Discretion* project.

[18] This is how the Miao women call each other. See Wang, *Memory on Hands,* op. cit.

[19] Michel Foucault, "On Other Spaces", in Nicholas Mirzoeff (ed.), *The Visual Culture Reader,* London and New York: Routledge, 1998. The concept of Heterotopia *(Hétérotopie)* was expressed during Foucault's lecture "Des espaces autres", 1967, in Michel Foucault, *Dits et écrits* (1984), vol. IV, "Des espaces autres", no. 360, Paris: Gallimard, 1994, pp. 752–762, quoted in Maria Antonietta Trasforini, *Lontane da dove. Artiste fra centri e periferie nei mondi dell'arte*, in Emanuela De Cecco (ed.), *Arte-mondo. Storia dell'arte, storie dell'arte*, Milan: Postmedia, 2010. Trasforini refers to the artists Marina Abramovic, Maya Bayevic, Mona Hatoum, Shirin Neshat (who often work in their places of origin in an implicit or explicit relation with other places). For the final quoted part: Marie Louise Pratt, *Imperial Eyes: Travel Writing and Transculturation,* London and New York: Routledge, 1992.

[20] Around the richness of Miao symbols, see Xiaomei Wang's "Gewo and Other Patterns" chapter published in this book, p. 113.

[21] In his chapter "On Ethnographic Surrealism", James Clifford indicates similar strategies of "fragmentation and juxtaposition of cultural values" through the practice of *collage*, used both in ethnography and Surrealism in the 1920s and 1930s in France. See Clifford, *The Predicament of Culture*, op. cit., pp. 117–151.

[22] Richard Wilhelm (ed.), *The I Ching, or, Book of Changes*, London: Routledge & Kegan Paul, 1951 (*I Ging. Das Buch der Wandlungen*, Dusseldorf: Eugen Diederichs, 1924).

[23] See Gombojav Mend-Ooyo, *Altan Ovoo,* Ulaanbaatar: Mongolian Academy of Culture and Poetry, 2012.

[24] *Ibidem*, p. 83.

[25] Due to the multiple evocations of the sacred I decided to include within this publication, Federico Campagna's illuminating contribution on the miracle.

[26] Tiziano Terzani, *A Fortune-Teller Told Me*, Glasgow: HarperCollins UK, 1997 *(Un indovino mi disse,* Milan: Rusconi, 1995).

[27] See Mihály Hoppál, *Shamans and Traditions*, Budapest: Akadémiai Kiadó, 2007.

[28] Wang, *Memory on Hands*, op. cit., p. 278.

[29] Through the ancient looms and the skills of the Fondazione Arte della Seta Lisio in Florence.

[30] The paper patterns for apotropaic embroidery and textiles for new-borns have taken the form of a mandala, placed on the ground. This work and the others mentioned (besides the video *Travel Notes*) have been expressly produced for the homonymous exhibition (including *Curtain, Preface,* a series of archival documents and symbolic finds, plus a traditional horse-hoof print fabric described by the artist in her chapter "Traces of Taoism", pp. 38–39, published here) which I curated at MAD Murate Art District in Florence, from 7 June to 25 July 2018.

[31] Clifford, *The Predicament of Culture*, op. cit., p. 4.

[32] See Angela Sheng (ed.), *Writing with Thread: Traditional Textiles of Southwest Chinese Minorities,* exhibition catalogue (21 September – 30 November 2008), Honolulu: University of Hawai'i Art Gallery, 2008, p. 378.

[33] James Clifford refers to a possible but transient process of fading of the so called "authentic traditions", see Clifford, *The Predicament of Culture*, op. cit., pp. 1–17.

[34] James Clifford (in *The Predicament of Culture,* op. cit) claims that cultural hybridization is a subversive form of persistence, through which a future inventive is possible. In the same way, Francesco Remotti in his final chapter "Impoverimento e creatività" *(Impoverishment and Creativity)* opposes "all those despondency theories which have for so long characterised the twentieth-century anthropological thoughts and which have done nothing but see, in the impact with the West, effects of despondency", Marshall Sahlins' theory (1993: 7) according to which "not being able to capture the aspects of creativity, seeing ruins and cultural collapses everywhere, is undoubtedly a *subtle* way of making more *complete* the conquering of the world by capitalism". In Remotti, *Cultura. Dalla complessità all'impoverimento*, op. cit., pp. 289–299.

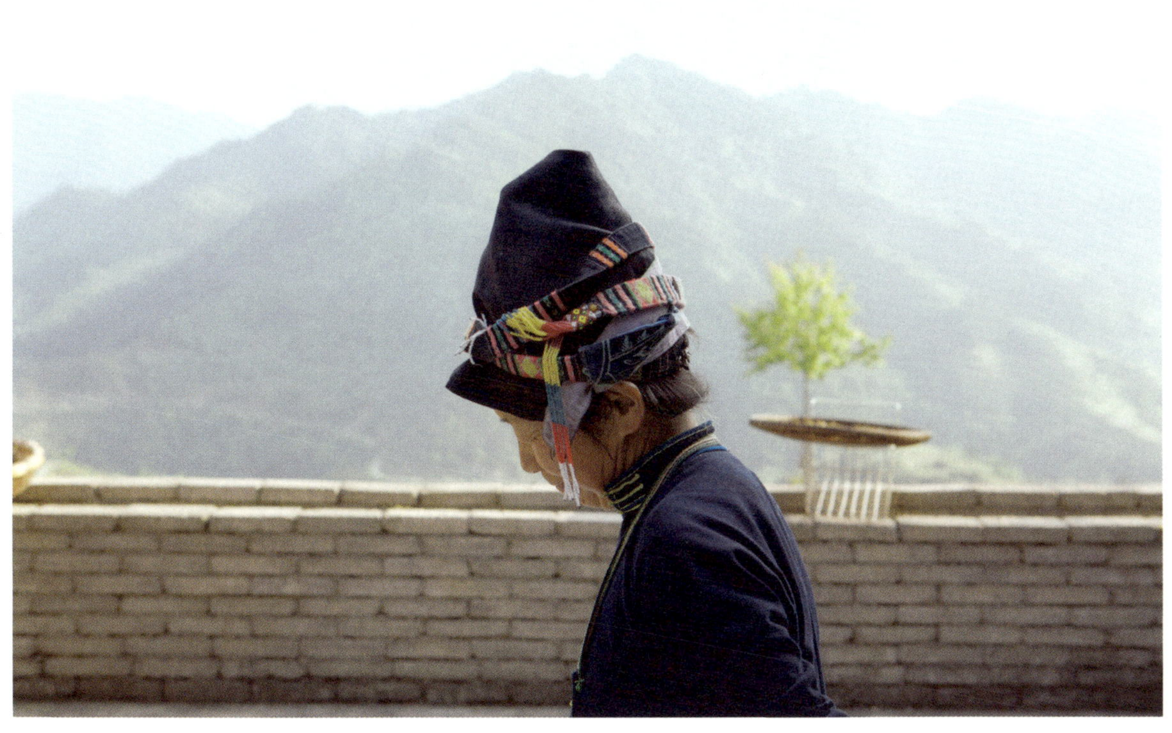

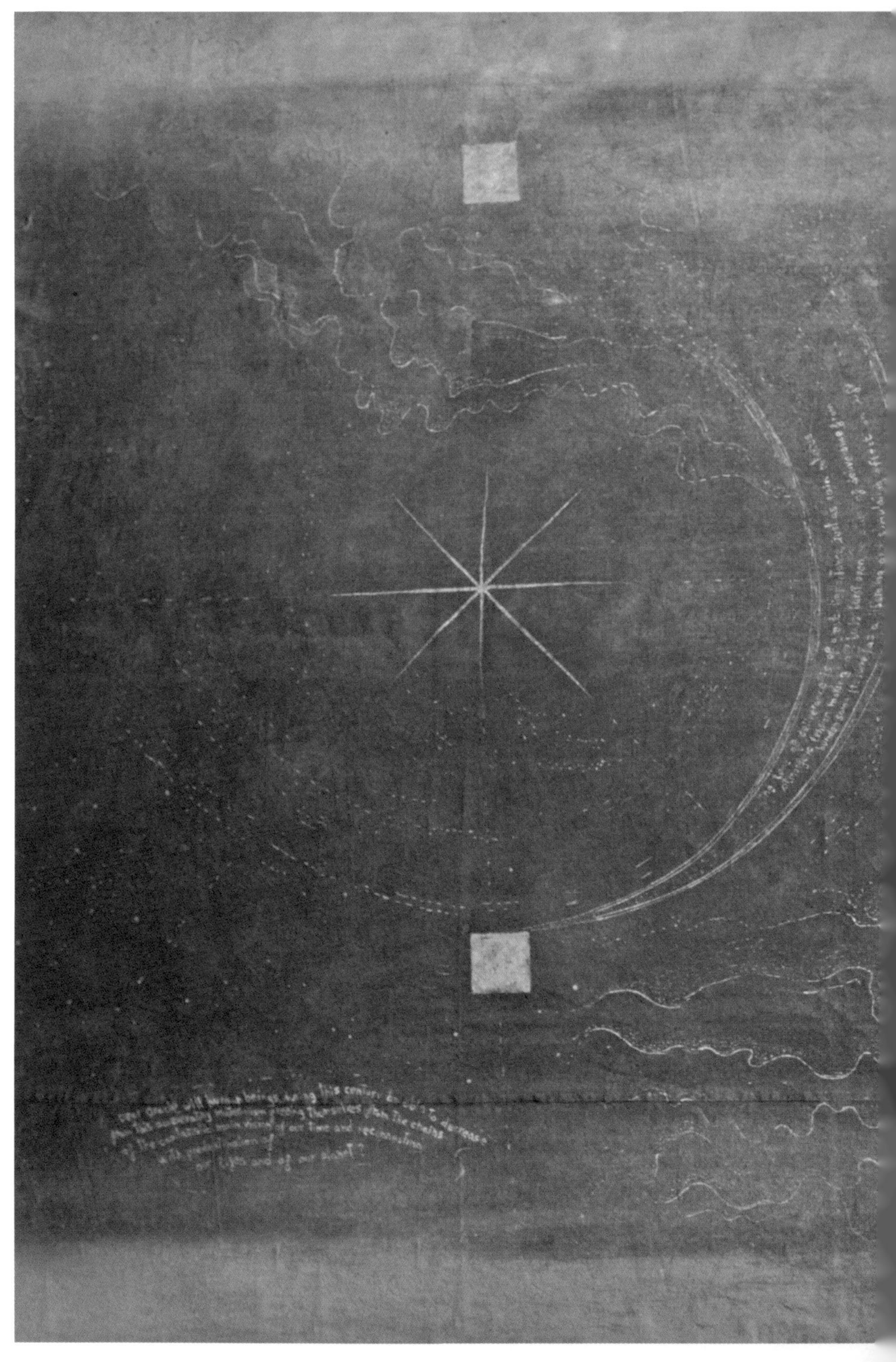

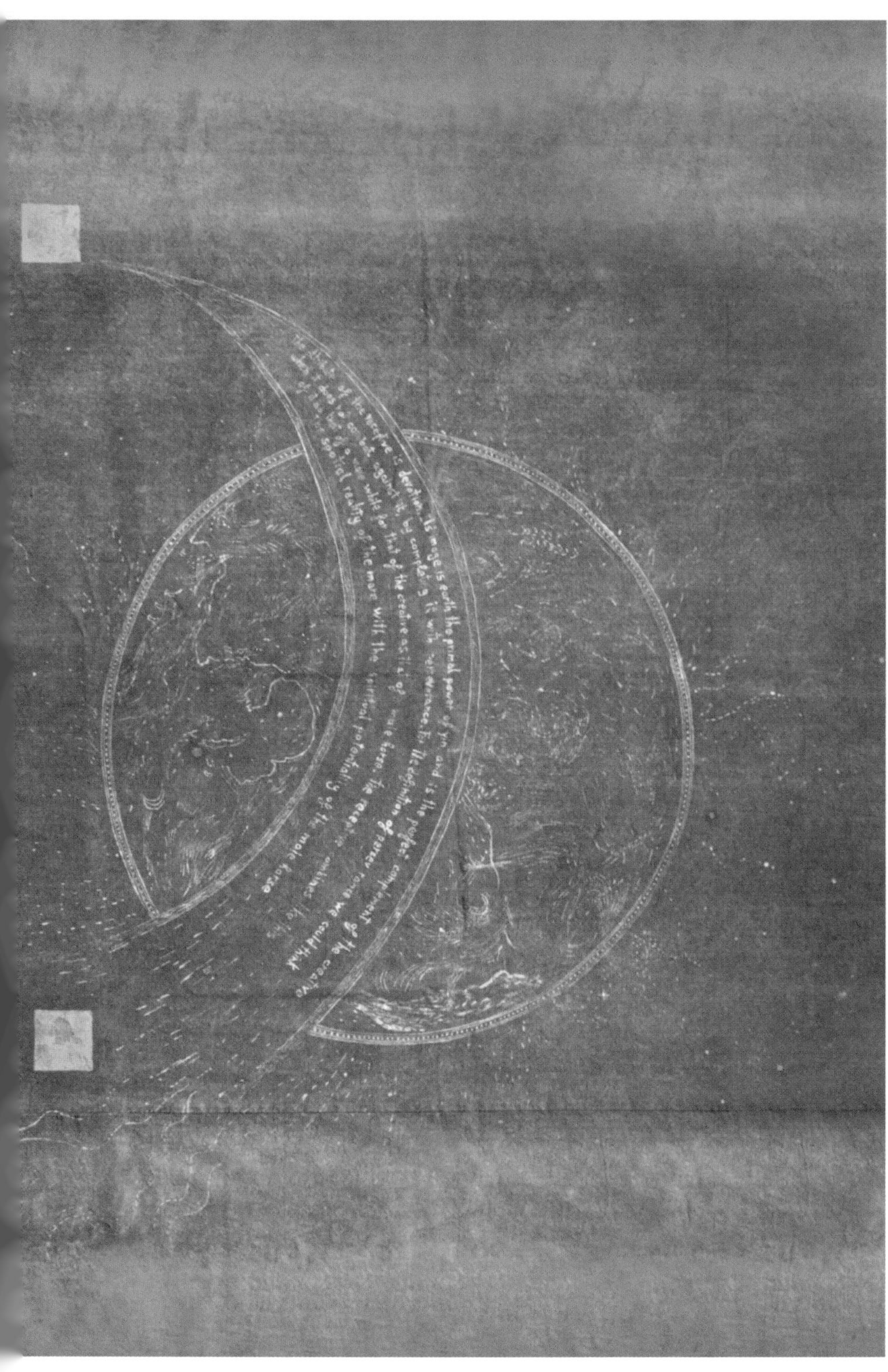

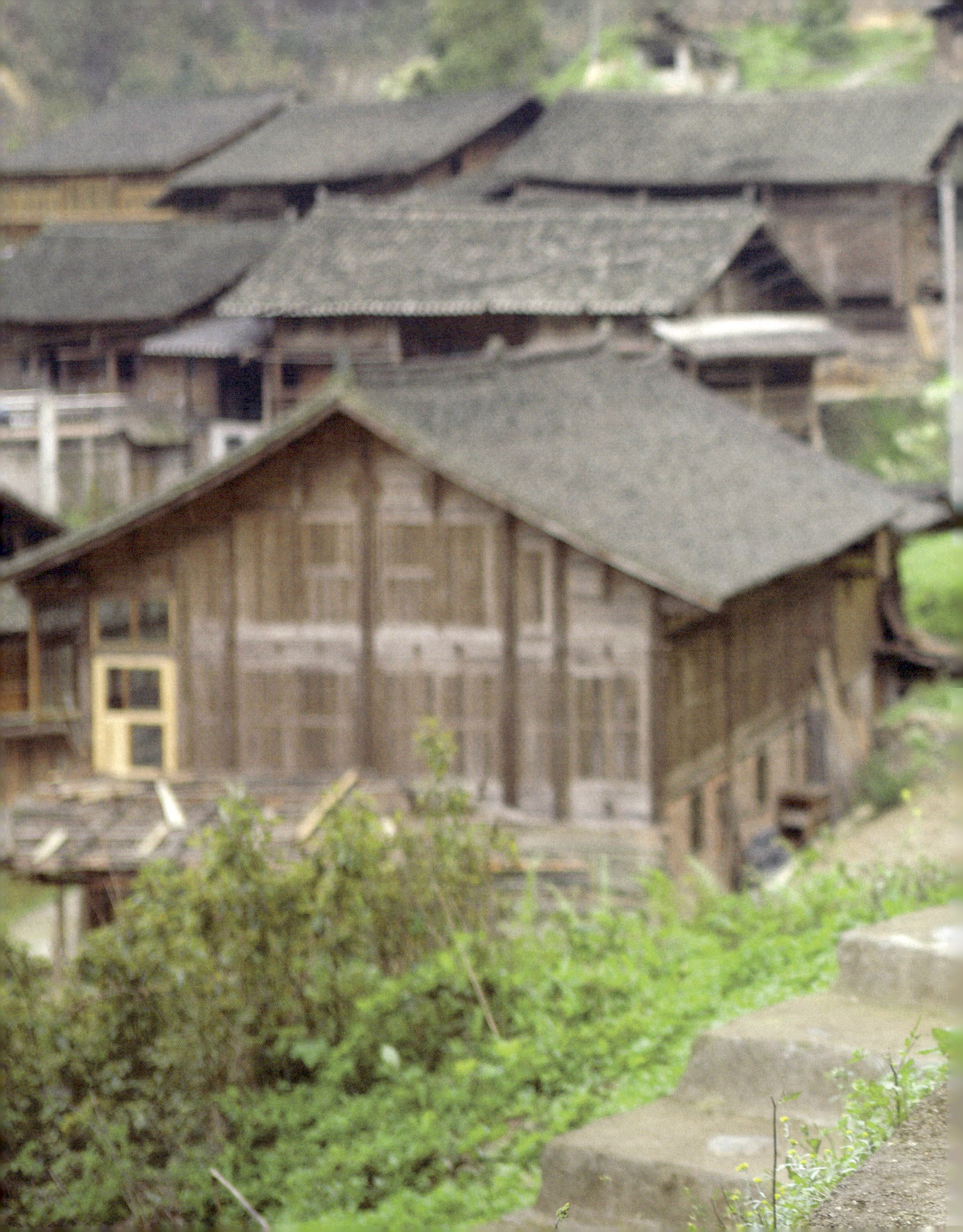

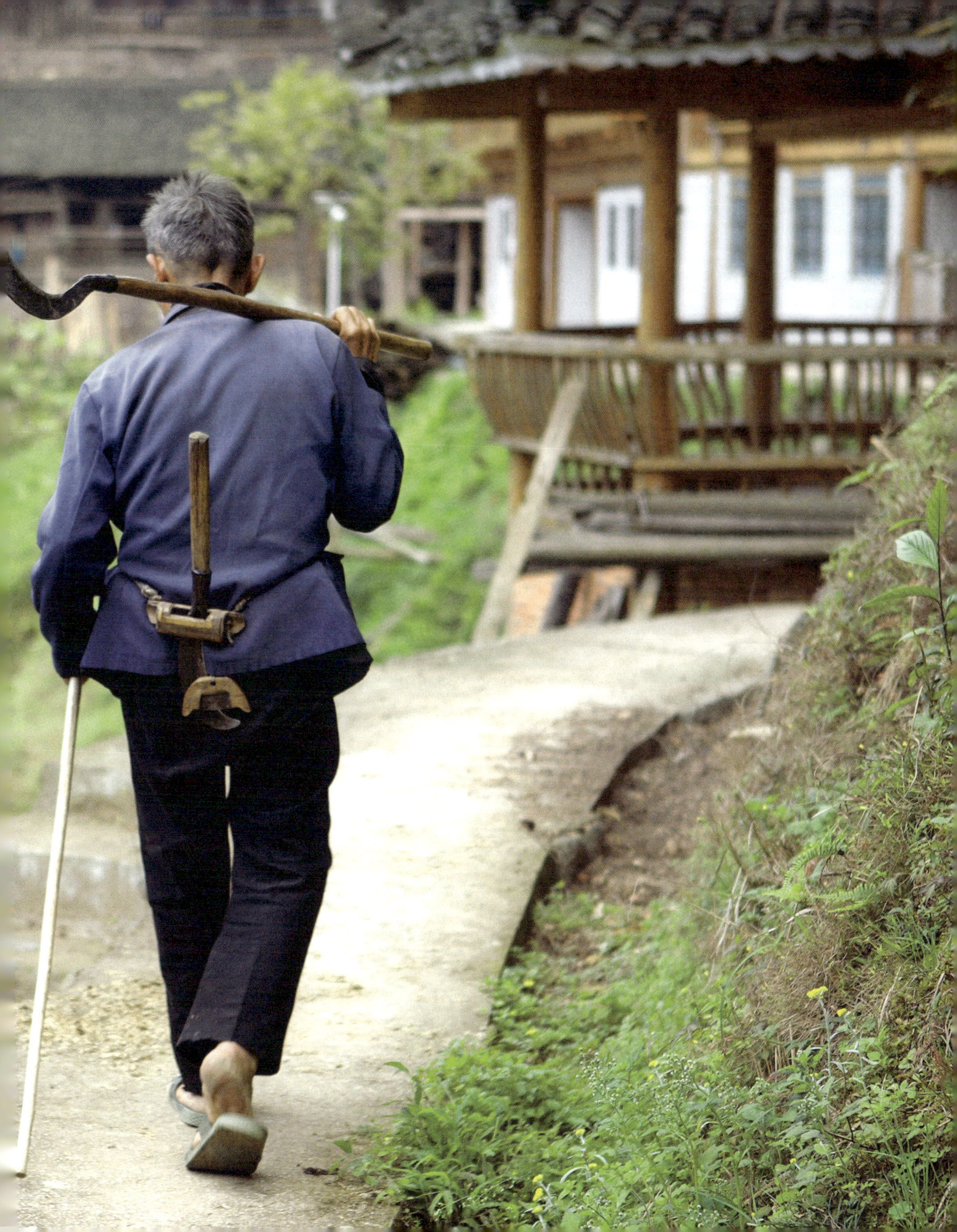

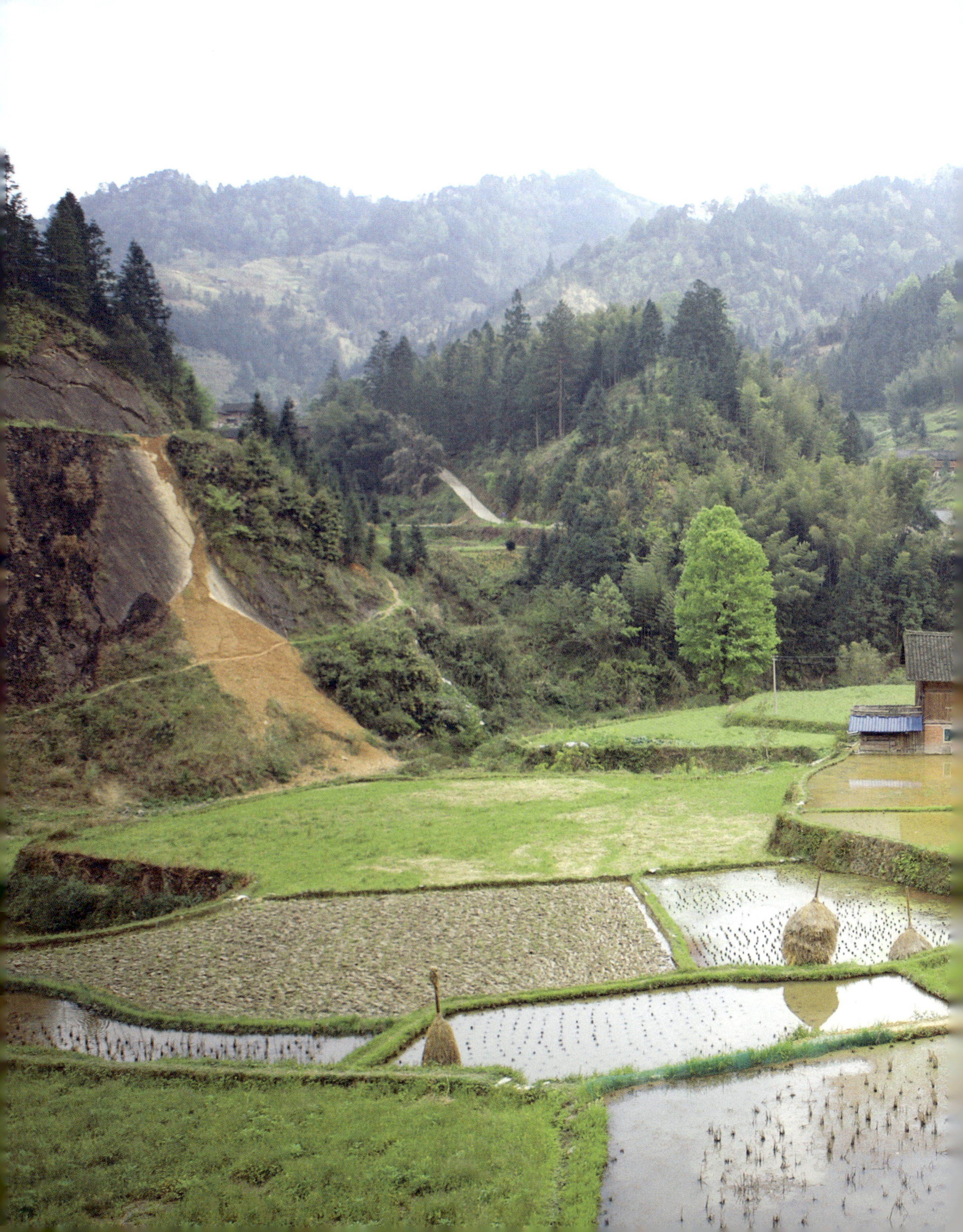

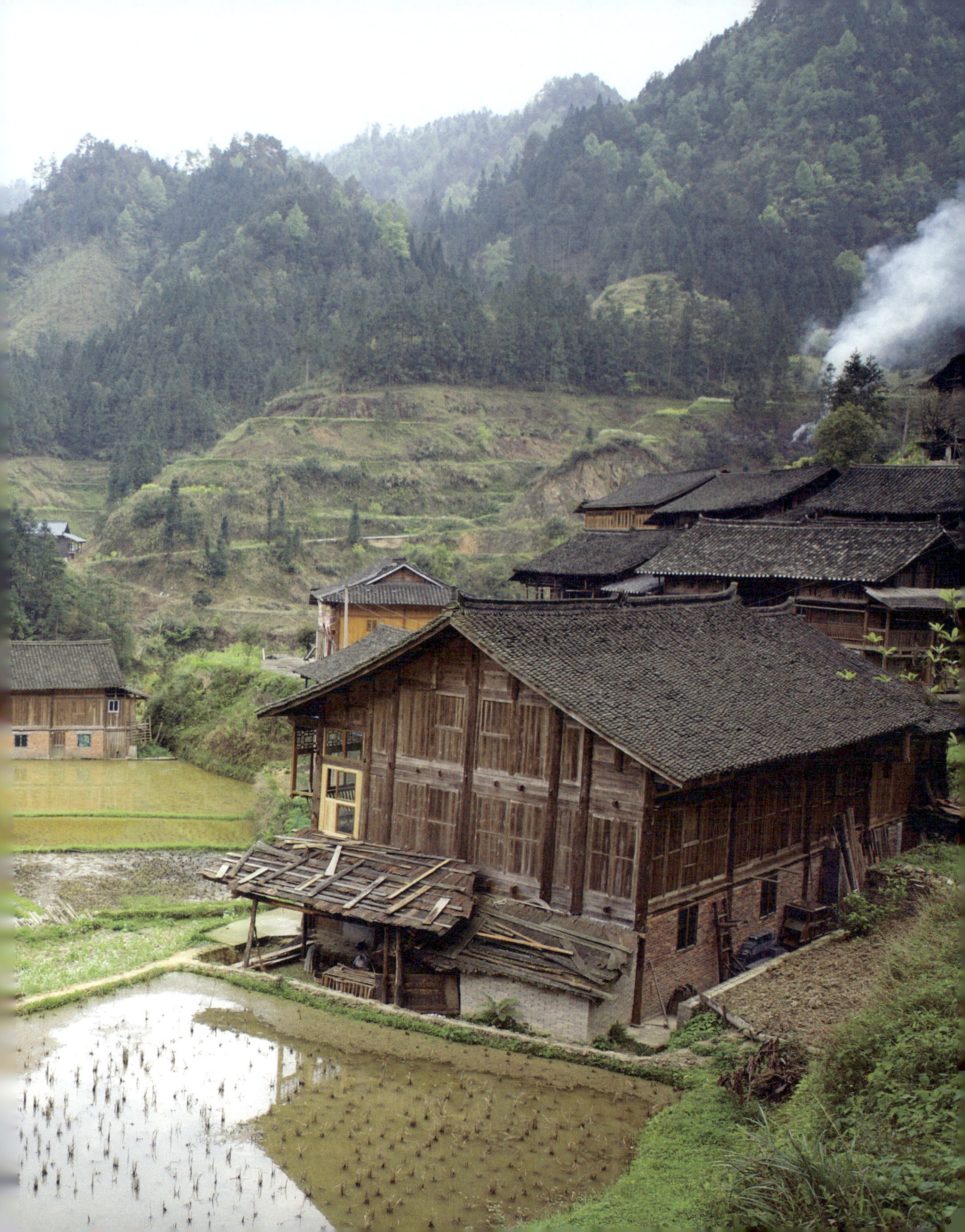

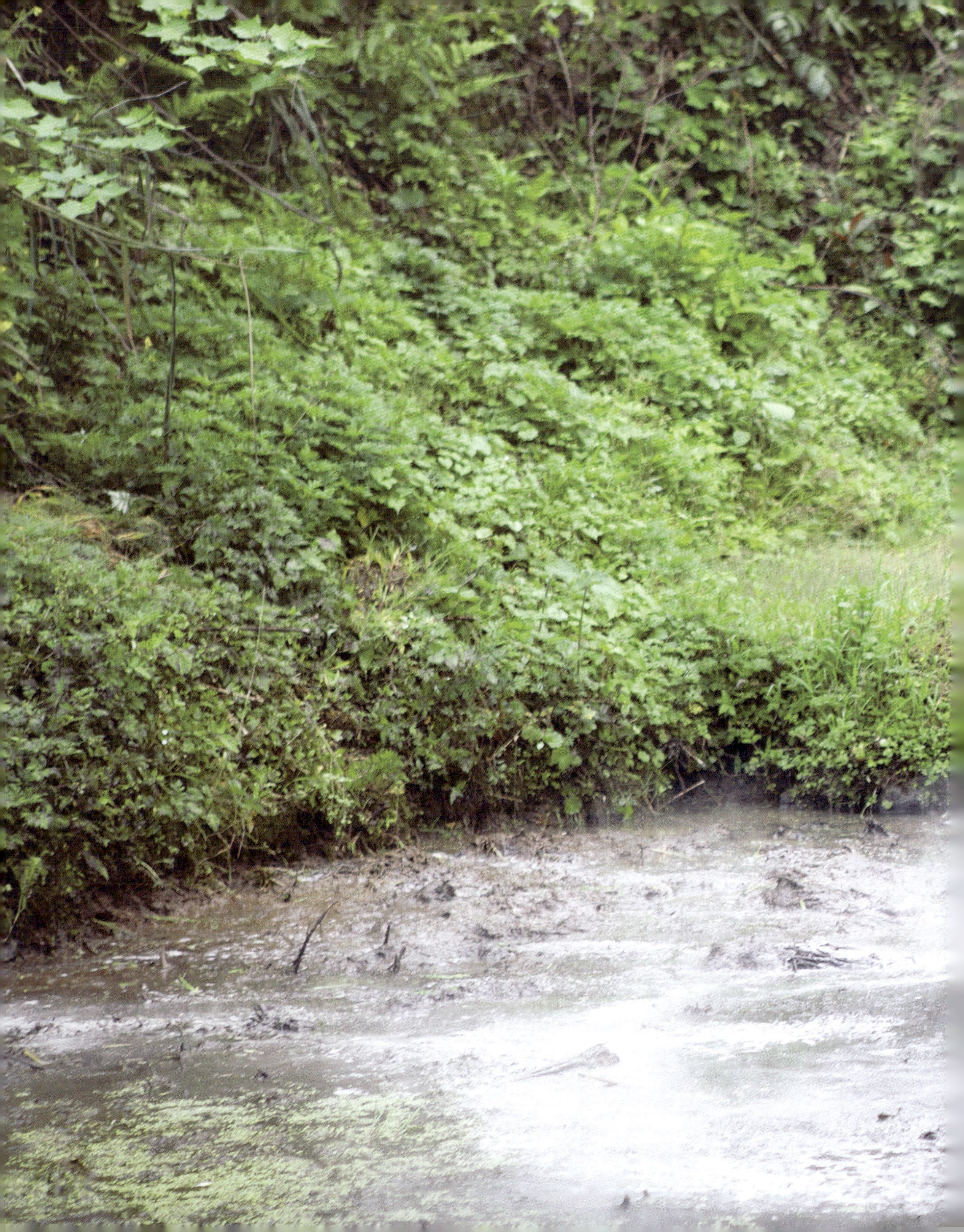

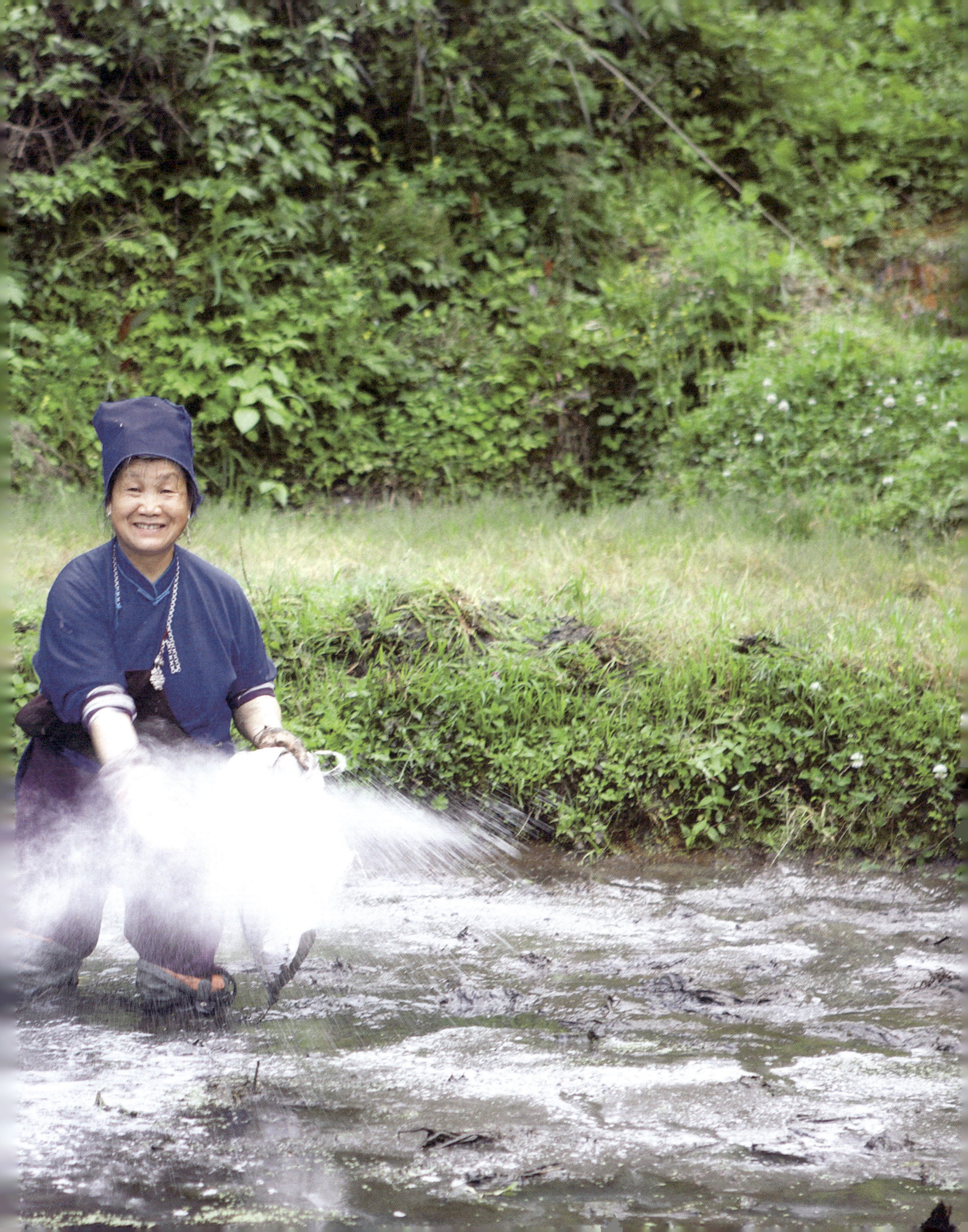

List of Works

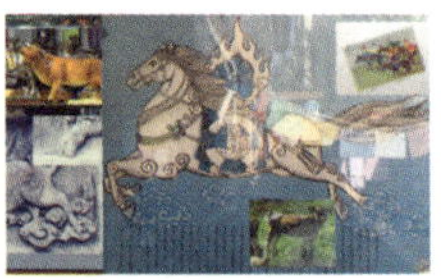

In Search for a Precise Shade of Blue #1, 2019
photographic collage, variable dimension

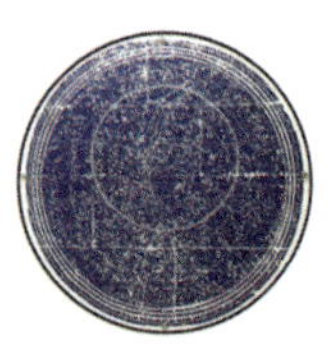

A Possible Future, 2016
photographic print on cotton paper
50.5 x 50.5 cm

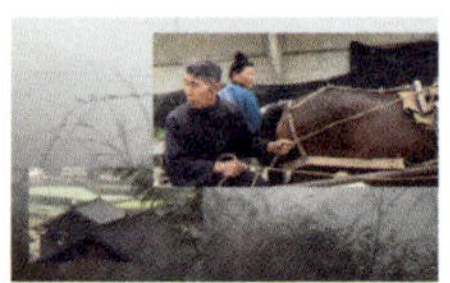

In Search for a Precise Shade of Blue #2, 2019
photographic collage, variable dimension

Rural and Ritual Life, 2017
pencil drawing on paper,
32 x 26 cm

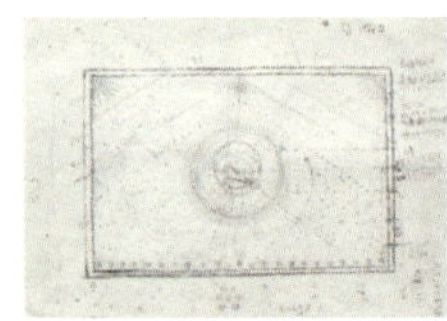

The Time of Discretion (Stage Curtain Drawing), 2016
pencil on acquarel paper,
26 x 36 cm

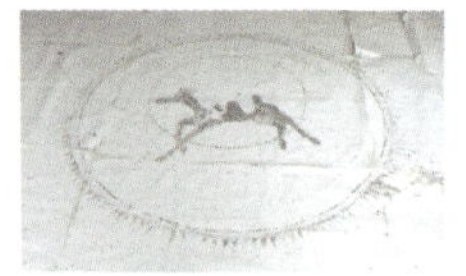

The Time of Discretion (Curtain Paper Pattern), 2016
paper, wax traces, 300 x 440 cm

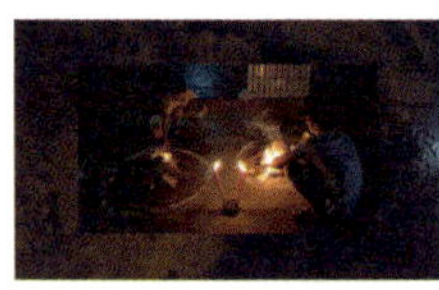

In Search for a Precise Shade of Blue #3, 2019
photographic collage, variable dimension

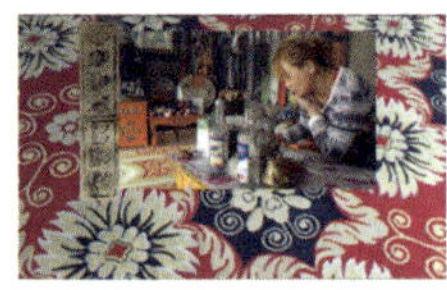

In Search for a Precise Shade of Blue #4, 2019
photographic collage, variable dimension

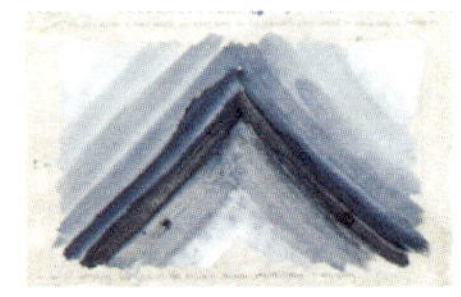

Untitled (Shades of Blue along Quotation by Tiziano Terzani), 2016
pencil writing and watercolor on rice paper, 19 x 28.8 cm

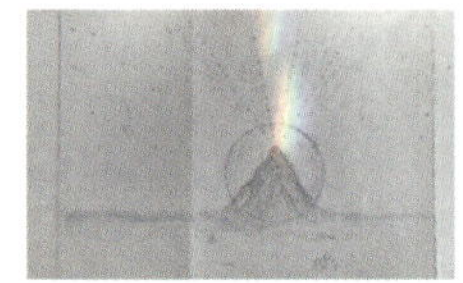

Wishes on the Altan Ovoo, 2016
pencil drawing on paper,
29.2 x 36 cm

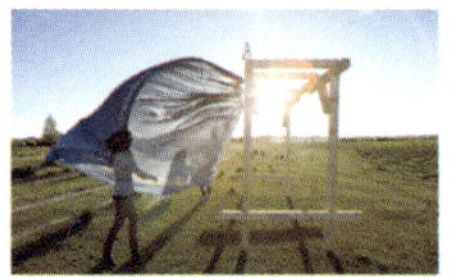

The Time of Discretion (Procession) #1, 2016
photographic print on fine art paper (baryta Hahnemühle), series of four, 72.7 x 102.7 cm, framed edition of 3

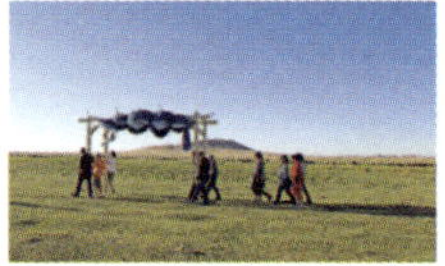

The Time of Discretion (Procession) #2, 2016
photographic print on fine art paper (baryta Hahnemühle), series of four, 72.7 x 102.7 cm, framed edition of 3

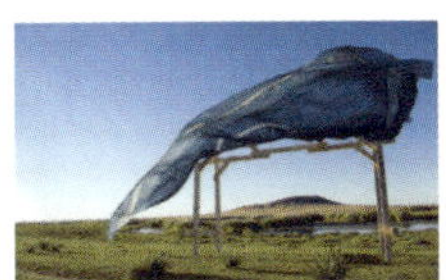

The Time of Discretion (Procession) #3, 2016
photographic print on fine art paper (baryta Hahnemühle), series of four, 72.7 x 102.7 cm, framed edition of 3

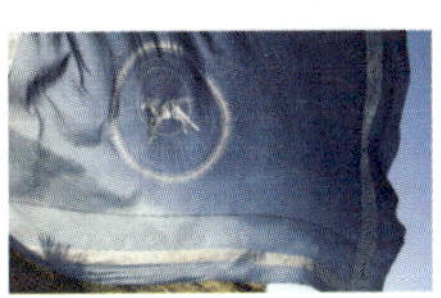

The Time of Discretion (Procession) #4, 2016
photographic print on fine art paper (baryta Hahnemühle), series of four, 72.7 x 102.7 cm, framed edition of 3

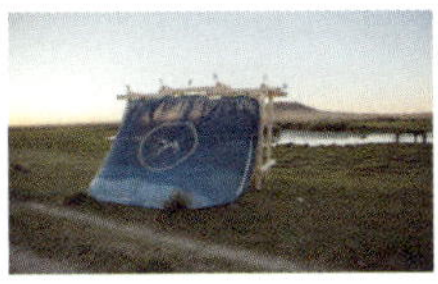

The Time of Discretion (Curtain), 2016
Dariganga, Land Art Mongolia Biennale, Mongolia, 2016
photographic documentation
installation: wooden structure (500 x 270 cm), 6 motorcycle mirrors, cotton fabric (500 x 370 cm), indigo, wax, 6 cotton and silk strings each of 300 cm long, 300 Chinese metal curtain hooks

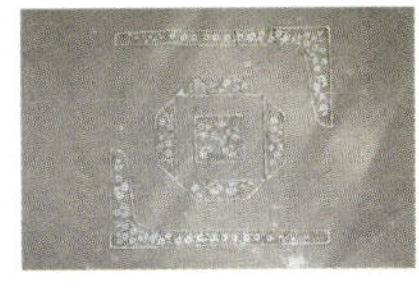

Elisir of Return, 2018
site specific intallation, MAD Murate Art District, Florence
Miao cut out papers with shapes of birds and flowers, variable dimensions

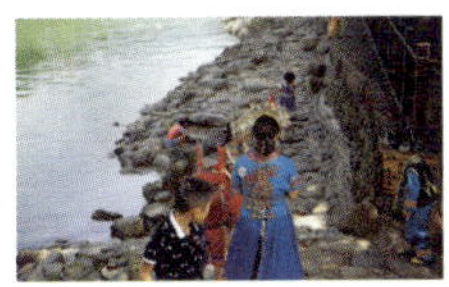

Elisir of Return #1, 2017/2018
photographic print on fine art paper (baryta Hahnemühle), series of seven, 39 x 53 cm, framed edition of 3

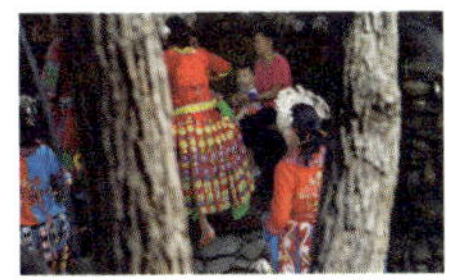

Elisir of Return #2, 2017/2018
photographic print on fine art paper (baryta Hahnemühle), series of seven, 39 x 53 cm, framed edition of 3

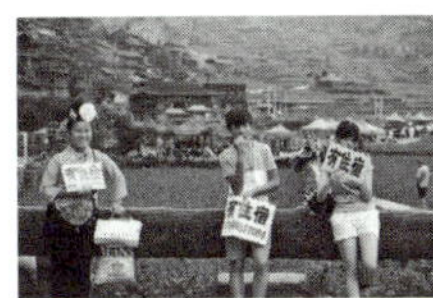

Elisir of Return #3, 2017/2018
photographic print on fine art paper (baryta Hahnemühle), series of seven, 23.7 x 15.8 cm
edition of 3

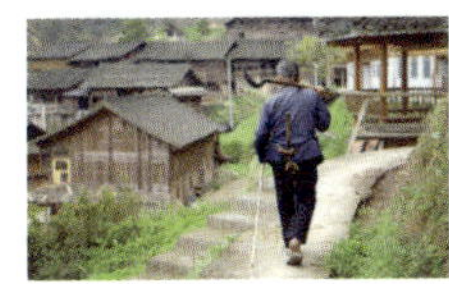

Elisir of Return #4, 2017/2018
photographic print on fine art paper (baryta Hahnemühle), series of seven, 39 x 53 cm, framed edition of 3

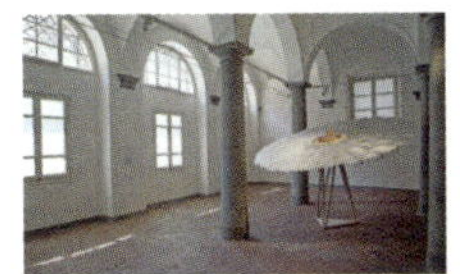

Toli, 2018
tin, 28 pieces, wood, ø 280 cm
site specific installation, MAD Murate Art District, Florence
Produced by PERCRO, Pisa

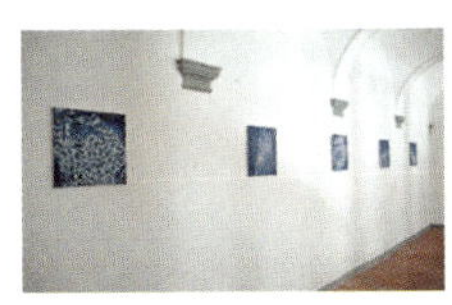

Crossing Destinies, 2018
installation view at MAD Murate Art District, Florence

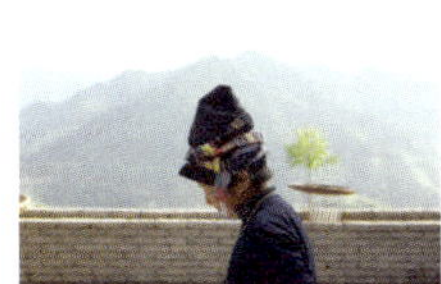

Elisir of Return #5, 2017/2018
photographic print on fine art paper (baryta Hahnemühle), series of seven, 39 x 53 cm, framed edition of 3

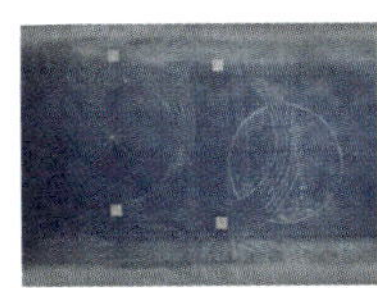

Preface, 2017
wax on raw silk fabric, indigo batik, 140 x 190 cm

Captions

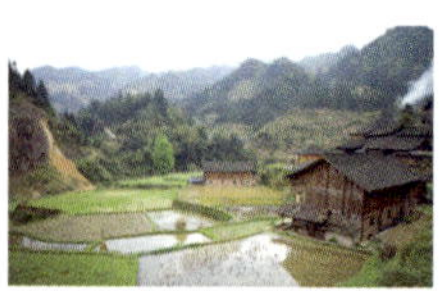

Elisir of Return #6, 2017/2018
photographic print on fine art paper (baryta Hahnemühle), series of seven, 39 x 53 cm, framed edition of 3

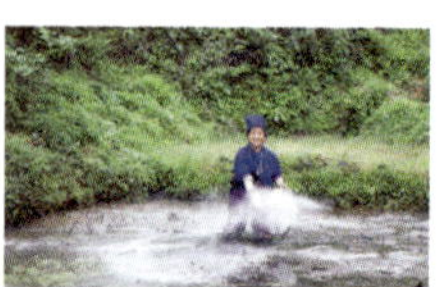

Elisir of Return #7, 2017/2018
photographic print on fine art paper (baryta Hahnemühle), series of seven, 39 x 53 cm, framed edition of 3

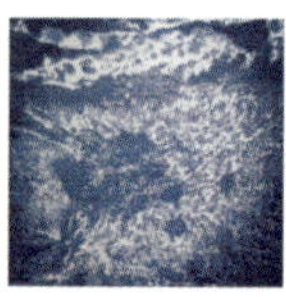

Crossing Destinies #1, 2018
series of five tapestries, cotton thread, natural indigo dye, each 60 x 62 cm

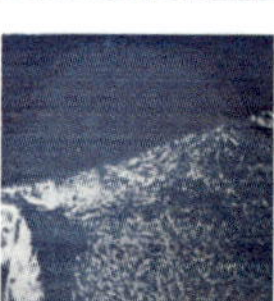

Crossing Destinies #2, 2018
series of five tapestries, cotton thread, natural indigo dye, each 60 x 62 cm

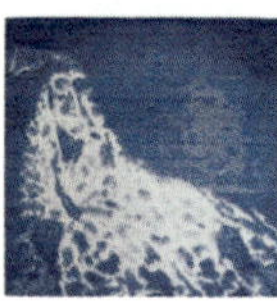

Crossing Destinies #3, 2018
series of five tapestries, cotton thread, natural indigo dye, each 60 x 62 cm

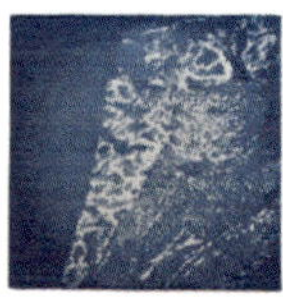

Crossing Destinies #4, 2018
series of five tapestries, cotton thread, natural indigo dye, each 60 x 62 cm

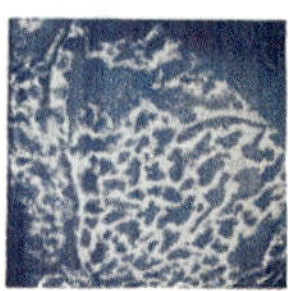

Crossing Destinies #5, 2018
series of five tapestries, cotton thread, natural indigo dye, each 60 x 62 cm

pp. 2–3
The Time of Discretion (film archive), 2016/2018
shamanic milk ritual, still from video

pp. 8–9
The Time of Discretion (film), 2019
I-Ching consultation, still from the short film
HD, color, sound, 24:53 min

pp. 12–13
Physical map of China (detail), n.d.

p. 14
Altan Ovoo, Dariganga, Mongolia, 2016
photographic documentation

p. 17
Ordos, Inner Mongolia, 2016
photographic documentation

p. 23
Mongolian home in cement, Grass Land, Inner Mongolia, 2016
photographic documentation

p. 28
The Time of Discretion (film), 2019
Miao cerimony jacket, still from the short film
HD, color, sound, 24:53 min

pp. 30–31
The Time of Discretion (film), 2019
still from the short film
HD, color, sound, 24:53 min

p. 33
Hanging item made of bird feathers, Qiandongnan Prefecture, Guizhou Province, China, 2017
photographic documentation

pp. 36–37
The Time of Discretion (film archive), 2016/2018
shamanic ritual, still from video

p. 41
Miao "Horse Hoof pattern", produced in late 1990s
cotton fabric, indigo batik
47 x 47 cm, artist's private collection

pp. 46–47
The Time of Discretion (film), 2019
preparing the hot wax, still from the short film
HD, color, sound, 24:53 min

pp. 50–51
Danzhai County, Guizhou Province, south west China, 8-15 August, 2016
photographic documentation

pp. 52
Danzhai, Guizhou Province, China, 2016

detail of wax drawing, photographic documentation

p. 57
Danzhai, Guizhou Province, China, 2016
detail of *Curtain* during a second immersion in the natural indigo dye, photographic documentation

p. 63
The Time of Discretion (film archive), 2016/2018
on the Transmongolica train, still from video

pp. 68–69
The Time of Discretion (film), 2019
still from the short film
HD, color, sound, 24:53 min

pp. 70–71
The Time of Discretion (film), 2019
still from the short film
HD, color, sound, 24:53 min

p. 72
Original Mongolian Shamanic Mirror called Toli, made around early 2000
brass, ø 15 cm, artist's private collection

p. 76
Altan Ovoo, Dariganga, Mongolia, 2016
photographic documentation

p. 79
Ulaanbaatar, Mongolia, 2016
detail of a wall painting in a temple
photographic documentation

p. 81
The Time of Discretion (film), 2019
shamanic ritual, south east of the Gobi Desert, still from the short film
HD, color, sound, 24:53 min

pp. 84–85
Altan Ovoo, Dariganga, Mongolia, 2016
photographic documentation

pp. 90–91
Dariganga, Land Art Mongolia Biennale, Mongolia, 2016
photographic documentation

p. 97
Dariganga, Land Art Mongolia Biennale, Mongolia, 2016
photographic documentation

p. 99
The Time of Discretion (film), 2019
still from the short film
HD, color, sound, 24:53 min

pp. 106–107
The Time of Discretion (film), 2019
still from the short film
HD, color, sound, 24:53 min

p. 108
Original Hmong Batik, made around early 2000
photographic documentation

p. 111
Xijang village, Guizhou, China, 2016
photographic documentation

p. 112
The Time of Discretion (film archive), 2016/2018
still from video

pp. 116–117
Qiandongnan Prefecture, Guizhou Province, China, 2017
photographic documentation

pp. 150–151
The Time of Discretion (film), 2019
still from the short film
HD, color, sound, 24:53 min

Annexes

Biography

Lisa Mara Batacchi
born in Florence, Italy
where she is based

Education

2011
BFA in visual arts – with honors, Accademia di Belle Arti, Florence

2004
BA – Fashion Design, Polimoda, Florence

Workshops

2012
Words... Action, with Christian Raimo, curated by 98weeks research/project space, Artissima 19, Museo della Resistenza, Turin

2010
Post Monument, Does the Sculpture Need a Camera?, XIV Biennale Internazionale di Scultura di Carrara, with Grzegorz Kowalski, curated by Fabio Cavallucci, Istituto del marmo Pietro Tacca, Carrara
The Materials of Thought, the Materials of the Work of Art, with Liliana Moro, Summer Academy, Salzburg

2007
Out Side Project on Invisibility, with Tanja Ostojic, different locations, Belgrade

Grants

2014
MOVIN'UP II session 2014 promoted by Ministry of Cultural Heritage and Activities and Tourism, General Directorate for Contemporary Art, Architecture and Urban Suburbs General Directorate for Performing Arts and GAI – Association for the Circuit of the Young Italian Artists

2010
Salzburg International Academy of Fine Arts award

Residencies

2017
ACAF Foundation, Shanghai

2016
Work In Progress residency, Textile Art Center, New York

2015
Clark House Initiative, Bombay
How We Want to Live? A project by Lu Cafausu with Ayreen Anastas, Rene Gabri, Adrian Paci, Luigi Coppola, FreeHome University, Lecce

2013
Incontri ad Eèa, curated by Alberto Di Fabio, Federica Forti, Ponza Island

Solo exhibitions, performances

2018
The Time of Discretion, curated by Veronica Caciolli, MAD Murate Art District, Florence

2017
The Time of Discretion. Act#05, curated by Valentina Gioia Levy for *Remembering the Future* directed by RikkeJørgensen, Art & Globalization Pavillion during the 57th Venice Biennale, Palazzo Rossini, Venice

2016
Soulmates (Within Time), Textile Art Center, New York

2015
Soulmates (Within Time), curated by Sumesh Sharma, Clark House Initiative, Bombay
Santa Caterina VS Art Verona = Performing, curated by Viaindustriae, Independents, Art Verona, Verona

2014
Soulmates (Within Time), curated by Ermanno Cristini, riss(e), Zentrum, Varese
Reduction from River to Stream, public art installation, curated by Forward, Florence
Victoria's Recipes, promoted by Nessiah festival, Royal Victoria Hotel, curated by Federica Forti, Pisa

2013
A Day Will Come in Which We Will All Be Poets, curated by Spela Zidar, Lato gallery, Prato

2010
Linger On, curated by Giovanni Surace, CAD Centro Arte e Design, Calenzano

2009
Traces of Sleep, galleria Alessandro Bagnai, curated by Start Point, Florence

Group shows

2018
What If It Did Not Happen? Something Else Cairo Off Biennale directed by Simon Njami and Moataz Nasr, Cairo
Art & Connectography. Remapping Global World through Art, Manifesta12 collateral event, curated by Art & Globalization, Palermo

2016
Animism, Dust space, Milan,
Catching the Axis – in between the Sky and the Earth, Land Art Mongolia Biennale, curated by Valentina Gioia Levy, Italian Embassy, UMA gallery, Ulaambaator

2015
Sviluppo di un poliedro irregolare nello spazio, curated by Imagonirmia, Treviso
Oltre città, curated by Giacomo Bazzani, Villa La Magia, Quarrata
ZOON, curated by Luca Scarabelli and Samuele Menin, Castello Visconteo, Abbiategrasso
Vitamine. Tavolette energetiche, curated by Monaldi Laura, Museo Novecento, Florence
Nuovi animali sociali, curated by Valentina Goia Levy, Villa Ada, Rome

2014
Disseminazioni, curated by Gino Giannuizzi, Casa bianca, Bologna
The Wall (archives) #10, a project by Pietro Gaglianò, Assab One, Milan
Terranauti, curated by Ilaria Mariotti, Angelika Stepken, Villa Romana, Villa Pacchiani, Pisa
Re-Birth Day. Io vedo, Io guardo, curated by Annalisa Cattani, Novella Guerra, Imola

The Wall (archives) #9, a project by Pietro Gaglianò, Casa Sponge/ Palazzo Giannini, Pergola
The Celebration of the Living (Who Reflect upon Death) collab project by Lu Cafausu, San Cesario di Lecce
Incontri ad Eèa, curated by Maria Ida Gaeta, Casa delle Lettarature, Rome
Motivi di famiglia, curated by Paolo Toffolutti, SPAC, Villa di Toppo Florio, Udine
Dimenticare quel corso artificiale di pensieri, Casa bianca, curated by Lisa Batacchi, Virginia Zanetti, Alessandro Laita and Gian Maria Tosatti, Bologna

2013
Finte nature, curated by Giacomo Bazzani, Mac,n museum, Monsummano Terme, Pistoia
A First Step towards Coincidences & Meetings Part V, b-a-d contemporary, Pietrasanta
The Wall (archives) #8, a project by Pietro Gaglianò, in collaboration with B.go Loreto/Spazio Permanente, CRAC Centro Ricerca Arte Contemporanea, Cremona
Acqua, curated by Carles Marco, Vivai Cioncolini/ Balestri/Trenti, Montevarchi
Love, video selection, curated by Stefano W. Pasquini, Melepere gallery, Verona

2012
A First Step towards Coincidences & Meetings Part II, Spazi Indipendenti, ArtVerona, curated by Cristiano Seganfreddo, Verona
Ephemera. Documenti, Ornamenti e Pizzini, curated by Luca Scarabelli, Riss(e), Varese
Quasi una lotteria, curated by a certain number of books.+Riss(e), VIR Viafarini-in-residence, Milan
A First Step towards Coincidences & Meetings Part I, SomethingLikeThis, Florence

2010
B/label, curated by Irene Balzani, Irene Innocente, Privat Flat #Brucia babilonia, Florence
The Materials of Thought the Materials of a Work of Art, curated by Liliana Moro, Hohen Salzburg Fortess, Salzburg
Sul disegnare, curated by Lorenzo Bruni, ViaNuova Arte Contemporanea, Florence

2009
Hallucinatory Sleep Paralysis, curated by Francesco Funghi, Sara Vannacci, studio MDT, Prato
Start Point, Istituto degli Innocenti, Florence

2008
Genius Loci, curated by Federica Forti, Forte Umberto I, Palmaria Island

2007
Out Side Project on Invisibility, curated by Dejan Atanackovic, Ex Turkish Bath, Belgrade

Talks/Lectures

2018
Lisa Batacchi for *Collective Identity* an educational project, Palazzo Strozzi, Florence

2017
Practicing Slowness and Disappearance from Capitalistic Ideology. Lisa Batacchi, Anna Mapoubi, Valentina Gioia Levy, Arts & Globalization Pavillion during Venice Biennale, directed by Rikke Jørgensen, Palazzo Rossini, Venice

2015
Roma incontra il mondo, Lisa Batacchi, Elena Bellantoni Mariana Ferratto, Giorgio De Finis, Elena Giulia Rossi, curated by Valentina Gioia Levy, Villa Ada, Rome

2014
Symposium - *Terranauti #Prolog: Navigating in the Art System. Dialogues with International Curators, Gallerists and the Director of a Public Museum*, curated by Ilaria Mariotti & Angelika Stepken,Villa Romana, Florence

2013
Talking about SLT art initiatives invited by Prof. Cecilia Guida, Accademia di Belle Arti, Florence

Personal workshops

2017
The Time of Discretion, ARTS CAN DO educational project invited by ACAF Foundation, Shanghai

2014
Victoria's Recipes, as part of *ORIENTamenti: Reshaping Past Traditions*, art platform by Wafa Hourani, Siena Art Institute, Siena

Curatorial / Art Initiatives

2013
A First Step towards Coincidences & Meetings Part IV, *Oh books.*, Giancarlo Norese, Oh Petroleum, Pietro Gaglianò, SomethingLikeThis, Florence

2012
A First Step towards Coincidences & Meetings Part III, Pierfabrizio Paradiso, SomethingLikeThis, Florence

2011
Coordination of *Attimi fondamentali*, Superstudio, curated by Alberto Salvadori, Museo Marino Marini, Florence

Publications

2016
G. Bonomi, *Il corpo solitario. L'autoscatto nella fotografia contemporanea*, Soveria Mannelli: Rubettino

2014
E. Fantin, L. Negro, G. Norese, C. Pietroiusti, L. Presicce (eds.), *Besides, it's Always the OthersWho Die*, Vienna: verlag für moderne kunst nürnberg | kmd – kunsthalle marcel duchamp no. 15

2010
Case d'arte. Guida ai luoghi della creatività, Florence: viol'Artedizioni

2008
Fiori e cioccolata, dvd, Com.Records

Exhibition Catalogues

2019
V. Caciolli, "Eternal Return to the Origins", in V. Gensini, A. Triandafyllidou, *Global Identities. Postcolonial and Cross-Cultural Narratives*, Milan: Mousse Publishing

2016
Catching the Axis, in between the Sky and the Earth, Land art Mongolia Biennale, self publishing

2015
G. Bazzani, *Come se lo facessimo noi*, Pisa: Pacini editore
L. Monaldi, *Vitamine. Tavolette energetiche*, Florence: Polistampa

2014
A. Stepken, I. Mariotti, *Terranauti. Quelli che arrivano, quelli che restano, quelli che vanno*, Pisa: Pacini editore
A. Di Fabio, *Incontri ad Eèa*, Ponza: self publishing

2013
C. Marco, *Acqua arte contemporanea*, Florence: Aska edizioni
G. Bazzani, *Finte naure. Una nuova scena artistica toscana*, Pisa: Pacini editore
C. Cosma (ed.), *La semantica delle pere*, Florence: Sensus luoghi per l'arte contemporanea, self publishing

2012
Art Verona, Veronafiere catalogue, Poggibonsi: Carlo Cambi editore

2008
F. Forti, *Genius Loci. Mostra d'arte ambientale itinerante*, Arma di Taggia: Athena Edizioni

Newspaper articles

2018
G. Rau, "Tra Oriente e Occidente il tempo di Lisa Batacchi", *La Repubblica*, June 7

2015
R. Gehi, "Stitch on the move", *Mumbai Mirror*, June 14, p. 12

2014
"Festival Nessiah. Protagonista la cucina ebraica", *Il Tirreno*, December 5
"Montelupo F.no, Una mostra di arte all'interno del mercato dell'usato", *La Nazione*, Empoli, April 27

E. Cristini, G. Brivio, "La coindizione di un azzardo", *boite magazine*, #12

2012
S. Rebora, "Non c'era, adesso c'è. Something like this", *Artribune Magazine*, Anno II, no. 10, Nov.–Dic.

2009
"Start Point", Primo piano Firenze: *La Nazione*, May 19, pp. 4–5

2008
C. Ricci, "Genius Loci", Non solo mare, *La Nazione*, August 14, p. 21
V. Bartarelli, "Un dialogo fitto e incessante fatto di segni", *Exibart on paper*, no. 52, Oct., p. 53
A. Montevedi, A., "Genius Loci sull'Isola di Palmaria", *My Media#19*, July/Sept., pp. 50–53
M. Costanzo, "Genius Loci", *La Palmaria*, *Rd'A*, y. 2, no. 5, pp. 47–52

Web Articles

2018
G. Rau, "Il mondo alle Murate ai confini della realtà", *La Repubblica*, February 13
B. Biondi, "Sarà un laboratorio dinamico, aperto a giovani artisti. La nuova stagione artistica del Museo Novecento e delle Murate (...)", *il Nuovo Reporter #Arte*
V. Silvestrini, "Tutte le novità da Le Murate di Firenze. Intervista a Valentina Gensini", *Artribune*

2017
L. Lunghi, "Lisa Batacchi", *Muse Contemporanee*

2016
L. Galdo, "LAM 360°– Land Art Mongolia. La quarta edizione della Biennale in Mongolia. Intervista a Valentina Gioia Levy", *LuxFlux*, Rivista no. 60/2016
"Biennale Land Art Mongolia. Il racconto di Lisa Batacchi", *Artribune*

2015
G. D'Acquisto, "Roma incontra il mondo 2015 a Villa Ada", *Marie Claire*
H. Marsala, "Italiani in trasferta. Lisa Batacchi a Bombay con Movin'Up", *Artribune*
R. Gehi, "Stitch on the Move", *Mumbai Mirror*, June 14
L. Binazzi (UFO), L. Batacchi, "Coltivare l'eccezione e non la regola", for *Voglia di '68* rubric on *UnDo.Net* curated by Ermanno Cristini

2014
"Al via la seconda tappa del progetto Terranauti", Livorno, *Il Tirreno*

"Da Riss(e) A Zentrum. Tre mostre", *ATP Diary*
"Festival Nessiah. Protagonista la cucina ebraica", *Il Tirreno*, December 5
G. Pagano, "Il gusto per l'incontro. L'artista Lisa Batacchi al festival Nessiah", *radioeco*
G. Rau, "Un lavatoio come ponte sull'Arno: l'installazione di Lisa Batacchi", *La Repubblica*, September 11

2013
H. Marsala, "Lisa Batacchi. Da Palmaria a Ponza", *Artribune*, March 23
L. Lorenzon, "Incontri ad EèA. La residenza di Lisa Batacchi", *BCome blog*, July 23
"Encounters in Eèa", *Flash Art International on line* #311, July–September
H. Marsala, "Artisti in vacanza sull'isola di Ponza", *Artribune*, July
M. Innocenti, "Cinque artisti e mille corrispondenze", *Artribune*, May 27
S. Rebora, "E il crowdfunding approda anche a teatro", *Artribune*, May 4
Rebora, S., "Lisa Batacchi e il cerchio perfetto", *Artribune*, January
"La semantica delle pere", *UnDo.Net*

2012
S. Rebora, "Dopo il salotto artistico ad Art Verona", *Artribune*, November 23
S. Rebora, "Artisti senza galleria né curatori", *Artribune*, September 28

2010
"Sul disegnare", *Toscana Oggi*
"Sul disegnare", *Exhibart*

2009
"Hallucinatory sleep paralysis", *UnDo.Net*

2008
V. Bartarelli, "Genius Loci", *Exhibart*, September 5
L. Larcan, "Genius Loci, arte contemporanea nella natura selvaggia di Palmaria", *La Repubblica.it*, August 1

The Time of Discretion

A Project by
Lisa Mara Batacchi

Supported by

ITALY

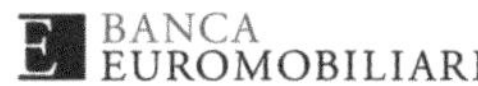

Banca Euromobiliare

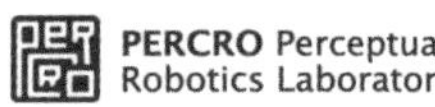

PERCRO Laboratory,

Scuola Superiore Sant'Anna, Pisa

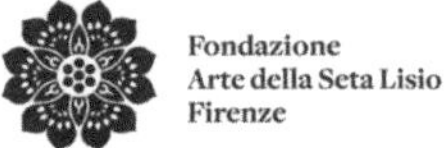

Fondazione Arte della Seta Lisio

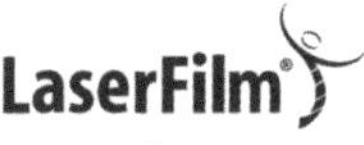

Laser Film S.R.L.

SOMETHING
LIKE THIS

SomethingLikeThis, Florence

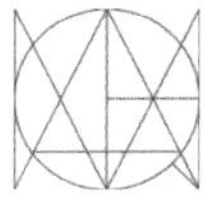

Imagonirmia, Treviso

MONGOLIA
LAM 360° Land Art Mongolia Biennale
Italian Embassy, Ulaanbaatar

Curators

LAM 360° LAND ART MONGOLIA BIENNALE
Valentina Gioia Levy

PALAZZO ROSSINI, VENICE
Rikke Jørgensen (Arts & Globalization)
Valentina Gioia Levy

INSTITUTIONAL SOLO SHOW MAD MURATE ART DISTRICT, FLORENCE
Veronica Caciolli

Cultural Partners

CHINA
Blue Flower Court Yard, Guiyang

The Time of Discretion Short Film

Post Production
Laser Film S.R.L., Rome

The Time of Discretion Book

Publisher
Silvana Editoriale

Edited by
Veronica Caciolli

Graphic Design by
Lisa Mara Batacchi

Contents
Lisa Mara Batacchi
Sumesh Sharma
Federico Campagna
Valentina Gioia Levy
Xiaomei Wang
Veronica Caciolli

Translations
Kathryn Lake

Photo Credits Documentation
All photos by Lisa Mara Batacchi with exception of:
Injinaash Ing, pp. 100–101
Pekka Niittyvirta, pp. 88, 90–91, 94–95
Vibha Galhotra, still from video, pp. 2–3
Edgar Endress, pp. 76, 82–83, 84–85

Special Thanks to
Veronica Caciolli, Valentina Gioia Levy, Sumesh Sharma, Federico Campagna, Xiaomei Wang, my husband Stefano Maurizi, my parents Joni and Paolo Batacchi and my brother David, Gioia (Ho Min), Julie Peters Deseract, Giancarlo Norese, Leda Lunghi, Sara Horowitz, Tim Schernau, Chunyen Yang, Ning batik factory, Na Jin Yang (Lala) and Guang Lian Yang (Napon), Wendy Hu, Dashdondog Badam, Enhmaa Borhuu & family, Eya Ganbat and family, Muuji Batmunkh and family, Julie Holyoke, Arch. Lorenzo Giorgi, Herman Finch Collection, Pamela Giorgi

Many Thanks for the Support to

ITALY
Antonio Lombardi (BancaEuromobiliare), Prof. Massimo Bergamasco and his assistants Alessandro Filippeschi, Alessandro Nicoletti (Laboratorio PERCRO, Sant'Anna, Pisa), Eva Basile, (Fondazione Arte Della Seta Lisio), Andrea Di Nardo (director of Laser Film, Rome), famiglia Mantoni, Pier Fabrizio Paradiso (Ass. Imagonirmia), Valentina Gensini (director of MAD Murate Art District, Florence)

MONGOLIA
Andrea De Filip, Italian Ambassador, Ulaanbaatar

SWEDEN
Arts & Globalization

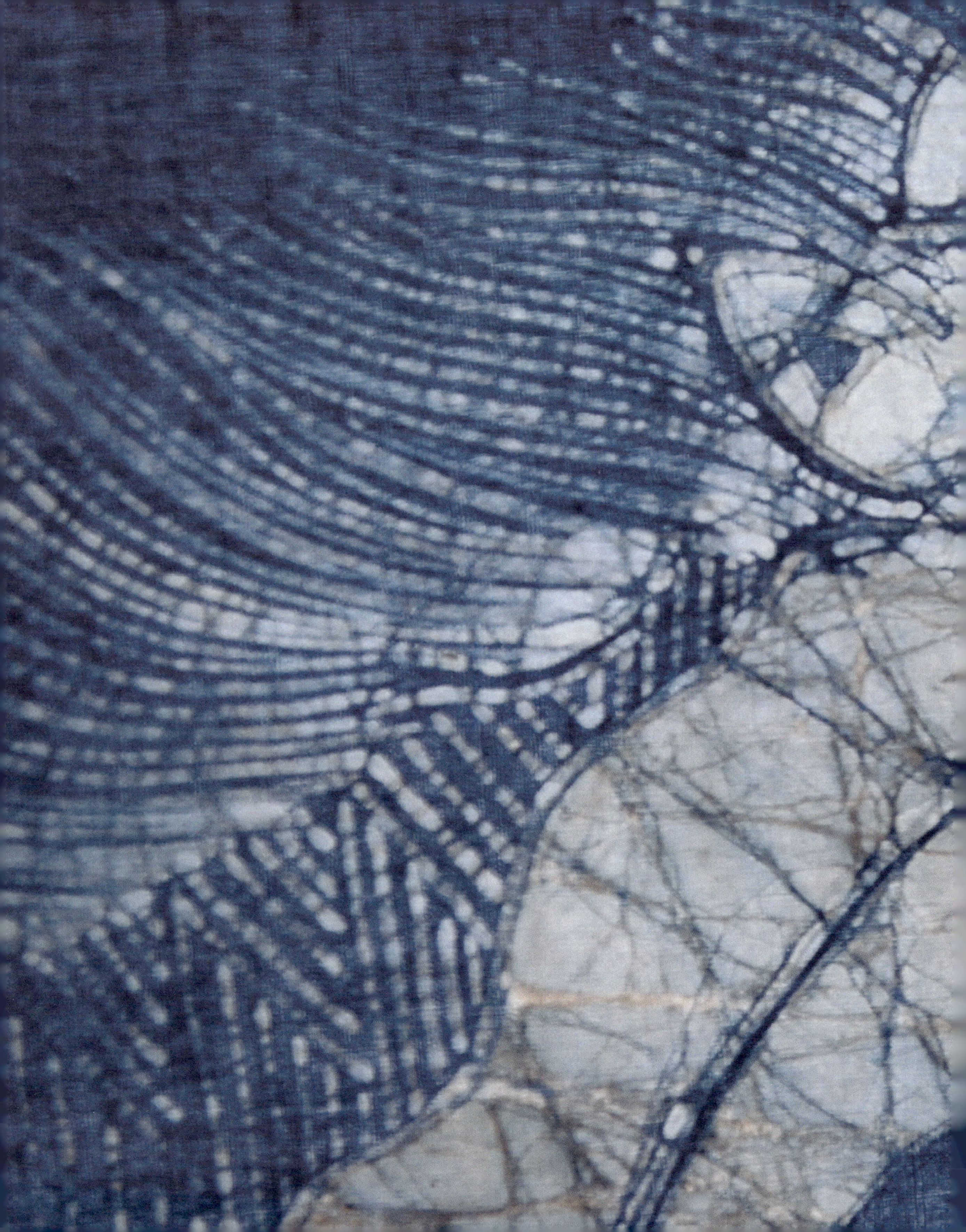

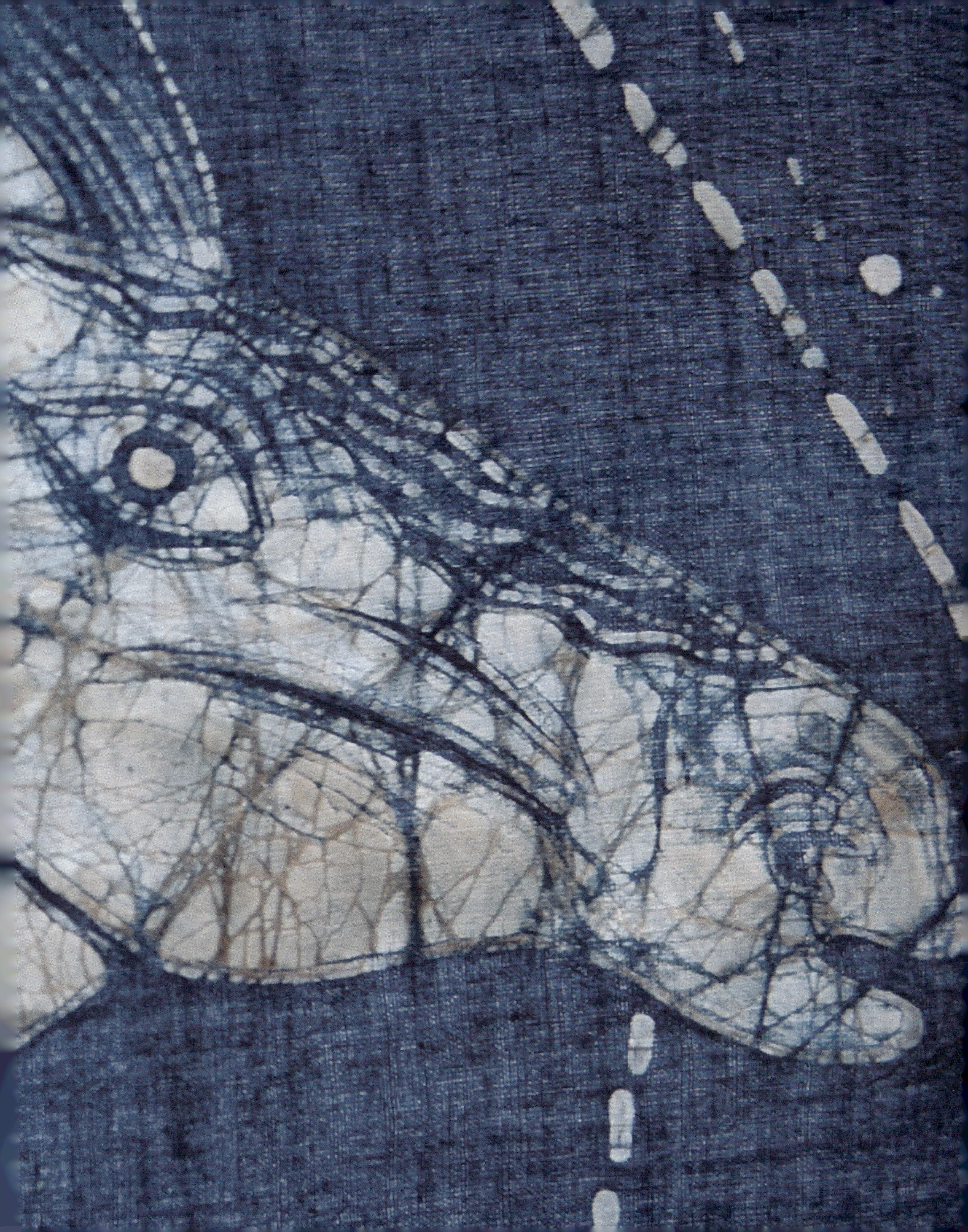

Cover
Preface, 2017
detail

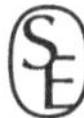

Silvana Editoriale

Direction
Dario Cimorelli

Art Director
Giacomo Merli

Editorial Coordinator
Sergio Di Stefano

Copy Editor
Filomena Moscatelli

Layout
Nicola Cazzulo

Production Coordinator
Antonio Micelli

Editorial Assistant
Ondina Granato

Photo Editor
Alessandra Olivari, Silvia Sala

Press Office
Lidia Masolini, press@silvanaeditoriale.it

Silvana Editoriale S.p.A.
via dei Lavoratori, 78
20092 Cinisello Balsamo, Milano
tel. 02 453 951 01
fax 02 453 951 51
www.silvanaeditoriale.it

Reproductions, printing and binding
in Italy
Printed by Grafiche Pacini, Ospedaletto (Pi)
January 2020

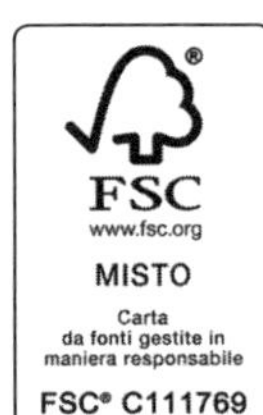